D0629595

PEDDLING PROSPERITY

ALSO BY PAUL KRUGMAN

The Age of Diminished Expectations

Currencies and Crises

Rethinking International Trade

Geography and Trade

PEDDLING PROSPERITY

*Economic Sense and
Nonsense in the
Age of Diminished
Expectations*

PAUL KRUGMAN

W·W·Norton & Company
New York   London

Copyright © 1994 by Paul Krugman
All rights reserved
Printed in the United States of America
First Edition

The text of this book is composed in 11/13 Berkeley Old Style Book
with the display set in Gill Sans Condensed and
Berkeley Old Style Medium.
Composition and manufacturing by the Haddon Craftsmen, Inc.
Book design by Margaret M. Wagner.

Library of Congress Cataloging-in-Publication Data
Krugman, Paul R.
Peddling prosperity : economic sense and nonsense in the age of
diminished expectations / Paul Krugman.
p.   cm.
Includes index.
1. Keynesian economics.   2. Supply-side economics.
3. Economics—Political aspects.   I. Title.
HB99.7.K77   1994
330.15′6—dc20   93–29965

ISBN 0–393–03602–2

W. W. Norton & Company, Inc.
500 Fifth Avenue, New York, N.Y. 10110
W. W. Norton & Company Ltd.
10 Coptic Street, London WC1A 1PU

1 2 3 4 5 6 7 8 9 0

The ideas of economists and political philosophers, both when they are right and when they are wrong, are more powerful than is commonly understood. Indeed, the world is ruled by little else. Practical men, who believe themselves to be quite exempt from any intellectual influences, are usually the slaves of some defunct economist. Madmen in authority, who hear voices in the air, are distilling their frenzy from some academic scribbler of a few years back . . . soon or late, it is ideas, not vested interests, which are dangerous for good or evil.

—JOHN MAYNARD KEYNES
The General Theory of Employment, Interest, and Money

Contents

Preface

An Indian-born economist once explained his personal theory of reincarnation to his graduate economics class. "If you are a good economist, a virtuous economist," he said, "you are reborn as a physicist. But if you are an evil, wicked economist, you are reborn as a sociologist."

A sociologist might say that this quote shows what is wrong with economists: they want a subject that is fundamentally about human beings to have the mathematical certainty of the hard sciences. And without doubt there is too much mathematics in the economics journals, because mathematical elaboration is a time-honored way of dressing up a banal idea. But good economists know that the speaker was talking about something else entirely: the sheer difficulty of the subject. Economics is *harder* than physics; luckily it is not quite as hard as sociology.

Why is economics such a hard subject? Part of the answer has to do with complexity. The economy cannot be put in a box. Physics does very well at explaining simple, contained systems: planets orbiting the sun, electrons jumping between the orbits of a hydrogen atom. It has a much harder time when trying to cope with the complexities of nature in the wild: weather forecasting, even with massive expenditure on satellites and supercomputers, remains an inexact business. And when climate modelers are asked to answer a speculative question, like the prospects for global warming, they produce a range of answers (and a set of bitter disputes) as wide as that of economic forecasters asked to assess a policy initiative.

Another reason economics is hard is that the critical sociologist is right: it involves human beings, who do not behave in simple, mechanical ways. Economists understand hyperinflations, those spectacular monetary aberrations in which prices rise by more than 50 percent per month, pretty well. I would argue, in fact, that they understand hyperinflations about as well as meteorologists understood hurricanes before they were able to simulate them on supercomputers: that is, the principles and the rough magnitudes are well explained by the theory, even if it's hard to make precise forecasts. But a hurricane today is the same as a hurricane a thousand years ago; hyperinflations are something new under the sun, because they couldn't happen until societies shifted from metallic to paper money. And each hyperinflation is a little different from the last, partly because governments learn lessons (though not necessarily correct ones) from history.

In spite of these difficulties, however, we actually do know quite a lot about economics—more than we know in any other social science—because economics studies human beings in their simplest (if least edifying) activities. The marketplace is special among social interactions in that it is subject to certain logical regularities. Every sale is also a purchase; this seemingly trivial observation implies a whole series of accounting principles, some of which still surprise many people (like the fact that a country which attracts an inflow of capital from abroad necessarily runs a trade deficit). Obvious opportunities for profits are rarely overlooked; this equally trivial-seeming observation leads to such surprising conclusions as the random-walk theory of stock prices.

Because the exchange of goods and services for money and

each other is a less complex, perhaps less human activity than other social interactions, economics lends itself both to the development of theory and to the testing of that theory to a greater extent than other social sciences. If economics were a subject of purely intellectual interest like astronomy it would be regarded as a quietly progressive field, one in which there has been a steady accumulation of knowledge over the past two centuries.

But economics is not astronomy, because its conclusions have a direct impact on government policies that affect almost everyone. In an ideal world this would mean that large numbers of people would care about economics enough to study it closely. In our imperfect world it means that people care about economics only enough to know what they *want* to believe.

Politicization is, of course, not unique to economics or even to social science. Creationists prefer not to believe in evolution, and they remain a powerful force well over a century after Darwin. A dangerously large number of people prefer not to believe that the HIV virus causes AIDS. In the physical and biological sciences, however, the demonstrable successes—antibiotics work, atom bombs explode—and the impressive equipment used for research tend to make it easy to define the boundary between serious ideas and pseudoscience.

In the social sciences, it is much harder to draw this line. Partly this is because one cannot perform controlled experiments: evidence in social science is always historical evidence, and history is complicated enough that its lessons are seldom unambiguous. Partly it is because social science studies people; and since we think we know ourselves, we all tend to think that we already know the answers.

The result is that while there is a steady accumulation of knowledge in economics, there is also a constant market for doctrines that play to popular prejudices, whether they make sense or not. In times of economic distress, the search for politically useful economic ideas—which often means ideas that are demonstrably wrong, but that appeal to those impatient with hard thinking—takes on a special intensity.

This book tells the story of the interaction between economic ideas and politics during one such period: the long stagnation of living standards since 1973, the period that in an earlier book I called the "Age of Diminished Expectations." It has been a time of serious and important debates about economics: broadly speaking, during the first decade conservatives mounted a powerful challenge to the case for government activism, while since then that case has been revived in a more sophisticated form. But it has also been the age of the policy entrepreneur: the economist who tells politicians what they want to hear. The way that a small group of "supply-siders," preaching a doctrine that even conservative economists regarded as nonsense, came to dominate American economic policy is one of the wonders of our age. The story of the "strategic traders," who are in effect the liberal counterparts of the supply-siders, is still unfolding.

When I began to write this book, it was intended as a more or less partisan tract. At that time conservatives still held the White House, and I am a liberal—that is, I believe in a society that taxes the well-off and uses the proceeds to help the poor and unlucky. And I was angry over the way that bad economics and spurious claims of success were being used to justify a program that helped the rich and hurt the poor while doing nothing positive for the economy. As I worked on it, however, the shape of the book changed. It was not just that the Democrats won the 1992 election, making a pure critique of conservative economics a little less timely. It was that as I tried to make sense of the economic debates of recent decades, it became clear to me that the fault line between serious economic thinking and economic patent medicine, between the professors and the policy entrepreneurs, is at least as important as the divide between left and right.

While this is a book with a message, however, it is also a collection of what I hope are interesting stories, both about the economy and about economists. Never mind the boring talking heads inexplicably favored by public television: economics *can* be exciting. To my mind, the Keynesian explanation of how reasonable actions by individual firms and families can cumulate to create the tragedy we call a recession has a kind of terrible beauty; the

strange history of how a few eccentric economists and their jour-
nalist allies created the supply-side revolution is dismaying, but it
is also funny. My hope is that reading this book will help convince
at least some readers that the ideas of serious economists are not
only a better guide to the truth than the easy slogans of the policy
entrepreneurs; they are more interesting, too.

PEDDLING PROSPERITY

Introduction:
Looking for
Magicians

██████████

Sometimes the magic works, sometimes it doesn't.

For a generation after World War II, America had (as Tom Wolfe put it) a "magic economy." Some of the magic was measurable: in less than thirty years, everything doubled. That is, the real earnings of the typical worker, the real income of the typical family, consumption per capita, all were twice as high by around 1972 as they had been in the late 1940s. But the numbers alone fail to convey the astonishing sense of affluence and economic optimism that pervaded the country. People worried about many things—social upheaval, nuclear war, the environment—but they took it for granted that the economy would continue to deliver an ever higher material standard of living.

In 1973 the magic went away.

Of course it wasn't really that sudden. Acute observers saw signs of an end to the great postwar wave of growth in the late 1960s, and with the benefit of hindsight we can now see that productivity growth, the engine that drives rising living standards, was beginning to sputter as early as 1965. Nor did the public perceive quickly that there had been a fundamental change in the trend. For a while it seemed that our economic malaise was the result of a few individual pieces of bad luck: the energy crisis that followed the 1973 Arab-Israeli War, and the "stagflation"—inflation and recession combined—of the next two years. It wasn't until 1978 or 1979 that the public began to develop a really deep sense of unease about its economic future. And this unease was broken by occasional bursts of optimism, like the euphoria when Ronald Reagan proclaimed "morning in America" in 1984.

Yet year by year, the depressing news continued to come in. In 1991, the typical family had a real income only 5 percent higher than its 1973 counterpart, and it achieved that income only by working longer hours: most workers were bringing in *lower* take-home pay than in 1973. Poverty had risen by any measure, and was reaching alarming levels among children. A few already well-off people had done very well during the 1980s, yet the recession of the early 1990s had struck fear into the hearts even of the affluent.

And the psychological change in the end reached deeper than the numbers themselves can convey. Despite disappointing growth, in per capita terms America in the early 1990s was a substantially richer country than it had been in the 1960s or even in 1973. Yet the end of optimistic expectations about the future left it feeling far worse. In the 1960s, Michael Harrington felt that he had to write *The Other America* to remind the affluent majority that there were still a lot of poor people in our country. Would anyone need that reminder today? The best-selling non-fiction book of 1972 was Charles Reich's *The Greening of America,* about the glorious cultural possibilities opening now that the economic problem was solved. By contrast, books about American economic woes—Lester Thurow's *Head to Head* and Michael Crichton's *Rising Sun*—topped the non-fiction and fiction lists, respectively, in 1992. And Bill Clinton's advisers had no difficulty in choosing a campaign theme for that year's election: "It's the economy, stupid," read the celebrated banner in his headquarters.

Why did the magic economy go away? Hundreds of books have been written on that topic. This isn't one of them—although I'll devote part of a chapter to some plausible stories and take a number of stabs at the issue along the way. But let me cut to the chase: the real answer is that *we don't know*. There are a lot of stories out there. Most of them, including the ones that have achieved the widest currency, are dead wrong on logical or factual grounds. There are some less popular stories that could be right— but if you are honest with yourself, you will admit that nobody, yourself included, knows which if any of these stories actually is right.

The problem is that "We don't know" is not a very encouraging answer. It's especially unsatisfying for politicians faced with an increasingly pessimistic and angry electorate. For them, the question of why the magic went away and how to get it back isn't an academic exercise. Their jobs depend on finding an answer—not necessarily an answer that is right, but at least one that will convince enough of the voters that they can make things better.

So what do you do when the magic isn't working? You look for a new set of magicians.

This is a book about that search. Or, to be more exact, it is a book about the interplay between economists and politicians, about how politicians try to find economists with ideas that they can package, and how economists both develop ideas and try to translate ideas into political influence.

It's a complicated story in detail, because the ideas involved are subtle, wrong, or both. If they're subtle, we need to spend a while understanding them; if they aren't we need to spend a while understanding why they're wrong. Although the discussion of ideas will be complicated, however, the book has two simple themes.

One theme is a familiar one: there are cyclical swings in ideology, from left to right and back again. The 1970s saw an astonishing rise in the influence of strongly conservative ideas in economics (as well as in other areas), a rise that was only certified by the 1980 victory of Ronald Reagan. Yet from an intellectual point of view, 1980 was really the conservative high-water mark. Even though the Republican Party easily held on to the White House in the elections of 1984 and 1988, the conservative ideology that had brought it to power was steadily decaying, a decay that was similarly only certified by George Bush's 1992 defeat.

But there is also a less familiar, and equally important theme: that there are two different kinds of "economists." We can call them professors and policy entrepreneurs; politicians, unfortunately, nearly always prefer the latter.

Politicians and Economists

Current mythology has it that politicians simply do the bidding of interest groups. The popular vision has politicians bought and sold by the lobbyists in Washington. Other observers, like John Kenneth Galbraith, see our political process as a faithful representation of the interests of the only part of the electorate that matters—the relatively well-off top 20 percent of the income distribution. In either case, what politicians do is seen as hardly at all influenced by ideas, since it merely reflects the interests of powerful constituents of one sort or another.

The truth is more complicated. On some issues there are interest groups who know what they want and have the clout to get it, never mind the logic—lumber companies who log on federal land or sugar growers sheltered behind their import quota aren't interested in the theory of the case. But on many issues, especially the big ones, voters do not have a clear vision of where their interests lie. What politicians try to do is define that vision for them, in a way that rebounds to their own benefit.

Nobody has been more successful at defining a public vision than Ronald Reagan. His theme was simple: middle-class Americans are overregulated and overtaxed, groaning under the weight of Big Government. He illustrated his theme with powerful images: welfare queens driving Cadillacs, huge rooms full of bureaucrats each taking care of a single Indian. Yet the images were fantasies—nobody has ever found a welfare queen in a Cadillac, or a bureaucrat whose job is to look after a single Indian. And the overall picture was highly questionable: Americans pay lower taxes than residents of any other advanced country, and most of those taxes go to pay for popular middle-class programs like Social Security and Medicare. In effect, Reagan built his political success on the basis of a compelling mythology that had relatively little to do with reality.

As the example of Ronald Reagan shows, real political success comes not simply from appealing to the interests that people currently perceive but from finding ways to redefine their perceived interests, to harness their discontent in favor of changes that you can lead. In the 1980s conservatives succeeded in defining a vision of what was wrong with America—Big Government, excessive taxes—that resonated with the American public and gave them an extended lease on power. Smart liberals understood early on that while they could win an election if they got lucky, they could only really break the conservative hold by coming up with a new vision that could redefine for the voters what they wanted. In other words, politics on the grand scale is not about interests but about ideas.

But where do ideas about economics come from? They come, of course, from economists—where by an "economist" I mean someone who thinks and writes regularly about economic issues. But not all economists are alike, and in fact the genus includes two radically distinct species: the professors and the policy entrepreneurs.

THE PROFESSORS

By "professors," I mean the academic economists. Not everyone you see introduced on TV as an economist is a member of this group. In fact, very few of them are. If you watch your TV economists early in the morning, you will mostly see the business forecasters, the people whose job it is to make confident, but nearly always wrong, pronouncements about what will happen over the next few months. (Academics scornfully call what these people do "up-and-down economics.") If you watch them on the evening or weekend talk shows, what you mostly get are the policy entrepreneurs. You will almost never see an economist whom the academics themselves regard as important or interesting. For example, neither Robert Lucas, without question the most influential economic theorist of the 1970s, nor Paul Romer, arguably the most influential theorist of the 1980s, has ever appeared on any public affairs program.

So, who cares? If academic economists are invisible to the public, do they matter? They certainly matter less than they themselves like to imagine. But their ideas do make a difference, enough to make it worthwhile to look at who they are and why they think the way they do.

The most obvious thing about the professors is, of course, that they are professors—a species that, like penguins or ostriches, is inherently faintly ridiculous. In America's academic system, professors of economics get tenure and build the reputations that give them other academic perks by publishing, and so they publish immense amounts—thousands of papers each year, in scores of obscure journals. Most of those papers aren't worth reading, and many of them are pretty much impossible to read in any case, because they are loaded with dense mathematics and denser jargon.

It's easy to be cynical about the motivations of the people who write these papers. You don't progress as an economics professor by solving the real problems of the real economy, at least not in any direct way. Instead, you progress by convincing your colleagues that you are clever. In an ideal world you would demonstrate your cleverness by developing blindingly original ideas or producing definitive evidence about how the economy actually works. But most of us can't do that, at least not consistently. So professors look for more surefire approaches. And thus the most popular economic theories among the professors tend to be those that best allow for ingenious elaboration without fundamental innovation—ways to show that you are smart by putting old wine in new bottles, usually with fancier mathematical labels.

And yet, however ridiculous the professors may sometimes appear, their work isn't all academic games.[1] After all, everything that I just wrote about academic economists could be said equally well about university physicists or medical researchers—but physics and medicine have made startling progress over time. Close up, it's all ego, pettiness, and careerism; back up, and you see an enterprise that steadily adds to our knowledge.

Believe it or not, the same is true about academic economics. It's a primitive science, of course. If you want a parallel, think of medicine at the turn of the century. Medical researchers had, by that time, accumulated a great deal of information about the human body and its workings, and were capable of giving some critically useful advice about how to avoid disease. They could not, however, cure very much. Indeed, the doctor/essayist Lewis Thomas tells us that the most important lesson from medical research up to that time had been to leave diseases alone—to stop the traditional "cures," like bleeding, that actually hurt the patients.

The parallel with economics isn't perfect, but it's not too far off. Economists know a lot about how the economy works, and can offer some useful advice on things like how to avoid hyperinflations (for sure) and depressions (usually). They can demonstrate to you, if you are willing to hear it, that folk remedies for economic distress like import quotas and price controls are about as useful as medical bleeding. But there's a lot that they can't cure. Above all, they don't know how to make a poor country rich, or bring back the magic of economic growth when it seems to have gone away.

Those limitations are a big problem for politicians, who want to hear positive answers. A few smart politicians (or at least their staffs) carefully trawl the academic waters, looking for ideas that

---

[1]One favorite line of attack by critics of academic economists is to look through the journals for paper titles that sound silly. But a whimsical title may head a very serious paper. For example, Martin Anderson's *Impostors in the Temple* gives a list of obviously trivial papers that includes Sherwin Rosen's 1981 piece "The Economics of Superstars," a brilliant and prophetic analysis of the reasons why modern information technology tends to increase income inequality.

can turn into issues that can turn into votes. But for the most part the politicians find the academics lacking.

Why? The usual answer is that so much of what academics write is dense and technical. But many of the most influential academics are quite capable of writing clear, non-technical English when the occasion calls for it. Harvard's Martin Feldstein, who did much to legitimize criticisms of the burden of taxation during the 1970s, has written dozens of lucid articles in non-academic magazines. Princeton's Alan Blinder, who helped carry the liberal torch during the 1980s, wrote a regular column for *BusinessWeek* and a graceful primer on the U.S. economy. Many academics are incomprehensible, but there is no shortage of economists with fine academic reputations who are quite capable of making simple, relevant policy points.

No, the problem that the politicians have with the professors is not one of failure to communicate; it is one of failure to say what politicians want (need) to hear, especially when they are trying to seize power from other politicians. And necessity is the mother of invention: a different group, the policy entrepreneurs, has arisen to fill the gap.

THE POLICY ENTREPRENEURS

In the mid-1980s the Center for Strategic and International Studies (CSIS), a Washington think tank, began running a telephone "alert system" for media callers. That way, when a newspaper or television show called the Center looking for a quote on some policy issue, a knowledgeable staffer could always be found, even on nights and weekends. After all, publicity was the Center's lifeblood.

CSIS may be unique in being so aggressive about courting the press, but it is not unique in its motivations. The people who work at CSIS, and at dozens of similar institutions, are part of a new class, neither professors nor politicians, that has come to play a key role in the interplay between ideas and policies: the policy entrepreneur.

What is a policy entrepreneur? He or she is, like the professors, a professional intellectual, but an intellectual of a different sort. He may be an academic by background: Arthur Laffer and Lester Thurow both have Ph.D.'s in economics and appointments as economics professors. More often they are based in Washington think tanks or in unorthodox university environments like Harvard's Kennedy School. What distinguishes entrepreneurs is not so much where they come from, however, as the language they speak and the audience to which their speech is addressed.

A professor writes mostly for other professors. If he should happen to write for a wider public, no matter how well and simply he may write, he will always have in the back of his mind the reaction of his colleagues, which will inhibit him from saying things that sound good but which he and they know to be wrong. And lurking behind his words, no matter how simple, are usually concepts that a broad audience does not understand.

The entrepreneur, however, writes and speaks only for that broader audience. And as a result, his or her writings suffer from none of the professor's inhibitions. They offer unambiguous diagnoses, even where the professors are uncertain; they offer easy answers, even where the professors doubt that any easy answer can be found.

You can get a pretty good idea of the difference just by looking at the titles of what the professors and the policy entrepreneurs write. In the 1970s, the conservative public finance expert Martin Feldstein expounded his influential views on how the tax burden was slowing economic growth in papers with titles like "Inflation and Corporate Profits Taxation"; only a journalist-turned-economics-entrepreneur like Jude Wanniski would have the nerve to present an exaggerated version of these views in a book called, simply, *The Way the World Works*. In the 1980s, Paul Romer wrote path-breaking papers about economic growth under self-deprecating titles like "Crazy Explanations of the Productivity Slowdown"; only a lawyer-turned-economics-entrepreneur like Robert Reich would have portrayed himself as a second Adam Smith by publishing somewhat similar ideas under the title *The Work of Nations*.

As you might guess, it is mostly policy entrepreneurs who sell books to the general public; it is mostly policy entrepreneurs who appear on television. After all, that is what they do professionally. And their rapport with their audience isn't inhibited by an underlying awareness of facts and concepts that do not appear in what they say. What the public sees in them is what it gets; and what it gets generally plays to its preconceptions.[2]

A professor can try to play entrepreneur—after all, the rewards in both money and a sense of importance can be huge. Ultimately, however, she is at a disadvantage, because she is too constrained by her obscure professorly ethics. Some professors manage to transcend these limitations, but in so doing they cease to be professors, at least in the minds of their colleagues. And in general it seems that it is easiest to become a policy entrepreneur if your mind has not been clouded by too much knowledge of economic facts or existing economic theories—only then can you be entirely sincere in telling people what they want to hear. As a result, most of our influential economic policy entrepreneurs, right and left, have their professional roots in journalism or law rather than economics.

From a politician's point of view, such entrepreneurs are extremely useful. They, much more than the professors, offer a source of those visions that can transform voters' perception of their interests. Above all, in a time of economic disappointment, they are willing to claim to know how to get the magic back. And of course policy entrepreneurs are much less likely than professors to get their backs up over a matter of professional pride or disagreement.

Yet politicians are neither wholly cynical nor by any means fools. They need their entrepreneurs, they lean on them, yet they

[2]There is a general rule that if you see an expert on television a lot, he or she probably isn't much of an expert—if nothing else, real experts are too busy doing research to be on that many shows. And the qualities that make for good TV are not closely related to those that make for good research. This observation is not unique to economics; for example, Stephen Hawking, whose *A Brief History of Time* was a best seller and who has been the subject of a number of adoring documentaries, is *not* the world's leading physicist.

distrust them—as operators, issue surfers themselves, they know that ideas that sound good don't necessarily really make sense. They want reassurance that their preferred pundits, unlike the other side's, really do know what they are talking about.

And so the entrepreneurs are themselves invariably insecure— hankering after a seal of intellectual respectability. They want to be professors, too. And out of this comes a peculiar posture: the entrepreneurs simultaneously look for support for their ideas among the professors, and denigrate the usefulness of the professors themselves. This almost Freudian conflict between professors and pundits is always ready to break out; it may be suppressed for a while when a group of entrepreneurs and a group of professors share a common political aim, but it always flares up again.

Consider, for example, the case of John Kenneth Galbraith. The general educated public—the public that watches McNeil/Lehrer or reads The New Yorker—thinks of Galbraith as an important economic thinker. Although Galbraith is a Harvard economics professor, however, he has never been taken seriously by his academic colleagues, who regard him as more of a "media personality." The contrast between public and professional perception became particularly acute in 1967, when Galbraith made a grand statement of his ideas about economics in The New Industrial State, a book that he clearly hoped would come to be regarded as being in the same league as John Maynard Keynes's General Theory or even Adam Smith's Wealth of Nations. The book was rapturously reviewed in the popular press, but it met with indifference from the academics. Galbraith's book wasn't what they considered real economic theory.

Not incidentally, the academics were right in believing that The New Industrial State could safely be ignored. History has not treated the book kindly. Galbraith began it in self-conscious imitation of Adam Smith's memorable description of a pin factory, with an account of the 1964 launch of the Ford Mustang. Starting from that example, he argued that technology was pushing us inevitably into an age of ever greater dominance by giant corporations.

These corporations would be able, through market research and advertising, to predict and indeed control demand for their products; they would be run by technocratic managers who would be increasingly independent of the stockholders who nominally owned the companies. And like the automobile companies, they would be virtually immune to the vagaries of market forces.

Need it be pointed out that none of this was remotely on target? The role of giant corporations in the U.S. economy has been shrinking, not rising, for the past two decades, with the great bulk of job growth among smaller firms. Many of our biggest companies—from Sears to IBM—have been spectacularly unable to get consumers to buy their wares. Those supposedly autonomous managers, far from being able to ignore stockholders, now live in terror of buyouts from investors willing to promise stockholders a higher return. And nobody, least of all the auto companies, has been insulated from the market.

The important point is not, however, that Galbraith was wrong (although it is interesting that his popular reputation as an economic guru seems not to have suffered at all from his errors). It is that after the failure of *The New Industrial State* to legitimize him as a serious thinker, he turned to increasingly bitter attacks on his fellow professors, ranging from his remarkably ill-informed *Economics in Perspective* (1987) to his more enjoyable 1992 novel *A Tenured Professor*.

The example of Galbraith is not an accidental one: in many ways, Galbraith broke important new ground in the relationship between politics and economics. He was the first celebrity economist (where the definition of a celebrity is the usual one: someone who is famous for being famous). His rise as a policy entrepreneur was one marker of the growing dominance of style (which he has in abundance) over substance in American political discourse, even among those who imagine themselves to be well informed about public affairs.

And yet Galbraith's influence never reached into the actual determination of policy. John F. Kennedy brought him into his administration, but literally put him as far from economic policy as possible by making him Ambassador to India. The actual architects of Kennedy's economic program were professors through and through. Indeed, Kennedy was the first President to elevate the chairman of the Council of Economic Advisers, an organization staffed by professors on leave, to cabinet rank; and his Council contained not one but two future winners of the Nobel Prize (James Tobin and Robert Solow).

It was only in the 1970s, faced with a desperate need to offer the public magical solutions, that politicians really began to take policy entrepreneurs seriously.

The Plot

We have seen the cast of characters for this book. Now let's look at the plot.

Act I, Scene I

It is the late 1960s. Whatever the great social and political divisions in America, there is broad agreement on economic policy: a combination of active management of the economy to achieve high employment, and a welfare state based on progressive taxation. Though a Republican, Richard Nixon declares that "we are all Keynesians now," and presides over a substantial expansion of social programs.

Among economists, however, the pendulum is swinging to the right. First Milton Friedman at the University of Chicago, then many other economists, offer new theories and evidence that seem to undermine the Keynesian faith that active government management can reduce or even stabilize unemployment. Their skepticism is given weight by the emergence of stagflation in the 1970s. Meanwhile, other economists, notably Harvard's Martin Feldstein, are starting to document the adverse effects of taxes and government programs on the incentives to work, save, and invest. As growth in U.S. living standards falters after 1973, the work of these economists becomes increasingly influential.

Act I, Scene II

It is the late 1970s. A powerful conservative political movement has arisen. The ideological core of this movement is a group of so-called supply-siders, who combine a rejection of Keynesianism with a belief that sharp tax cuts will produce a tremendous surge in economic growth, so much so that one need not worry about offsetting these cuts by reducing expenditures. The supply-siders draw some legitimacy for their ideas from economists like Martin Feldstein; but the supply-siders themselves are primarily journalists and political staffers, with only a few renegade professors.

When Ronald Reagan runs for President, he bases his campaign on supply-side ideas. Even fellow Republicans are aghast: George Bush calls it "voodoo economics." And the Republican establishment is sure that once in office, Reagan will turn to real experts for advice. But they are wrong: he goes through with the supply-side program. The policy entrepreneurs of the right have seized power.

Act II

It is the 1980s, and the conservatives are in power. They remain in power for twelve years, and the record is not encouraging. There is no spectacular collapse, no "hard landing," just a consistent failure to live up to promises. Economic growth does not accelerate—the magic does not come back. And new problems become increasingly apparent. Income distribution becomes rapidly more unequal, so that most Americans share little of the modest growth in income and many see their incomes decline. And for the first time in American history, the country begins to run large peacetime budget deficits. Much of this has very little to do with Ronald Reagan or George Bush, but the right claimed to have the answers, and failed to deliver. When a recession emerges at the beginning of the nineties, the hold of the conservative vision on voters' perceptions is broken.

Faced with a lackluster record in power, the policy entrepreneurs of the right change roles, from prophets to spin doctors. They take it upon themselves to deny that anything has gone wrong; they celebrate imagined achievements and proclaim triumph. Meanwhile, the conservative professors retreat into academicism.

ACT III, SCENE I

Even as the supply-siders are driving toward power, the pendulum of academic economics is swinging left. New theories of industrial organization, international trade, economic growth, and the business cycle emerge: all of these theories suggest that markets are less perfect, and the role of the government less malign, than the now reigning political orthodoxy would have it. By the mid-1980s, while the right surveys the political landscape in triumph, the world of academic research is fermenting with ideas like "strategic trade policy" and "new Keynesian macroeconomics"—ideas deeply at odds with doctrinaire laissez-faire principles.

As the failure of conservative economic policies to accelerate growth becomes apparent in the late 1980s, these new ideas begin to get some attention from the press and politicians. The ideas themselves are, however, relatively subtle and difficult to put into political slogans—even more so than the ideas of mainstream conservative economists during the 1970s. And the economists remain stubbornly professorial, refusing to lend themselves to any program that could serve as the core of a challenge to conservative simplicities.

ACT III, SCENE II

While liberal professors challenge conservative orthodoxy but fail to provide the kinds of answers that politicians want, a group of liberal policy entrepreneurs moves onto the scene. This group does not adopt a common label comparable to "supply-sider," but we can refer to their doctrine as "strategic trade." Strategic traders essentially view the United States as a giant corporation, competing with other countries in a global marketplace. And at least initially, the strategic traders assert that the magic can be put back into the U.S. economy with the same kind of strategic planning that had been fashionable among business consultants a few years before.

At a superficial level, the views of the strategic traders sound similar to those of the liberal economists. In fact, however, the economists are aghast at ideas that seem to them to be simplistic and dangerous. In the early 1980s there is an effective campaign by the economists to discredit strategic trade ideas. For the time being, it works: Democratic candidates for President in 1984 and 1988 run on conventional economic platforms. They also lose badly.

By the early 1990s, strategic trade is back. As the public becomes disillusioned with conservatism, it looks for a new vision, and finds the simplicities of strategic trade much more palatable than the subtleties of the professors. Strategic trade tracts like Reich's *Work of Nations* and Lester Thurow's *Head to Head* are best sellers. And the Democratic candidate has a long association with leading strategic traders, indeed may be said to be one himself.

The liberal professors are also quieter this time: the long rule of the right has made them more anxious to see a Democratic victory than to police the intellectual quality of their party's arguments. Like the conservative professors who backed Reagan in 1980, they cannot believe that what they perceive as the silliness of the policy entrepreneurs with whom they are allied will be allowed to govern real policy.

But they, too, are wrong.

The Plan of This Book

This book is divided into three main parts, corresponding to the three acts of the play we have just described.

Part I traces the rise of the conservative economic ideology. It begins with the impressive intellectual achievements of conservative economists: their challenge to Keynesianism and their critique of high taxation and the welfare state. Then it turns to the rise of those spectacularly successful policy entrepreneurs, the supply-siders.

Part II reviews the record of conservatism in power. It focuses on three main issues: the lackluster record of economic growth, the rapid increase in income inequality, and the relentless growth of budget deficits. A main theme here is the moral and intellectual decline of conservatism, as policy entrepreneurs tried to rationalize a disappointing record.

Part III tracks the swing of the intellectual pendulum: the revival of Keynesianism, the emergence of a new, more interventionist economic theory—and the rise of the strategic traders, the liberal equivalent of the supply-siders.

It's not a particularly edifying story. If you're looking for a morality play in which the good guys win at the end, you won't find it here: there aren't really any good guys, and in any case there certainly isn't any end. Not too many years ago the supply-siders were riding high; today, they are in almost pitiful disarray. The strategic traders have taken their place, but the wheel of fortune will turn for them too. If there is any underlying trend in ideology, it is not to right or left but toward a sort of non-partisan dumbing-down. Meanwhile, luckily, the economy seems remarkably resistant to all policies: throughout the 1980s its underlying rate of growth hardly budged. And in a final irony, there were some signs that as the 1990s began the magic was coming back to the U.S. economy, every bit as mysteriously as it went away.

Yet it is not all foolishness. There were marvelous, fascinating intellectual debates among economists from the 1970s through the 1990s. Never mind whether the arguments from those debates got translated accurately into policy; they increased our understanding, and in the end that is what will really matter.

PART I

THE RISE OF CONSERVATIVE ECONOMICS

CHAPTER 1

The Attack on Keynes

In 1981 Senator Daniel Patrick Moynihan uttered a startling pronouncement: "The Republicans," he declared, "are now the party of ideas." Moynihan was and is a moderate Democrat. He once served in the Nixon administration, and he earned the ire of many 1960s liberals both by his willingness to talk about the disintegration of black families and by his authorship of a leaked memo suggesting that the race issue be treated with "benign neglect." By 1980, however, the rightward shift of American politics had put Moynihan's positions well to the left of center, so this was a self-punishing admission.

Why would Moynihan say such a thing? Because as an unusually bookish politician, a former Harvard professor who prided himself on his intellectual honesty, Moynihan felt compelled to admit the impact of conservative ideas on American social thought, above all in economics. His generosity was refreshing and also ironic; for it came just at the moment when conservatism was simultaneously seizing real power and losing its soul, experiencing a process of intellectual and moral debasement.

But the main purpose of this chapter and the next is to trace the sources of conservatism's growing intellectual dominance among serious thinkers between the 1960s and about 1980. I want to show what it was that made the challenge from the right the dominant force in American economics and to a lesser extent in other fields for more than two decades. We will examine the coarsening and cheapening that happened to that challenge on the way to Washington, and the inward turning of its academic wing, in later chapters.

In this chapter, I will trace the rise of conservative thought in one crucial area: the rise of skepticism over government management of the business cycle.

The Business Cycle

There are many economic puzzles, but there are only two really great mysteries.

One of these mysteries is why economic growth takes places at different rates over time and across countries. Nobody really knows why the U.S. economy could generate 3 percent annual productivity growth before 1973 but only 1 percent afterward; nobody really knows why Japan surged from defeat to global economic power after World War II, while Britain slid slowly into third-rate status. At any given time there are always policy entrepreneurs willing to claim that they have all the answers; but we'll come to that story in later chapters.

The other mystery is the reason why there is a business cycle—the irregular rhythm of recessions and recoveries that prevents economic growth from being a smooth trend. It was in challenging the orthodox, Keynesian view of business cycles that conservatives first forced a major rethinking of economics.

To get some idea of just how important the business cycle is, look at Figure 1. The solid line in that figure traces the output of

the U.S. economy since 1973 (specifically, gross domestic product in 1987 dollars). The broken line shows a more abstract concept: the economy's "potential" output. This is an estimate of what
the economy could have produced in each year if it had been at
more or less full employment, defined for these purposes as a 5
percent unemployment rate. We'll turn in Chapter 4 to the question of how this potential output measure is constructed; for now,
take it on faith that the measurement of potential output is one of
the more solid and uncontroversial pieces of modern economic
analysis.

What we see in the figure is that potential output has grown
pretty steadily (at about 2.5 percent per year). Actual output has,
however, grown much less steadily. Indeed, sometimes output
actually falls, producing a gap between actual and potential output
that can exceed 10 percent; then it closes the gap with a spurt of
rapid growth. Those periods when output slumps below potential
are what we call recessions; those periods when it grows rapidly
and closes the gap are what we call recoveries.

Now think about what happens in a recession, such as the
prolonged slump from 1990 to 1992. If you believe that markets

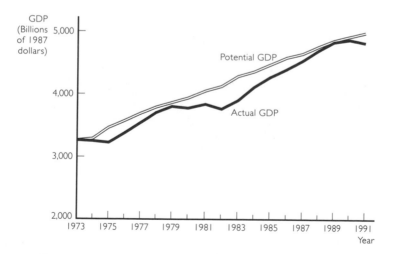

Figure 1. The actual output of the economy often falls below its potential.

are a pretty effective way to organize economic activity, you should be disturbed by the sight: a free-market economy in which large amounts of productive capacity are sitting idle, apparently being wasted. Factories stand unused, or on reduced shifts, even though they could be producing valuable goods and indeed were in full operation only a few months before. Willing workers cannot find jobs. Shops are half empty, though they had only recently been crowded with consumers. What is going on? We are all taught to understand the principle that markets match supply with demand; yet during a recession there seems to be supply everywhere, demand nowhere.

The phenomenon of recessions puzzled many economists in the early years of this century, and led many of them to produce their worst work. Thorstein Veblen went from his brilliant *Theory of the Leisure Class* to write a really terrible book (*The Engineers and the Price System*) purporting to explain economic slumps. Joseph Schumpeter, whose magnificent vision of the "creative destruction" inherent in capitalist growth continues to inspire many economists, wrote a turgid, almost meaningless two-volume study, *Business Cycles*. Marxists gleefully seized upon the biggest recession of all, the Great Depression of the 1930s, as evidence of the irrationality of capitalism; yet they never offered a good explanation of why and how such things happen, just assurances that socialism would cure them.

It fell to the British economist John Maynard Keynes to provide a clear story about what happens during a recession, and some useful advice about how to get out of one.

Let me give my own version of Keynes's story, which will set us up for an understanding of the attack on that story later posed by Milton Friedman and his successors.

Keynes's Theory of Recessions

Imagine for the moment an economy that is chugging along happily at full employment. All factories are working full shifts, all workers have jobs. (In reality this never happens, because there is always enough friction and uncertainty in the world to ensure that some factories are closing and some workers can't find jobs; but that isn't important at this stage of our story.) Alongside the smoothly functioning "real" economy will be a smooth financial flow, as firms earn money from their sales, pay out their earnings in wages and dividends, and households spend these receipts on new purchases from the firms.

But now suppose that for some reason each household and firm in this economy decides that it would like to hold a little more cash. There are a number of reasons, which we need not go into, why people hold some of their funds in the form of currency or bank deposits backed by currency rather than in other assets that yield higher returns. The important point is that sometimes they decide that they would prefer to hold more cash than they were holding a little while ago. Keynes argued, in particular, that this happens when businessmen lose confidence and start to think of potential investments as risky, leading them to hesitate and accumulate cash instead; today we might add the problem of jittery households who worry about their jobs and cut back on purchases of big-ticket consumer items. Either way, each individual firm or household tries to increase its holdings of cash by cutting its spending, so that its receipts exceed its outlays.

But as Keynes pointed out, what works for an individual does not work for the economy as a whole, because the amount of cash in the economy is fixed. An individual can increase her cash holdings by spending less, but she does so only by taking away cash that other people had been holding. Obviously, not everyone can do this at the same time. So what happens when everyone tries to accumulate cash simultaneously?

The answer is that income falls along with spending. I try to accumulate cash by reducing my purchases from you, and you try to accumulate cash by reducing your purchases from me; the result is that both of our incomes fall along with our spending, and neither of us succeeds in increasing our cash holdings.

If we remain determined to hold more cash, we will react to this disappointment by cutting our spending still further, with the same disappointing result; and so on and so on. Looking at the economy as a whole, you will see factories closing, workers laid off, stores empty, as firms and households throughout the economy cut back on spending in a collectively vain effort to accumulate more cash. The process only reaches a limit when incomes are so shrunken that the demand for cash falls to equal the available supply.

That is Keynes's story. It's pretty simple, yet it has caused an astonishing amount of confusion; somehow even intelligent people seem to find it difficult and abstract. As it happens, however, we can illustrate the essence of Keynesianism with an example that is, literally, childishly simple.

INFANTILE KEYNESIANISM

Nobody can hold a picture of the reality of the U.S. economy, with its hundreds of thousands of firms and hundred million workers, in his or her head. Inevitably we must rely on models—that is, some kind of simplified representation that we hope gets at the essence of the question we are trying to answer. Part of what distinguishes professors and policy entrepreneurs is the kind of model that they prefer. Policy entrepreneurs generally prefer their models in the form of metaphors: for example, they may describe the U.S. economy as being like a corporation, competing in the world marketplace. Professors generally prefer their models mathematical. Each of these preferences has disadvantages: mathematical models can be constricting, leading you to ignore what you haven't figured out how to represent as an equation; metaphorical models can all too easily create a false impression of understanding and sophistication, and those who rely exclusively on metaphor often fail to notice that their fine phrases are covering crude conceptual or factual mistakes.

In the physical and biological sciences, however, there is a third kind of model: the experimental model. My personal favorite example is the work of the great meteorological theorist Carl-Gustaf Rossby, who found that the essential features of global weather can be simulated by placing a pan filled with water on a slowly rotating turntable and gently heating its rim. Experimental models can allow you to see, on a small scale, the essence of events that occur in the vastly larger and more complex real world.

Unfortunately, experimental models are hard to come by in economics, for obvious practical and moral reasons. There is a limited literature on experimental auctions and other market mechanisms, some anti-poverty schemes have been tried out with pilot projects, and so on; but how could you experimentally produce recessions and recoveries?

Well, it turns out that a group of Washington, D.C., professionals inadvertently created a sort of experimental macroeconomy during the 1970s. Their unhappy experiences are described in a whimsical article by Joan and Richard Sweeney in the *Journal of Money, Credit and Banking* (February 1977), entitled "Monetary Theory and the Great Capitol Hill Baby-Sitting Co-Op Crisis."

Here's the story. A group of young professional couples with children formed a baby-sitting co-op: that is, they set up an arrangement to look after each other's children. Any such arrangement requires some method to make sure that the burden gets fairly allocated. What this co-op did was introduce a self-regulating bookkeeping system, by issuing scrip: coupons worth one hour of baby-sitting. Every hour of baby-sitting would involve a transfer of a coupon to the baby-sitters from the baby-sittees.

If you think about it a bit, you will realize that such a system requires that there be a fair amount of scrip in circulation. Couples cannot predict exactly when they will want to go out, or when they will be free to baby-sit for others, so on average they will want to keep a reserve of coupons available in case they want or need to go out several times before earning some more scrip by sitting for others.

After the co-op had been in existence for some time, it got into trouble. For reasons that we needn't get into, the number of coupons in circulation per couple became rather low. This had peculiar consequences. Since on average members of the co-op had fewer coupons in hand than the reserve they wanted, couples tried to increase their reserves by baby-sitting more and going out less. But one couple's decision to go out is another couple's opportunity to baby-sit, so the increased caution of the co-op's members about spending their coupons made it increasingly difficult to find chances to earn coupons—which further reinforced the mood of caution. The result was a sharp fall in the volume of baby-sitting actually taking place: couples sat glumly at home, unwilling to take a night out until they had accumulated more scrip, unable to accumulate more scrip because nobody else was going out either.

In other words, the baby-sitting co-op had managed to get itself into a recession.

Since the co-op consisted primarily of lawyers, it was hard to convince its officers that the problem was essentially monetary. Instead, at first they tried regulatory solutions—for example, instituting a rule requiring that each couple go out at least twice a month. Only after a considerable time did the co-op increase the quantity of scrip in circulation. When it did, the results were (to the lawyers) miraculous: couples began going out more, making baby-sitting opportunities more plentiful, which made couples still more willing to go out, and so on.

Of course the story didn't end there. The expansion in the supply of scrip was overdone, leading to incipient problems of inflation . . .

The moral of this story is that the study of recessions and recoveries is not some deep or mystical subject. The details are complex; but understanding the essence of what happens can be, well, child's play.

KEYNES AND ECONOMIC POLICY

It should be pretty obvious that the Keynesian analysis of recessions offers not only a story about why recessions happen, but some guidance about what to do to end them.

The first, and most obvious, thing to do is to make it possible for people to satisfy their demand for more cash without cutting their spending, preventing the downward spiral of shrinking spending and shrinking income. (That's the solution that worked for the baby-sitting co-op.) The way to do this is simply to print more money, and somehow get it into circulation. Keynes whimsically suggested hiding bottles full of cash where enterprising boys might find them; Milton Friedman was later to offer the image of currency dropped randomly from helicopters. Fortunately for the dignity of monetary policy, there is a more respectable method: in a so-called open-market operation, the Federal Reserve buys U.S. government debt, paying for it with newly created money, which is thereby injected into the economy and put into circulation.

Keynes's analysis suggested, then, that a developing recession can be cured through an expansionary monetary policy: by increasing the supply of money, the monetary authority (in the United States, the Federal Reserve) can induce firms and households to resume the smooth, circular flow of spending and production that keeps the economy near full employment.

A good example of this Keynesian prescription in practice came in the aftermath of the stock market crash of 1987. During one terrifying week in October 1987, stock prices abruptly plunged, falling 23 percent in five days—slightly worse than the fall following Black Thursday in 1929. This crash was both a reflection of declining investor confidence and a potential cause of a further fall in confidence, and in the face of a passive Federal Reserve this loss of confidence could quite easily have led to a severe economic slump. But the Federal Reserve was not passive. It aggressively expanded the money supply, to such good effect that there was no slump at all: output actually rose faster in the year after the crash than in the year before. (And the stock market itself recovered and soared to new heights.)

So the usual and basic Keynesian answer to recessions is a monetary expansion. But Keynes worried that even this might sometimes not be enough, particularly if a recession had been allowed to get out of hand and become a true depression. Once the economy is deeply depressed, households and especially firms may be unwilling to increase spending no matter how much cash they have; they may simply add any monetary expansion to their hoard. Such a situation, in which monetary policy has become ineffective, has come to be known as a "liquidity trap"; Keynes believed that the British and American economies had entered such a trap by the mid-1930s, and some economists believed that the United States was on the edge of such a trap in 1992.

The Keynesian answer to a liquidity trap is for the government to do what the private sector will not: spend. When monetary expansion is ineffective, fiscal expansion—such as public works programs financed by borrowing—must take its place. Such a fiscal expansion can break the vicious circle of low spending and low incomes, "priming the pump" and getting the economy moving again. But remember that this is not by any means an all-purpose policy recommendation; it is essentially a strategy of desperation, a dangerous drug to be prescribed only when the usual over-the-counter remedy of monetary policy has failed.

Throughout the thirties, Keynes and his intellectual allies campaigned unsuccessfully for large-scale public works spending to lift the Anglo-American economies out of the Depression. They never got their wish, because too many objections were always raised. Eventually, however, the Depression was ended by the one kind of public works program that even conservatives are willing to support: a war.

This, then, in a highly simplified nutshell, is the Keynesian theory of recession and recovery. The theory remains one of the great achievements of economic thought.

Like any major intellectual contribution, Keynes's ideas were bitterly criticized. To many people it seems obvious that massive economic slumps must have deep roots. To them, Keynes's argument that they are essentially no more than a problem of mixed signals, which can be cured by printing a bit more money, seems unbelievable. (It is reported that Franklin Roosevelt, early in his administration, received a memo suggesting a large monetary expansion to fight the Depression. He is supposed to have dismissed it with the comment, "Too easy.")

Leftists have also long been uncomfortable with Keynes. Since Marx, they have regarded the business cycle as evidence of the instability and ultimate unsustainability of capitalism; they are dismayed at the suggestion that it is a technical problem that can be fixed without any major change in institutions.

The greatest hostility to Keynes has, however, always come from the right.

Why do conservatives hate Keynesian economics? Part of the answer is that they dislike Keynes the man—aesthete, homosexual, and member of the dread Bloomsbury group. Indeed, the historian Gertrude Himmelfarb, attacking Virginia Woolf and her friends, has been explicit in tying the rejection of Keynesian economics to the Republican concern for family values: "There is a discernible affinity between the Bloomsbury ethos, which put a premium on immediate and present satisfactions, and Keynesian economics, which is based entirely on the short run and precludes any long-term judgements. . . ." This is silly stuff—can you see anything licentious in the theory described above? Yet Ms. Himmelfarb's remarks should be viewed as symptomatic of one strand in the conservative opposition to Keynesianism, which is opposed not so much to the logic of his ideas as to what conservatives perceive as their moral implications.

More seriously, conservatives have disliked Keynes because of the justification he seems to have given for an expanded role of government. Keynes's theory of a recession sees it as a situation in which private markets have gotten into a kind of traffic snarl, a snarl that government action can help untangle. He himself was no socialist, nor were most of his followers; they saw their ideas as a way to make capitalism run better, not a reason to replace it. Yet conservatives have always regarded Keynesian economics as the thin end of the wedge for a wholesale intrusion of government into the marketplace, and have searched for alternatives and refutations to Keynesianism.

And in this they were very successful. From the 1950s through the 1980s, Keynesian ideas were subjected to an increasingly withering conservative critique, to such an extent that by 1982 Edward Prescott of Carnegie-Mellon University would proudly declare that students at his university never heard Keynes's name. We need to understand the force of that critique to understand why, for so long, the intellectual right had the intellectual left on the run.

Milton Friedman I: Monetarism

Milton Friedman may well be the world's best-known economist. He has turned his unprepossessing stature and manner into a trademark persona: a feisty conservative David battling the Goliath of Big Government. But his influence is not merely a matter of skill at propaganda. It rests on the long campaign that he waged against the ideas of Keynesian economics, a campaign that eventually bore fruit in radical changes in both economic ideology and real-world economic policy.

Friedman has always been a strong advocate of free-market policies—he first became well known with a pamphlet criticizing postwar rent controls. It's therefore likely that Friedman's initial distaste for Keynesian economics had a strong political motivation. Keynesian theory almost inevitably points the way to a more active, interventionist government than Friedman and his colleagues at the University of Chicago could stomach, a government that tries to "finetune" the economy by pumping money in or pulling it out, starting and stopping public works projects. And some of Keynes's followers—like Friedman's followers a few decades later—were far cruder and more extreme than their idol. There was a time in the 1940s and 1950s when a sort of vulgar Keynesianism was used to justify a huge array of statist policies around the world, perhaps most damagingly in newly independent nations which all too eagerly used their new powers to strangle their still fragile private sectors. So, Milton Friedman and his friends would have had good political reasons to attack Keynes even if they had been unable to find good economic arguments.

But they had some pretty good economic arguments, too.

The first stage of Friedman's attack on Keynes was his effective though somewhat slippery critique of the idea that monetary and fiscal policy can be actively used to smooth out the business cycle. Friedman argued that such active policy is not only unnecessary but actually harmful, worsening the very economic instability that it is supposed to correct, and should be replaced by simple, mechanical monetary rules. This is the doctrine that came to be known as "monetarism."

Friedman began with a factual claim: most recessions, including the huge slump that initiated the Great Depression, did not follow Keynes's script. That is, they did not arise because the private sector was trying to increase its holdings of a fixed amount of money. Rather, they occurred because of a fall in the quantity of money in circulation.

Why was this claim important? Because it undermined the case for active efforts to stabilize the economy. If economic slumps begin when people spontaneously decide to increase their money holdings, then the monetary authority must monitor the economy and pump money in when it finds a slump is imminent. If such slumps are always created by a fall in the quantity of money, then the monetary authority need not monitor the economy; it need only make sure that the quantity of money doesn't slump. In other words, a straightforward rule—"Keep the money supply steady"—is good enough, so that there is no need for a "discretionary" policy of the form, "Pump money in when your economic advisers think a recession is imminent."

And Friedman went on to argue that discretion does more harm than good. One might make this point simply by arguing that any policy that relies on good advice from your economists is unlikely to work very well! Aside from general distrust of his colleagues, however, Friedman had a more solid point. He argued that the historical record shows that changes in monetary policy do not get reflected in the economy until quite some time after they occur—and that the length of time they need to take effect is itself rather unpredictable. In what came to be a famous phrase among economists (who are admittedly short on eloquence), he claimed that monetary policy works with "long and variable lags." And as a result of these long and variable lags, monetary policy that tried to smooth out the business cycle would actually end up making it worse.

Consider the following analogy. Imagine that your house is heated by a furnace that is controlled by a thermostat. Such a system works through feedback. When the house gets a little too warm, the thermostat shuts off the furnace; the house then cools down until the thermostat turns the furnace on again; it warms up; and so on. If this feedback works quickly enough, the effect will be to keep the temperature of the house fairly even, fluctuating within only a narrow range.

But suppose that the feedback is slow. Suppose, for example, that you have old radiators that take twenty minutes to respond to the furnace, and that the thermostat has been put in a remote room that is the last part of the house either to warm up or to cool down. Then, instead of keeping the temperature of the house even, the system will make it fluctuate wildly. Let the house be a little too warm: then the thermostat will shut off the heat, and will not turn it on again until the main part of the house is freezing; it will then set the heat blasting, and will not turn it off until the main rooms are excessively hot; and round again. The temperature in the house would have been more stable if you threw away the thermostat and simply kept the furnace running at a constant rate.

Friedman argued that this was what was happening to monetary policy. Suppose that a recession began to develop. Friedman argued that it would take a while before the Federal Reserve would become aware of the recession and convinced that action should be taken. Then this action would itself be slow in affecting the actual economy, so much so that instead of helping to stop the recession it would all too often reinforce an already excessive subsequent boom; when the Fed realized this, it would pull back, helping to plunge the economy into a new recession; and so on.

By trying to help, the Fed would actually be making matters worse.

What Friedman therefore proposed was that the Fed abandon any active monetary policy and instead follow a strategy more or less equivalent to that of leaving the furnace on a constant setting: keep the money supply steady, growing slowly at a rate consistent with stable prices and long-run economic growth, which for the United States meant 3–4 percent per year. Friedman argued that the inherent stability of the private economy was such that given this kind of monetary rule, the business cycle would be considerably less of a problem than it had been with active efforts to combat it.

If active monetary policy was to be ruled out, active fiscal policy looked even further out of line. If a monetary rule was already keeping the economy stable, then an attempt to stimulate employment through public spending (or, for that matter, through tax cuts—an important point we'll have to remember) would accomplish nothing of value. All that it would do would be to force the government to borrow, pulling savings away from private investments into the purchase of government debt; so instead of a net economic expansion, expansionary fiscal policy would produce "crowding out" of productive investment.

You can see why conservatives, opposed to a large role for the state, would like this analysis. Friedman was telling them that a government that rejected Keynesianism, that abandoned any effort to manage the business cycle and instead adhered to a simple monetary rule, would not only be less intrusive but would actually preside over a more stable economy.

But was Friedman right? He certainly scored some points. Changes in the money supply have played much more of a role in creating recessions, including the Great Depression, than the crude Keynesians who flourished in the 1950s were willing to admit. Monetary policy does require a long and uncertain time to take effect, and has therefore sometimes made matters worse instead of better. And attempts to end recessions with government spending programs all too often end up delivering their peak effect in the middle of the next recovery instead, when they can and do crowd out private investment. So, much of his critique was right.

Yet at a fundamental level monetarism was and is unconvincing to serious thinkers. Friedman's claims about the dominant role of money in business cycles, for example, rested rather heavily on his willingness to play games with the definition of "money." Money is traditionally defined either as what the Federal Reserve actually issues—cash in circulation plus the reserves held by banks—or as the total sums that can be used directly as a means of payment, cash plus checking accounts. Friedman, however, always insisted on broader definitions of money, so-called monetary aggregates, that include a variety of deposits and financial instruments, among them things like savings deposits (on which you can't write checks) and money market accounts (which often have large minimum check sizes). Such broad monetary aggregates are more like measures of the size of the whole financial sector than they are measures of the availability of cash or close substitutes for cash.

Now the problem with this kind of broad measure is that you start to have trouble distinguishing cause and effect. If you find that a Friedman-type broad definition of money always declines in recessions, does this say that monetary policy caused the recession—or does it just say that during a recession everything in the economy, including the size of the financial sector, tends to go down?

The central case in point is the onset of the Great Depression. In the United States, the Depression began as a sharp but not catastrophic recession in 1929–1930, then turned into an incredible plunge that left output a third lower than its 1929 peak. Friedman attributed this plunge to a sharp contraction in his monetary aggregates, implying that the economic collapse was the result of bad Federal Reserve policy rather than any inherent instability of the private sector. But the Federal Reserve did not actually pull money out of the system. What happened instead was that a wave of bank failures, which proved self-reinforcing as it led to runs on banks that might otherwise have survived, generated fears about the safety of deposits of all kinds. Families began hoarding currency instead of putting their money in banks; banks that survived the first panic began holding large quantities of cash in their vaults, so that they could pay off nervous depositors and head off any incipient run; and so although the actual amount of cash in circulation had not fallen, it supported a much smaller volume of deposits.

Now, what does this say about monetary policy? In his role as monetarist propagandist, Friedman told the story as if it were the following: "The Federal Reserve contracted the money supply, plunging a private economy that would otherwise have been pretty stable into a depression." This sounds like a strong argument for the proposition that markets should be left alone. But his actual story was: "The Federal Reserve failed to inject cash into the economy as the banking system was collapsing of its own accord; if the Fed had injected enough cash to stabilize my preferred monetary aggregate, the slump would have been much milder." In fact, Friedman accepts the principle that the Federal Reserve should have been doing *something;* he only argues that it should have aimed at stabilizing a broad monetary aggregate, not the still broader target of the economy itself.

And once we are talking about tactics rather than the basic philosophy of economic policy, it becomes hard to justify a rigid monetarist position. Of course the Fed should beware of trying to overmanage the economy in such a way that it actually makes matters worse, but does that necessarily mean that 3 percent growth in the target monetary aggregate is the best policy? It is hard to make that case either on logical grounds or on the record—especially as financial deregulation and innovation have made the definition of what is and is not money (money market funds? credit card limits?) ever harder to spell out.

On the whole, the monetarism for which Friedman first became famous seems clever, brilliantly argued, but shallow—and perhaps even a bit disingenuous. Friedman's writings from that period have the feel of a smart man who knows what he wants to believe looking hard for supporting arguments. And I think it is fair to say that up until the late 1960s Friedman and his followers, while influential, were regarded by many of their colleagues as faintly disreputable.

But at the end of the 1960s Friedman found another, even more effective, line of attack on Keynesianism.

Milton Friedman II: Stagflation

Keynesian economics suggests that it is usually pretty easy to get out of a recession: Just print money, and watch the wheels of commerce start to spin again. By providing enough cash, one should be able to get the economy back to a high level of employment.

But what happens if a government, for whatever reason, continues to print money in large quantities even when the economy is at full employment? (The usual reason governments do this is to finance a budget deficit.) The answer is obvious: Once there are no longer idle factories and workers to draw into production, printing money will no longer raise production; it will simply raise prices.

Now Keynes always understood this. Keynes's first great book was not his famous *General Theory of Employment, Interest and Money,* but his *Tract on Monetary Reform* (1923), an analysis of the hyperinflations that exploded in much of Europe after World War I. Thus Keynesian economics never called for expanding the economy without limit. Instead, it called for expanding the economy up to full employment, but no further. And it called for reining in the money supply when necessary in order to prevent inflation.

But the simple prescription, "Expand the economy up to full employment, but not beyond," runs into difficulties when you try to put it into practice. Some of the difficulties are technical: for the reasons emphasized by the monetarists, in the real world it is not possible to steer the economy very accurately. More fundamental is the problem of defining "full employment."

In my presentation of Keynes's story about a recession, I began by imagining an economy in which all factories are busy and all willing workers are employed, then noted parenthetically that in reality this never happens. Here is where that qualification becomes important. In the real world, change and uncertainty prevent the economy from ever achieving truly full employment. Some workers are always being fired, temporarily laid off, or quitting, no matter how good conditions are; new workers are always looking for their first job, or returning to the labor force after an absence. Labor market statistics, which count as unemployed all those who are looking for a job but have not yet found or taken one, therefore show some unemployment even in the midst of a runaway boom. At the height of the "Massachusetts Miracle," when McDonald's was offering twice the minimum wage and trying to entice senior citizens out of retirement, the measured unemployment rate in Massachusetts was still 2.7 percent. Since 1973, the national unemployment rate has never dipped below 5 percent.

What this means is that there is no obvious line to tell us that the national economy is at full employment. At 7 percent unemployment there is clearly a lot of unused capacity; at 6 percent much less; at 5 percent the economy begins to look overheated; but there is no clearly marked red line.

Correspondingly, there is no sharp dividing line at which expanding the money supply stops raising output and starts raising prices. Instead, there *seems* to be a relatively smooth tradeoff between unemployment and inflation. (We'll see shortly why Friedman argued that the apparent tradeoff is an illusion.)

In 1959 A. W. Phillips of the London School of Economics noted that in long-term British statistics there was a visible relationship between the unemployment rate and the rate of change of wages. In years in which the unemployment rate was very high, wages had fallen; in years in which it was low, wages had risen, and the lower the unemployment rate the higher the rate of wage increase. American economists quickly found a similar relationship in U.S. data. This so-called Phillips curve seemed to quantify the tradeoff between unemployment and inflation. Figure 2 shows what the tradeoff looked like in the 1960s. The evidence seemed to suggest that price stability would require something like a 7 percent unemployment rate, but that if the country was willing to accept an inflation rate of 3 or 4 percent, it could achieve an unemployment rate of only 4 percent.

The discovery of the Phillips curve seemed to suggest a more discretionary view of policy than the original Keynesian prescription of "Expand the economy up to full employment." Since full employment was no longer precisely defined, a value judgment appeared to be involved instead: "Expand the economy up to the point where you think that the cost of higher inflation outweighs the benefit of lower unemployment."

Now it also happens to be the case that the costs of inflation, at least at modest rates, are elusive. Suppose, for example, that we compare two imaginary economies, one with stable prices and one that is identical except that it has 5 percent inflation. If every price and wage in the second economy simply rises 5 percent faster than in the first, why should anyone care? After all, everyone's real income will be exactly the same.

Meanwhile the costs of unemployment are very clear. So it

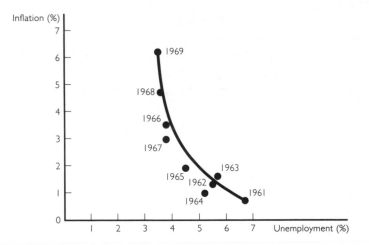

Figure 2. During the 1960s, it seemed that there was a tradeoff between unemployment and inflation . . .

seemed to be a natural conclusion from the orthodox economics of the 1960s that government policy should accept a persistent inflation rate of, say, 4 or 5 percent as an acceptable price for keeping unemployment low. This conclusion was actually written into law: the much-ignored Humphrey-Hawkins bill of 1978 in fact requires the U.S. government to seek to achieve a 4 percent unemployment rate. And some economists went even further. For example, in 1968 Lester Thurow advocated a national policy of 3 percent unemployment, accepting the inflationary consequences, as a necessary condition for getting minority groups out of the vicious circle of poverty.

Of course nothing like this happened. Since 1973 the unemployment rate has never fallen below 5 percent, and has risen as high as 10.7 percent. And yet we have hardly had stable prices: inflation since 1973 has averaged 6.2 percent annually, going as high as 13 percent.

Milton Friedman was not surprised. In 1968, in one of the decisive intellectual achievements of postwar economics, Friedman not only showed why the apparent tradeoff embodied in the idea of the Phillips curve was wrong; he also predicted the emergence of combined inflation and high unemployment, which Paul Samuelson dubbed "stagflation."

Friedman was not the only economist to criticize the Phillips curve. From about 1965 on, there had been a growing sense among economists that there was something fishy about the idea of a long-term tradeoff between unemployment and inflation. Ideas very similar to Friedman's were expressed at about the same time and with considerably more rigor by Edmund S. Phelps, an "economist's economist" at Columbia who was not particularly political. But Friedman took center stage by choosing to unveil his theory of stagflation in a highly visible way, in his presidential address to the American Economic Association.

Friedman began, like Keynes, with a thought experiment. Suppose, he asked, that I were to double the quantity of money in circulation—but also to double all prices and wages. What would happen to the unemployment rate?

The answer, pretty clearly, is nothing. If all prices and wages are twice what they were, and the quantity of money in circulation has also kept pace, nothing *real* about the economy has changed. In effect, all that has happened is a change of accounting units—as if the British, instead of using pounds sterling worth (at time of writing) about 2 German marks, were to use marks instead. Nobody thinks that would matter, and neither would Friedman's hypothetical doubling of money and prices.

So far, Friedman was enunciating a familiar proposition, generally known as that of the *neutrality of money*. But now he went on to turn it into a crucial policy idea.

How can it be, asked Friedman, that if I could double the money supply without any real effects, an increase in the money supply by the Federal Reserve *does* have real effects? Why is it that a 5 percent increase in the money supply does not immediately raise prices by 5 percent, but instead raises prices (initially, at least) by only a little and leads to a rise in output instead? His answer was startling: An increase in money does not get reflected one-for-one in prices because firms and workers are *fooled*. Workers set their wage demands too low, because they underestimate the coming rate of inflation. Firms set their prices too low because they underestimate the coming rise in their wage and supplier costs. Perhaps no single worker or firm makes a very big mistake, but all the mistakes are in the same direction, and they cumulate, because my price is part of your cost, and vice versa. The end result is that a 5 percent rise in the money supply raises prices much less than 5 percent, and correspondingly raises output instead.

According to Friedman, the apparent tradeoff between output and inflation seen in the Phillips curve in effect represents the history of occasions in which unexpectedly high or low inflation caught markets off guard. Observations of low unemployment represent cases in which markets were surprised by unusually high inflation; observations of high unemployment cases of surprisingly low inflation.

And now comes the moral of the story: You can fool all of the people some of the time, but you can't fool them all of the time. Suppose that the government of a country were to try to follow the advice of some 1960s economists and to trade off, say, 5 percent inflation for 3 percent unemployment. This might work for a little while; but according to Friedman, markets would soon catch on. Workers and firms would start to build that 5 percent inflation rate into their expectations, so that to surprise them you would have to have more than 5 percent inflation—and anything less would represent a surprise in the opposite direction, leading to a recession. After a while you would need to accept 5 percent inflation just to keep unemployment at a level that used to be associated with stable prices, and 10 percent inflation to get what you used to be able to achieve with 5.

Thus Friedman argued that any attempt to use the Phillips curve to trade off higher inflation for lower unemployment would cause that curve to disappear: you would end up paying a higher and higher price in inflation for low unemployment, and when that price became unacceptable, you would discover that inflation would persist even in the face of high unemployment.

And that's just what happened. Figure 3 shows what happened to the unemployment-inflation relationship from the 1960s through the 1980s. What looked like a stable Phillips curve from 1960 to 1969, as the economy went through a long phase of expansion, fell apart as inflationary expectations got built into the economy. A recession from 1969 to 1971, induced deliberately by the Nixon administration in an effort to control inflation, was notably unsuccessful. During the 1970s the economy managed to have both high unemployment and high inflation.

So Friedman was right, on a very big issue. His insight deservedly raised his prestige and that of the Chicago School of economics to new heights, and gave his earlier, monetarist critique of Keynesianism new respectability. But it is important to realize the limits of what Friedman's analysis of stagflation achieved.

What Friedman showed was that it was not possible to use monetary expansion to aim for some arbitrary target of "full em-

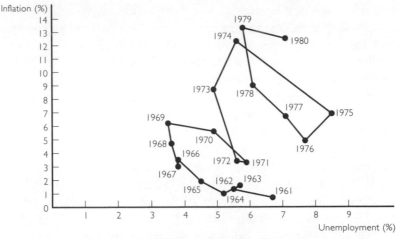

Figure 3 . . . But that tradeoff fell apart, just as Milton Friedman had predicted.

ployment" without leading ultimately to unacceptable inflation. The best one could hope for was to try to keep the economy near the unemployment rate that it tended to achieve when the actual rate of inflation was more or less the same as that which workers and firms expected. Friedman dubbed this the "natural rate"; other economists, disliking the implied satisfaction with, say, 6 percent unemployment, have used such terms as the "non-accelerating-inflation rate of unemployment," or NAIRU. Most estimates of the natural rate in the 1990s place it at 6 percent or a little lower.

The conclusion that one can at best try to achieve the natural rate was a bucket of very cold water on the heads of economists who had gotten carried away with the possibilities of government management of the economy. But one can accept this conclusion without at all accepting the larger Friedman claim, that the government should get out of the business of economic management altogether.

The point is that nothing in Friedman's natural rate argument suggests that the private economy, left to its own devices, tends to keep unemployment more or less stable near the natural rate. *On average* the economy should more or less achieve the natural rate, but it may oscillate wildly around it; one may still advocate Keynesian policies to try to stabilize the economy. Friedman would then presumably argue that such policies will do more harm than good, for the usual monetarist reasons. As we have seen, the monetarist argument—as opposed to the natural rate story—is more clever than convincing.

There is, however, an extension of Friedman's argument that completes the conservative case against Keynesian economics: the "rational expectations" argument of Robert Lucas and his disciples. This is an argument that Friedman himself has never endorsed, perhaps because he is at root too sensible to buy into its assumptions. But during the 1970s the theory of rational expectations was so influential that it seemed as if Keynesian economics might be pushed completely into oblivion.

Rational Expectations

When Keynes published his theory of the business cycle, some conservative economists argued that there was no need for government policy to combat recessions because recessions would be self-correcting. Their argument went as follows: In the face of high unemployment, wages and prices will tend to fall. This fall in wages and prices will increase the *real* supply of money—that is, the given stock of money in circulation will have steadily rising purchasing power. And this expansion in the real supply of money will in turn lead to an economic expansion.

Keynes did not deny the logic of this so-called classical argument; he was willing to concede that in the long run economic slumps would be self-correcting. But he regarded this self-correcting process as very slow, and as he pointed out in a widely quoted but rarely understood remark, "In the long run we are all dead." What he meant was: Recessions may eventually cure themselves. But that's no more a reason to ignore policies that can end them quickly than the fact of eventual mortality is a reason to give up on living.

One might have thought that Keynes had thereby killed the

case for inaction in the face of recessions. But in the 1970s, Robert Lucas, an economist at the University of Chicago, offered a renewed version of the classical argument. He combined the Friedman-Phelps theory of inflation and unemployment with another idea, that of "rational expectations," to suggest that Keynes's long run might not be so long after all.

Lucas's name, unlike Friedman's, is hardly a household word. He is neither a prolific writer nor easy to read; although he can write clear, forceful English when he chooses, he prefers to express himself through dense mathematics, leaving it to others to popularize his ideas. Where Friedman used his academic notoriety as a stepping stone to a wider public role, Lucas has in recent years seemed to retreat to safe, increasingly technical issues of theoretical economics. And yet for most of the 1970s there was little question that Robert Lucas was having more impact on economic thought, both through his own writings and through the extraordinary devotion of his intellectual disciples, than any other working economist. Above all, he became identified with a much stronger form of Friedman's argument against active monetary policy. Where Friedman argued that such policy would *in practice* do more harm than good, Lucas argued that *in principle* it could do nothing but harm.

To understand Lucas's argument, let's replay our original Keynesian recession scenario. We suppose that for some reason everybody in the economy decides that they want to hold more money, and are prepared to cut spending in order to accumulate more cash.

Now a follower of Lucas would point out that there need not be an economic contraction in this scenario. Suppose that every firm immediately cuts its prices, and that every worker immediately reduces her wage demands. Then the purchasing power of the money in circulation will be increased, satisfying the demand for more cash without any need either for a slump or for government intervention to increase the money supply.

Why, then, are there sometimes recessions? Lucas echoed Friedman in asserting that recessions happen because people get confused. I know that I am trying to increase my money holdings, but I don't know that you are trying to do the same thing. I see that the demand for my product has fallen, but I don't know whether this is a temporary event specific to me, which does not call for a price cut, or a general deflation, which does. And so I hesitate, or equivocate, reducing my prices only a little. And everyone else does the same, so that initially there is an economic slump.

The recession is, however, self-correcting as soon as people realize that it really is a general slump. Once they realize that everyone is trying to hoard cash, and that the falling demand they face is not specific to them, firms will cut their prices to the point where the natural rate of unemployment is restored. The long run, claimed Lucas, is not when we are all dead; it is when we all understand the economic situation.

What is left for monetary policy in this story? One might think that there is still a role. After all, the recession that follows the increase in money demand may be no more than a product of people's confusion, but it is real and painful nonetheless. Why not seek to cut it short by providing cash rather than waiting for prices to fall?

Here is where "rational expectations" come into the story. The concept of rational expectations, originally introduced by Richard Muth in the early 1960s, was a strategy for economic modeling. Muth suggested that we should normally assume that firms make efficient use of all the information available to them. They may make mistakes, because the future is always uncertain, but we should beware of any model that supposes that they make systematic, predictable mistakes.

Lucas pointed out that the hypothesis of rational expectations implies that if firms are confused about the appropriate price to charge for their products, this is honest, reasonable, *appropriate* confusion. They just cannot tell yet. And thus if we are to suppose that the monetary authority can improve on the outcome, it must be because it has better information than the firms do. But in general, argued Lucas, the Federal Reserve has no more to go on than the same kinds of information about business conditions that are available to anyone who can buy a good business newspaper. Thus monetary policy could not, he argued, actually hasten recovery from a recession.

Moreover, Lucas went on to argue that *any* predictable monetary policy would be ineffective. Suppose that it becomes known that the Federal Reserve typically increases the money supply by 1 percent every time the published unemployment rate goes up by 1 point. Then, claimed Lucas, firms will build that typical policy into their expectations and pricing policy, and every time the measured unemployment rate goes up they will mark up their prices accordingly, ensuring that the monetary expansion affects only prices, not output.

The only way monetary policy could "work," then, would be to be unpredictable—and the only way to be consistently unpredictable is to be random. A random monetary policy, however, would by definition make output more unstable, not less! So Lucas seemed to have shown that as a matter of sheer logic, activist government policy to stabilize the business cycle would either be ineffective or actually counterproductive.

At this point, readers may want to take a deep breath. Lucas's conclusions are far more sweeping than anything Friedman proposed, and his chain of logic seems much longer. Is it necessarily right?

The short answer is, of course, no. There are at least two weak links in the chain. The first is the proposition that a recession lasts only as long as firms are confused about the actual economic situation—in effect, that you can have a recession only as long as most people don't notice. This idea was implicit in the way that Friedman presented his natural rate argument, but it is something that few people other than economists find plausible (and it is possible to accept Friedman's views about stagflation without fully buying his notion that monetary policy works only by fooling people). The second weak link is the whole idea that firms set their prices by closely watching monetary policy or, worse yet, macroeconomic indicators that might help predict monetary policy.

The point is that unlike Friedman's argument, which seemed on reflection more sensible than the view that one can cheerfully choose a point on the Phillips curve, Lucas's theory seems to fly in the face of our workaday perceptions about how firms and households really behave. That observation does not by itself amount to a refutation of his theory, but it suggests that something is wrong; in Part III of this book we'll try to figure out specifically what's wrong with the Lucas view, and how setting it right brings us back to Keynes.

What's important at this stage is to realize that however strange Lucas's logic may seem to the layperson, for a period of a decade or so his ideas dominated academic discussion of the business cycle. The rational expectations approach swept all before it, pushing Keynesians into an intellectual corner from which they have only recently started to emerge.

How could such a difficult, technical intellectual structure acquire the force first of a crusade, then of a dogma? (And how could a man as reserved and quiet as Lucas take on for a time the role of Ayatollah?) There are probably three reasons.

First, Lucas's approach to macroeconomics seemed to offer a way to heal a deep wound in the heart of economic theory. Since the time of Keynes, economics has been split into two subdisciplines. Microeconomics, the study of how individual firms, households, and markets behave, is a field that operates by fairly strict intellectual rules. Firms are assumed to maximize profits, households to maximize their consumption. Market outcomes are carefully deduced as the "equilibrium" that results from the interacting decisions of rational economic agents. Meanwhile, macroeconomics, the study of business cycles, inflation, and unemployment, is full of ad hoc assumptions that, in the jargon of the field, are not "derived from microfoundations." For example, nobody ever gave a very good story about why there should be something like a stable Phillips curve. Macroeconomists just took an observed correlation and made a leap of faith that it represented a usable relationship. And they were wrong!

What Lucas seemed to be able to do was derive business cycles from microeconomic models. That is, he seemed to be able to tell a rigorous story in which rational firms and households, doing the best that they could in the face of limited information, ended up behaving in a way that yielded something looking like a Phillips curve. Edmund Phelps edited a book in 1970 hopefully entitled *Microeconomic Foundations of Inflation and Unemployment Theory;* for a number of years it seemed to many that Lucas was the man who could really build those foundations, who could create an equilibrium business cycle theory.

Second, the technicality and difficulty of Lucas's theory—a technicality that is barely hinted at by the exposition here—was, in the world of academic economics, an asset rather than a liability. It is cynical but true to say that in the academic world the theories that are most likely to attract a devoted following are those that best allow a clever but not very original young man to demonstrate his cleverness. This has been true of deconstruction-ist literary theory; it has equally been true of equilibrium business cycle theory. It turned out that Lucas's initial theory naturally led to the application of a whole new set of mathematical and statistical techniques. A first set of Lucas disciples made academic reputations developing these techniques; later waves of students invested large amounts of time and effort learning them, and were loath to consider the possibility that the view of the economy to which their specialized training was appropriate might be wrong. Indeed, Lucas himself has in the end seemed more interested in his techniques than in what he does with them.

Finally, we cannot ignore the role of political bias in making rational expectations macroeconomics attractive. A major part of monetarism's appeal was that it seemed to confirm the conservative prejudice that government activism is always a bad thing. There have without doubt been many conservative thinkers who would ordinarily have been repelled by the crudeness and border-line intellectual dishonesty of monetarism but were unconsciously moved to overlook its flaws because it fitted their political philosophy. Similarly, many thinkers who would have rebelled at the unrealism bordering on silliness of rational expectations business cycle theory were predisposed to overlook its flaws because of its powerful conservative implications.

The Situation in 1980

In 1980 an astute observer might already have noticed cracks in the facade of conservative macroeconomics. There was a quietly growing body of evidence contradicting Friedman's assertion that a steady growth rate for the money supply would mean a stable economy. Rational expectations macroeconomics was in the midst of a hidden conceptual crisis, and events would soon undermine its real-world credibility as well. But all of this was virtually invisible except to the cognoscenti. From the point of view of the outside world, and even of much of the economics profession, the picture was one of overwhelming conservative intellectual triumph.

The triumph went far beyond business cycle analysis proper. Keynesian economics had always stood for more than simply a policy of increasing the money supply in recessions and starting public works projects in depressions, even though that was all that it literally called for. Metaphorical implications matter more than specific policies in the world of politics, and Keynesianism had carried with it the metaphor of a market economy improved upon, made to work better than it could on its own, by judicious government intervention. In the hands of many liberals this metaphor in effect legitimized a wide range of government interventions. The apparent refutation of Keynes damaged the reputation of liberal economics in general, and correspondingly lent intellectual prestige to economic conservatives on all issues, even those quite remote from the specific problem of what to do about the business cycle.

In the end, this intellectual "penumbra" from the attack on Keynes was its most important practical consequence, because conservative macroeconomics was put into practice only briefly. Between 1979 and 1982 the Federal Reserve adopted, at least in principle, Milton Friedman's idea of targeting monetary aggregates rather than setting goals for the economy. Even this adoption of monetarism may have been disingenous—a matter of using the fine rhetoric of conservative macroeconomics to cloak a rather brutal policy of throwing the economy into a deep recession to control inflation. In any case, in mid-1982, as the economy plunged more deeply than anticipated, even the pretense of monetarism was abandoned, never to be resumed.

Still, as of 1980 the triumph of the attack on Keynes had, more than anything else, given not only economists but politicians the sense that the intellectual cutting edge in America was on the right, not the left; that, as Moynihan said, the right was the side with the ideas. And there was an idea that the right *did* succeed in putting into policy: namely, the idea that high taxes and excessive regulations were a major drag on U.S. economic growth.

CHAPTER 2

Taxes, Regulation, and Growth

The conservative assault on Keynesian economics was its highest intellectual achievement. The success of that assault in putting advocates of an activist government on the defensive did much to legitimize conservative economic ideology, even among those who knew or understood little of the debate. Yet as we will see when we turn from ideas to events, in the end monetarism and rational expectations had only a brief and limited impact on actual economic policy.

Where conservative ideas really had a large direct impact was in taxation and regulation policy. At the same time that one group of conservative economists was challenging the Keynesian notion that government had some positive role to play in stabilizing the business cycle, another group was arguing that government was the main obstacle to long-run growth. Like the challenge to Keynes, this challenge began at a high and impressive intellectual level—although like monetarism, the appeal of this new anti-government analysis also rested at least in part on the way it confirmed conservative prejudices. The level did not remain this high: the sophisticated public finance arguments of Martin Feldstein were eventually to give way to the crude and silly Laffer curve, the well-argued advocacy of airline and trucking deregulation to degenerate into the blanket anti-regulatory rhetoric of Dan Quayle. But in this chapter I want to focus on the impressive beginnings of the idea that taxation and regulation had become obstacles to growth. We'll turn to that idea's dismaying subsequent evolution later.

Of course, there would have been little market for conservative claims that government policy was frustrating economic growth if that growth had been satisfactory. And for a generation after World War II, growth had been not only satisfactory but extraordinary by historical standards. There were conservatives who claimed that government was too intrusive, taxes too high, incentives too weak, but nobody took them seriously. What made the conservative case suddenly timely was the gradual realization after 1973 that something had gone wrong—that the rapid growth in productivity and living standards that Americans had come to expect had somehow slowed to a crawl.

In this chapter, then, I will briefly describe the economic malaise that emerged in the 1970s, then turn to the emergence of a conservative diagnosis of that malaise.

The Productivity Slowdown

Depression, runaway inflation, or civil war can make a country poor, but only productivity growth can make it rich. In the long run, barring some catastrophe, the rate of growth of living standards in a country is almost exactly equal to the annual increase in the amount that an average worker can produce in an hour.

At the end of World War II, the productivity of U.S. workers was about 40 percent of what it is today—roughly comparable to the current productivity of Greek or Portuguese workers, a little less than that of Irish workers. We thought of ourselves as a rich country, because we were far richer than most other nations, and because things had improved greatly from the depths of the Depression. But only 54 percent of families owned cars, only 44 percent owned their own homes; even in 1950, 40 percent of the population lived below what we now consider the poverty line.

Over the next generation there was a remarkable change. By the early 1970s productivity had doubled, and living standards had risen in tandem. We had become a middle-class nation, in which 63 percent of families owned their own homes, in which there were as many private cars as families, in which only 10 percent of families were still in poverty.

Nearly everyone expected this growth to continue, or even to accelerate. *Fortune* magazine, in a special 1967 issue on the year 2000, forecast a continuing dramatic rise in living standards, guessing that real wages would increase 150 percent over the next quarter century. Popular books like Alvin Toffler's *Future Shock* or Charles Reich's *Greening of America* took rapid economic progress for granted, and worried only about the social changes that such progress might bring.

And then the machine stopped. In 1973 and 1974 the combined effects of long-building inflationary pressures and soaring oil prices led to record consumer price increases; the efforts of the Federal Reserve to contain that inflation with tight money led to the worst recession since the 1930s. Like recessions before and after, this slump was followed by a convincing recovery. As the recovery proceeded, however, it became increasingly obvious that it was not a recovery to the old trend. Productivity was simply not rising the way that it had for the previous twenty-five years.

That was twenty years ago. At this point we can distinguish three eras of U.S. productivity growth. From the late nineteenth century until World War II, productivity grew at about 1.8 percent on average each year—enough to double living standards roughly every forty years. From World War II until 1973, the average growth was a brisker 2.8 percent annually, enough to double living standards in twenty-five years. Since 1973, productivity has risen on average less than 1 percent annually, at a pace that would take eighty years to achieve the rise in living standards that took place in less than a generation after World War II.

This slowdown in productivity growth is one of the two central facts about the U.S. economy over the past twenty years. Coupled with the other central fact—the growing inequality of income distribution—the productivity slowdown turned the broad economic progress of the postwar generation into fitful advance or even decline for many Americans. By almost any measure the middle class is smaller now than it was in 1973, partly because some families have moved upward, but more because of an increase in poverty: poverty rates are 20 percent higher than they were in 1973, and are 40 percent higher among children. Automobile ownership has continued to rise, because more and more families need two cars to commute to the two jobs they need to make ends meet, but home ownership has declined. There is now a pervasive sense that the American Dream has gone astray, that children can expect to live worse than their parents.

With the benefit of hindsight, we can also see that the problem of stagnant productivity is a deep and intractable one. At this point, America's productivity problem has entered its third decade. Of its first twenty years, sixteen were spent under Republican administrations, twelve under administrations dedicated to the ideology of economic conservatism. So at this point productivity is a problem for that ideology: today's conservatives must defend their position against their own dismal productivity record. But in the 1970s, as the extent of the slowdown became apparent, they were on the offensive, with a series of powerful arguments that placed much of the blame for stagnating productivity on the government.

We'll get to the specifics of those arguments shortly. Let's look first, however, at several broad views about why the magic of rapid productivity growth went away.

Why Did Productivity Growth Slow?

In the first few years after the productivity slowdown became apparent, it was widely blamed on the worldwide rise in the price of oil. After a while, however, most economists abandoned this explanation. The dislocations associated with higher energy prices could have explained a few years of sub-par growth, but the size and persistence of the shortfall was too large to be explained even by something as important as the price of oil. Indeed, in the 1980s the price of oil was to crash, in real terms, right back to the levels of the early 1970s, without leading to any recovery of productivity growth. So something else was going on. But what?

In the 1970s, and still today, there were three main broad explanations of productivity slowdown. Let's call them technological, social, and political.

TECHNOLOGY AND THE PRODUCTIVITY SLOWDOWN

Technology in the broad sense—not just new kinds of hardware, but also "soft" innovations like just-in-time inventory management—is crucial to productivity growth. Indeed, since the seminal work of MIT's Robert Solow in the 1950s, analysts of long-run growth have been aware that long-run economic growth would grind to a halt without continuous technological progress, and that such progress is the main source of productivity increase.

The technological story of the productivity slowdown holds that this vital engine of growth ran out of steam, not because there was anything wrong with the basic structure of our economy, but simply because the technologies that were the basis of the postwar boom had pretty much reached their limits. The story runs as follows: Productivity grew rapidly after World War II through the elaboration of a set of ideas and techniques that had been around for a long time, but that required a sustained period of political and economic stability to be fully exploited. By the early 1970s, most of the possibilities inherent in existing science and technology had been explored, and so productivity growth fell off. In effect, the productivity slowdown can be attributed to an exhaustion of ideas.

"But wait a second," the reader may object, "haven't the last twenty years been a time of radical technological progress? What about personal computers, fax machines, mobile phones, VCRs? How can you claim that there was an exhaustion of ideas?"

This is a good point, but there is an answer. Economic historians have observed that it often takes a very long time before a new technology begins to make a major impact on productivity and living standards. For example, the crucial technological breakthrough that launched the Industrial Revolution was arguably Hargreaves's invention of the spinning jenny in 1764; yet the wholesale industrialization of Britain did not begin until around 1810, and real wages did not begin to rise significantly until the 1840s. Electric power was introduced in the 1880s, yet the historian Paul David has argued that it had little positive impact on productivity until the 1920s.

The reason for these long lags is that a technology often does not have its full impact when it is used in isolation; it is only when it becomes broadly applied and interacts with other technologies that its true potential can be exploited. An automobile is a plaything of the rich when it is a rare item; it becomes much more when there is a network of paved roads, gas stations and repair shops are universally available, and the biggest department stores are in suburban malls rather than traditional downtowns. And there is a circularity: the network of support and reinforcement that makes a technology fully productive is both a cause and a result of that technology's widespread use. So a new technology, no matter how marvelous, may have only superficial effects for decades, then flower as it finally reaches critical mass.

We may therefore argue that the generation after the war benefited from the interactive exploitation of some key technologies that had been in existence for a long time, indeed for the most part since before the *first* world war, but which could not come fully into their own during the long years of depression and war. Under the aegis of the *Pax Americana,* old ideas could be put into their fullest use, with dramatic effects on productivity.

Think of the twinned growth of the oil and transportation industries: superhighways, supertankers, and giant, super-efficient refineries did not involve any radical intellectual breakthroughs; even jet aircraft had been possible in principle since the 1930s. It was the implementation of known concepts, and the mutual reinforcement of growing linkages among these industries, that made rapid productivity growth possible. The same may be said of the nexus among private automobiles, refrigerators, and supermarkets that sharply increased productivity in the retail sector. Much of the productivity growth in manufacturing came from the replacement of the old-style multi-story, cramped factory—designed to allow a massive steam engine to power many machines, and to allow a single railway spur to deliver raw materials and take away shipments—with single-story, open-plan plants designed around electric power and road transport. The ideas were not revolutionary; their impact on productivity was.

The point is that by the late 1960s these technologies had, in many cases, started to approach their limits. Indeed, to a considerable extent things that we still think of as "modern" were introduced more than twenty years ago. It is somewhat startling, for example, to realize that the Boeing 747, still the flagship of airlines, was introduced in 1969; today's versions are improved, but not radically different. Bill McKibben, who subjected himself to a massive dose of television reruns for his book *The Age of Missing Information,* has pointed out a revealing fact: the houses shown in situation comedies from the early 1960s do not look particularly old-fashioned. Russell Baker has made the point even more strongly: "Why does 1940 still seem like yesterday, when back in 1940, 1890 seemed like the Dark Ages?"

In the late 1960s the management consultant Peter Drucker wrote a deeply perceptive book, *The Age of Discontinuity.* He pointed out that in spite of the rapid economic progress of the previous generation, the industrial structure of the economy, and even its leading firms, had changed relatively little since the 1920s; economic progress had come primarily from improvements within well-understood paradigms, not from radical innovation. And he also pointed out that this "continuity" could not continue: the old technologies were almost played out, and new technologies were emerging whose exploitation would require massive economic restructuring.

What he failed to point out was how long it might take before the new technologies bore fruit in broad-based economic progress.

Consider, for example, the office computer. Computers have been in widespread use in the business world since the 1960s, and personal computers sprouted everywhere in the 1980s, to the point that by 1991 about 60 percent of U.S. office workers had one on the desk. Yet simply adding computers to an office organized in traditional fashion may add little to productivity; it may simply lead to the repeatedly redrafted letter, laser-printed in elegant font, where a quickly dictated memo might have done the same job.

Many businesses now believe that in order to take real advantage of computers, it is necessary to reorganize the whole structure of office work, and for that matter the way that different parts of a corporation relate to the outside world. It's not enough to give each manager a personal computer. These computers must be linked into a network, preferably including the firm's suppliers and customers; and both the roles of employees and the lines of authority must be redesigned so as to induce workers and managers to use the electronic network to replace paper and personal contact. That is, the computer doesn't realize its full potential in an office designed around the flow of paper, in the same way that electric power didn't realize its full potential in factory buildings designed for machines powered by steam.

There were some signs that the "technology payoff" (to quote the title of a *BusinessWeek* story in 1993), the long-delayed economic reward from the widespread use of information-processing technology, was finally beginning in the 1990s. The point, however, is that through the 1970s and 1980s technological advances were impressive but, apparently, not all that fruitful.

The technological explanation of the productivity slowdown, then, asserts that by the early 1970s the set of technologies that had driven the postwar boom had been pretty much fully exploited, while the technologies that will eventually power another boom were not yet ready for prime time. It is essentially a fatalistic view. There are some policy activists who think that governments should try to anticipate the shape of the future that new technologies will bring, and force the pace with a collective campaign to move rapidly into the future. We'll discuss some modest versions of this vision in Part III. But unless you can muster a faith in the wisdom of government planners that few can feel nowadays, the technological view of the productivity slowdown cannot inspire much more than patience.

THE SOCIOLOGICAL EXPLANATION

The productivity slowdown dates from the early 1970s—just about a generation after World War II. Is there some significance in the fact that the postwar good years lasted for only one generation?

It is easy to think of reasons why. After all, it was the late 1960s and early 1970s that saw the large-scale entry of the baby boomers into the labor market. Simply because of the need to absorb large numbers of new entrants into the work force, the growth of the ratio of capital to workers slowed. But the baby boomers were not distinguished by numbers alone. This was the first generation raised in widespread affluence, the first generation that was reared according to the permissive dictates of Dr. Spock. Above all, it was the first generation to grow up watching television.

Anyone who was touched, one way or another, by the cultural winds of the 1960s finds it plausible that social factors played a significant role in the 1970s slowdown. Surely productivity must have been affected by a decade in which capitalism and work itself were denigrated, in which the mixture of high values and hypocrisy that holds society together seemed to lose its adhesive grip. This is not serious economic analysis, but one need not dismiss what one cannot measure.

For that matter, there were some quantifiable changes taking place during the 1960s that seemed to owe more to social trends than to narrowly defined economic forces, yet which certainly had a negative impact on growth. Educational standards as measured by test scores appear to have started a gradual decline in the late 1960s, a decline that has continued through to the present. Some of this decline represented the troubles of inner-city schools. But even middle-class education seems to have become less effective. It is widely claimed, for instance, that admission standards even at elite universities have dropped considerably—one supposed figure is that a third of today's typical entering class at Harvard would not have been admitted twenty years ago.

The decline in educational standards is not for the most part due to lower spending. While there are some distressed school districts where students must use old textbooks and sit on packing crates, on the whole teachers' salaries have kept up with earnings in private industry, and class sizes have gotten smaller. (Between 1960 and 1990 the number of students in primary and secondary education rose only 10 percent, but the number of teachers increased 70 percent.) Instead, the problems of our education system seem to be linked to problems of motivation—motivation of teachers, parents, and students. In our worst schools education is lost in a climate of violence, but even in more ordinary schools the traditional drive for excellence seems to have been lost.

Beyond education lies the problem of social collapse among important segments of our population. The size and misery of America's underclass is unique among advanced countries; most people believe that that underclass began to expand rapidly during the 1960s. The economic consequences of the underclass are not the most important issue, but it must surely be true that the expansion of the underclass has been a significant drag on U.S. growth.

So there is a plausible case to be made that social problems—

the loss of economic drive among the children of the middle class, the declining standards of education, the rise of the underclass— played a significant role in the productivity slowdown. This story is very different from the technological explanation; yet it has in common with that story a fatalistic feel. After all, while one may lament our social problems, few people have much faith in the ability of the government to provide solutions. And at any rate, social problems are not for the most part in the domain of *economic* policy. So the sociological explanation would seem to suggest that we should learn to live with slow productivity growth, not demand that the government somehow turn it around.

But this was not a verdict that economists were prepared to accept. On both the left and the right, they looked for explanations of slow productivity growth, or at least for ways to make that growth faster. And at first the interesting ideas were on the right.

*THE POLITICAL EXPLANATION OF THE
PRODUCTIVITY SLOWDOWN*

During the 1970s, there was a growing body of economic analysis that attributed the nation's economic difficulties largely to a third basic cause: the distortions and reduced incentives caused by taxes and regulations. We may call this the political explanation of the productivity slowdown; it said, in effect, that our economic troubles were the government's fault.

In the Reagan years the view that taxes and regulation were a drag on economic growth became a political dogma, treated by conservatives as revealed truth, needing only to be asserted, not demonstrated. But like the attack on Keynes, the conservative critique of taxation began as a serious intellectual movement, which commanded (and still commands) the respect of even the most liberal-minded economist.

Taxation, Incentives, and Growth

If you try to tax people, they will try to find ways to avoid paying. Some people will resort to simple fraud—hiding their income and cooking their books. Some will resort to elaborate legal evasions, arranging for paper losses to offset real gains. But in the United States the main way that people try to avoid taxes is by avoiding doing things that are taxed. Unfortunately, these things include working and investing.

Economists, left and right, have always agreed that the tendency of people to change their behavior to avoid taxes—in the jargon of the economists, the *distortion of incentives* associated with taxation—represents a hidden, extra cost of government. This is a basic truth. Unfortunately, during the ideological reign of economic conservatism, this basic truth became mixed up with a set of other ideas that range from half-truths to outright falsehoods, from the popular notion that the government wastes a lot of the money it collects (partly true) to the idea that most of the taxpayer's dollar goes to pay the salaries of useless bureaucrats (completely false).

To make sense of conservative arguments about taxation, we need to get back to the basics. What are the costs of taxation? Why did many economists in the 1970s come to the conclusion that these costs were higher than previously thought?

THE COSTS OF TAXATION

To think about almost any economic issue, it helps to start by imagining a much simpler economy than the one we actually live in. So, to think about taxes, let's start by thinking about an economy in which there is no saving or investment, in which the only economic decision that might be affected by taxes is how hard people work. And let's also imagine that the government of this hypothetical economy raises all its revenue by a simple proportional income tax. To make things concrete, suppose that the economy has a national income of $1 trillion, and that the government finances a $300 billion budget with a 30 percent tax on all incomes.

In the current political climate, there will probably be many readers who will assume that much of that budget must be wasted. But that's both unfair as a characterization of our actual government and unnecessary to the conservative economic case. So let's suppose instead that the government actually spends the money pretty well, getting things of value—defense, education, health care, and so on—in return for the $300 billion. Still, one needs to ask whether the value is sufficient to justify the cost. And the key point is that the true cost of $300 billion in government spending is considerably more than $300 billion.

To see why, suppose that the government decided to spend an extra $10 billion—1 percent of national income. You might think that it could pay for this spending by raising the tax rate 1 point, from 30 to 31 percent. But in fact, this would certainly not be enough, because a rise in the tax rate would induce at least some people to work less hard or work shorter hours. This decline in work effort would reduce the size of the tax base (that is, the amount of income to be taxed). In an extreme case, the rise in the tax rate would reduce work effort so much that revenue would actually fall. But even in a less extreme scenario, a 1 percent rise in the tax rate would on net increase the tax yield by *less* than 1 percent of national income. So, to raise an extra $10 billion, the government would have to raise taxes by more than 1 point. For the sake of the example, let's suppose that the necessary rise in the tax rate would actually be not to 31 but to 32 percent.

How much does this tax increase hurt taxpayers? The answer is that the true cost to them is close to $20 billion, not $10 billion. To see why, imagine an individual taxpayer with an income of, say, $100,000 before taxes. If she did not change her work effort in the face of a 2-point tax increase, her tax payments would rise by $2,000. That increase in what she would owe with unchanged behavior represents, to a first approximation, the real cost of the higher tax rate. It's true that she actually doesn't pay $2,000, because she limits her taxes by working less; but this is a poor compensation, since if she really wanted to trade less income for more time off, she would have been doing it in the first place.[1] Multiply her experience 10,000-fold, and we find that the government's decision to spend an extra $10 billion really costs the public almost $20 billion.

The basic point is that when the government tries to collect revenue, it drives a wedge between what people earn and what they get to keep. When someone works to earn an extra dollar, he raises gross national product by $1.00; but if he pays a 30 percent marginal tax rate, he gets to keep only $0.70 for himself. As a result, people tend to work too little.

This doesn't mean that government spending is a bad thing. All that it says is that the true costs of such spending are higher than the simple cash outlay. If you want to increase government spending, you must increase taxes and thus worsen the distortion of incentives. The extra distortion is a cost over and above the direct cost of the government program.

How serious an issue is this? In reality, government in the United States—local, state, and federal combined—does in fact take about 30 percent of our income in taxes. Furthermore, the reduction in the incentive to work is somewhat more than this number would suggest, because the U.S. tax system is designed to be somewhat progressive, that is, to make high-income people pay a higher share of their income in taxes than lower-income people. This seems reasonable on social grounds, but has the side consequence that the "marginal" tax rate—the rate you pay on the

---

[1]There's a tricky argument (known in the trade as the "envelope theorem") that says that the true cost to a taxpayer of a small tax increase is very closely approximated by the extra payments on the *pre-tax* income—even if the taxpayer manages to avoid much of the tax. It runs as follows: The work effort of our hypothetical taxpayer before the tax increase was optimal given the 30 percent rate. That is, the taxpayer chooses to work up to the point where the utility from a little more income is just equal to the disutility of the extra work needed to earn that income. If you think about it, this means that working less to avoid higher taxes brings only a small benefit compared with just accepting the higher burden: the extra loss in income is nearly as valuable as the gain in leisure time.

last dollar of your income—is higher than the average tax rate. If the economic program proposed by Bill Clinton in early 1993 passes, very high income individuals will pay a marginal federal tax rate of 46 percent, plus a few extra points for state and local taxes. This is not trivial: without any question, the negative effects of taxes on incentives are significant.

In the example I have suggested that the true cost of an extra $1 of government is nearly $2; this is more than most estimates actually suggest (a more typical estimate is something like $1.30). But the principle is certainly right.

By itself, however, acknowledging that taxes distort incentives tells us little about economic policy. After all, doing without a government and hence completely without taxes is not an option, so that there is no way to avoid imposing distortions on incentives. It's not an either-or argument. All that you can say for sure is that when choosing a structure of taxes and deciding what projects the government should undertake, one should in principle take into account the effects on incentives.

So, what did the conservatives add? They made a strong case that the distortions of incentives associated with taxes were larger than most economists had previously realized—and that these distortions were particularly concentrated, not on the incentives to work, but on those to save and invest.

TAXES, SAVING, AND INVESTMENT

In any given year, the U.S. economy devotes 15–20 percent of its income, not to current consumption, but to investment. Investment represents a decision to defer consumption now in order to be able to consume more at a later date. And it is a decision that, even more than work effort, is distorted by taxes.

To see why, suppose that today, *after* paying any taxes on my current income, I am deciding whether to consume or invest $1,000. Suppose that I know that if I invest the $1,000 for ten years, it will be worth $2,000. Then in effect I can trade $1,000 of current consumption for $2,000 of future consumption, or vice versa; and I can choose based on how much I value gratification today relative to gratification ten years from now.

Or rather, I could trade off $1,000 today for $2,000 later if there were no taxes. Because there are taxes, the tradeoff is not nearly that favorable. The reason is that if I invest $1,000 now to get $2,000 later, the tax authorities will consider the difference to represent income, and they will tax it. If my tax rate is 30 percent, I will find that my tradeoff is not the "true" $1.00 today for $2.00 later, but $1.00 for $1.70, instead.[2] The result? My behavior will be distorted: I will consume too much now, and invest too little in the future.

Again, this is not a controversial proposition. But during the 1970s, experts on public finance produced convincing theoretical analyses suggesting that the effective tax rates on certain kinds of investment in the United States had risen during the 1970s to punitive levels. Less convincingly, they also provided evidence that these rising tax rates had or would actually have a major effect in discouraging saving and investment, and thus in slowing economic growth.

The leading light in this movement was Martin Feldstein of Harvard University, who would later spend two years as chairman of Ronald Reagan's Council of Economic Advisers—and would achieve some notoriety as perhaps the least-listened-to economic adviser in U.S. history. But in the 1970s Feldstein was at the cutting edge of a new public finance that, whatever its conservative political implications, simply had to be taken seriously.

What Feldstein pointed out was that the tendency of taxes to discourage investment, bad enough in any case, had become much worse during the 1970s because of accelerating inflation. To see why, let's think of another numerical example. Suppose that I face a marginal tax rate of 50 percent, and I am trying to decide whether to consume some of my income or invest it for a year in a U.S. Treasury Bill. In a time of low inflation, a Treasury

---

[2]We could, of course, try to change the form of the tax system so as to remove this disincentive. Options include exempting capital income from taxes or a value-added tax.

Bill might pay, say, 4 percent interest. I would, however, get taxed on this interest, so that my net return on the investment would be 2 percent. This means that even with low inflation, taxes reduce my incentive to invest. But let's suppose for the sake of argument that this isn't a big issue, that cutting the rate of return on savings from 4 to 2 percent imposes only modest costs on the economy.

Now suppose that the economy is experiencing 10 percent inflation. Interest rates normally rise along with inflation; with a 10 percent inflation rate, we would expect the interest rate on Treasuries to rise to about 14 percent. If there were no taxes, this would leave the "real" return on investment—the increase in the purchasing power of a dollar invested for a year—unchanged, because 14 percent interest minus 10 percent inflation is still 4 percent.

But now comes Feldstein's point: the tax law counts all of the interest, not just the interest in excess of the rate of inflation, as income. At a 50 percent marginal rate, a 14 percent rate of return before taxes would mean only 7 percent after taxes—3 percent *less* than the rate of inflation. I actually get punished for saving! This is a much worse distortion of incentives than before; if putting money aside for the future actually yields a negative real rate of return, why bother saving at all?

Feldstein pointed out that throughout the tax system inflation was turning tolerable paper tax rates into very high effective rates. Corporations, for example, were supposed to pay a tax rate of 42 percent on their profits. Feldstein calculated, however, that when the effects of inflation were taken into account, the true tax on any profits from investing in equipment was more like 75 percent.

You don't need to be a Republican to accept that tax rates this high might discourage investment and hurt economic growth. But was the interaction between inflation and investment really a major villain in America's economic difficulties? There the evidence was less clear.

One piece of evidence came from statistical work by a Stanford professor, Michael Boskin. (Like Feldstein, Boskin was later to become a chairman of the Council of Economic Advisers, this time for George Bush. Unlike Feldstein, Boskin avoided public criticism of his boss's policies, even when he disagreed privately; this did not save him from being made a scapegoat for Bush's economic troubles.) Boskin found evidence that the overall rate of savings in the United States was more strongly influenced by the rate of return than most economists had previously believed.

More sophisticated evidence was produced by a very young Harvard economist, Lawrence Summers, who was regarded as a conservative at the time because of his strong advocacy of lower taxation on corporate earnings. (It turned out that he was not all that conservative, since he later popped up on the other side, as an economic adviser to both Michael Dukakis and Bill Clinton.) Summers showed that if a widely accepted model of consumption behavior—the so-called life cycle model—was correct, it implied large adverse effects on saving from the kind of effective tax rates that Feldstein was calculating.

By 1980, the work of Feldstein, Boskin, Summers, and others had convinced many economists that U.S. taxes were in fact a significant obstacle to investment. Nor was this all: another major U.S. policy, the Social Security system, was also discouraging saving and investment.

THE SOCIAL SECURITY ISSUE

In the days before the welfare state, poverty was one of the most frequent afflictions of the elderly. Those who had earned little during their working years had few savings, so that when they could no longer work they were often plunged into penury. Even as late as 1970, elderly people were twice as likely to be poor as the population at large.

The Social Security system was designed to change that. In effect, it guarantees a pension to anyone who has worked in his or her lifetime. The system became increasingly generous during the 1970s, and largely as a result of this generosity the poverty rate among the elderly fell sharply. Indeed, by 1990 the poverty rate among the elderly was less than half what it had been in 1969, and was lower than that of the population as a whole.

But Martin Feldstein suggested that this progress might be coming at a significant cost. He pointed out that the existence of the Social Security system reduced the incentives for people to save; since you could count on receiving Social Security payments after you stopped working, there was less reason to save on your own account.

Now, each of us does have an obligation to pay money into the Social Security system while we are working, so one might think that we are simply doing our saving in a different way—just as many workers in the private sector rely on pension funds rather than their personal assets to take care of them after retirement. But Feldstein argued that the Social Security system is not like a private pension plan, because it is "unfunded": it operates on a pay-as-you-go basis, in which the current contributions of workers are used to pay the benefits of retirees.

This is a pretty good arrangement for the retirees. Because both the work force and average wages tend to grow over time, each worker can expect to receive more in benefits than he could have gotten if his payments into the system had been invested in a private pension plan. In effect, Social Security gives each worker a gift from larger and richer future generations. It feels good; but it also encourages people to consume more and save less.

During the 1970s, Feldstein calculated that the net benefits that people currently alive could expect to receive from the Social Security system were as much as 40 percent of the value of all productive assets in the United States. So, if Social Security was really taking the place of private pensions or other private saving, it could be having a major effect in discouraging the formation of capital.

Labor Markets

The new conservative public finance suggested that the United States was imposing really high rates of taxation on savings and investment. But it also suggested, albeit with somewhat less force, that taxation was imposing serious distortions on labor markets.

Yet again Feldstein took the lead. As early as 1973 he suggested that the problems that the United States was having in reconciling full employment with low inflation might be the result of poor incentives. His target was unemployment compensation. This compensation has the effect, of course, of alleviating the pain of unemployment. Characteristically, Feldstein argued that there was a hidden cost to this laudable goal: because unemployment was less painful, the incentive for workers to moderate their wage demands was less, making it harder to control inflation. In the end, he argued, unemployment compensation, while making any given rate of unemployment less unpleasant, forced the United States to have higher unemployment than it would otherwise have had.

Other economists produced evidence suggesting that while the main distortions from taxes might involve their effects on savings and investment, they also had significant effects in reducing work effort. Economists have traditionally been skeptical about whether work effort is really seriously deterred by tax rates in the range that one sees in this country. Sophisticated statistical work seemed to show, however, that there was indeed a noticeable if not overwhelming effect, with a 1 percent rise in the tax rate reducing work effort by perhaps as much as one third of 1 percent.

TAXATION AND ECONOMIC GROWTH

Feldstein and his followers made a convincing case that the distortion of incentives due to taxation is a major economic issue. But just how major?

In the next chapter we'll turn to the "supply-siders," a movement of radical conservatives who believed that tax cuts would lead to a huge surge of economic growth. Most famous of these supply-siders was Arthur Laffer, who claimed that a tax cut would lead to so much more output that revenue would actually rise. The important thing to realize here is that neither Feldstein nor his followers made any such extravagant claims.

One example may make the point. In the Bush years, the centerpiece of conservative demands for further tax cuts was the idea of reducing taxes on capital gains; indeed, Republicans came to put almost religious faith in the power of a capital gains cut to energize the economy. But in 1980, Lawrence Summers, in a paper that made a very strong case for reducing the rate of taxation on corporations and investors, estimated that even a complete elimination of the tax on capital gains would take almost ten years to raise U.S. output by a single percentage point.

What the conservative public finance of the 1970s really suggested was that the U.S. tax system could use some reforming. It suggested that some tax rates were so high they were substantially distorting incentives, and thus that reducing those tax rates—and paying for those tax cuts either by raising other, less distorting taxes or by cutting spending—would be beneficial to the economy. There was nothing in the analysis or the evidence indicating either that taxes were at the root of America's economic difficulties or that lowering taxes would by itself get the country moving again.

In the world of politics, however, the actual content of an academic movement may be less important than the way it affects the tone of the discussion. During the 1970s there was a growing public sense of disillusionment with government, which first fed grass-roots tax revolts in California and Massachusetts, then helped elect Ronald Reagan. And there was also a determined effort by a few extremely conservative journalists and politicians to promote radical tax-cutting plans. No matter how careful the research of conservative public finance theorists like Martin Feldstein might be, in that political climate it was inevitable that it would be widely seen as basically confirming popular prejudices. There was a huge intellectual gulf between Feldstein or Boskin and the sweeping claims of Arthur Laffer; but in the public mind, they were in effect allies.

The Costs of Regulation

The most intellectually exciting area of the new conservative analysis of government policy focused on taxation. Yet taxes are not the only expense that government imposes on the public. Indeed, there has been a long-term trend away from taxing and spending as the principal instruments of government policy. Increasingly, over the course of the twentieth century, there has been a shift toward administrative measures: toward standards, requirements, and regulations that aim directly to shape private behavior in order to serve a presumed public interest.

Many economists, not all of them conservatives, have suggested that unnecessary or mishandled regulation involves more unnecessary costs than does taxation. Some of these costs have been part of the U.S. economy for a long time, even during the rapid growth postwar generation. But other costs of regulation arguably grew larger during the 1970s, as government came to play a larger role in environmental and safety issues. In fact, some economists suggested that it was increased regulation, not higher effective tax rates, that really explained the productivity slowdown.

By the 1990s the attack on regulation, like so much else, had become a knee-jerk reflex of conservatives. But it is worth reminding ourselves of how intellectually persuasive that attack seemed in its early years.

REGULATION OF COMPETITION

Economic theory tells us that monopoly power is bad for the economy. This is not simply a matter of fairness: the efforts of monopolies and cartels to keep prices high distort economic incentives, imposing efficiency losses very similar to those produced by taxation. The best answer to this problem is to encourage competition, and to make illegal any collusion to keep prices high. But some industries are "natural" monopolies: the technology of production or distribution pretty much ensures that each market is dominated by a single firm. Examples include electric power generation, local (but not national) telephone service, and local cable television.

In many countries, natural monopolies are reserved for publicly owned firms. In the United States, however, we have usually preferred to maintain private ownership of such monopolies, but to curb their monopoly power by setting maximum prices and minimum standards of service. This is an imperfect solution, but so are all the others. And in many cases it works pretty well. The obvious alternative—simply accepting monopoly power—appeals to diehard conservatives, but does not work nearly as well. (During the 1980s Reaganites in the United States and Thatcherites in Britain were prepared to make a leap of faith in the power of free markets, and turn such natural monopolies as cable and power over to unregulated private firms; I'll describe the debacles that resulted in later chapters.)

During the nineteenth century, the most important natural monopoly by far was rail transportation. There were some parts of the United States, such as the stretch between Chicago and New York, where the sheer density of traffic made it possible for a number of railroads to compete. In rural areas, however, especially those west of Chicago, farms and small towns all too often found themselves dependent on a single railroad that effectively controlled everything shipped either in or out. Thus more than one hundred years ago the Interstate Commerce Commission was formed to regulate railroad pricing. The same principle was then extended to other kinds of transportation, including trucking, airlines, and the pipelines that carry natural gas.

All of this was quite reasonable at first. But over time two things began to happen. First, the economy changed: as the United States shifted from rail to road, and as the volume of first truck and then airplane traffic increased, the transportation sector ceased to be as clearly characterized by natural monopoly. Indeed, by 1980 many economists (and not only conservatives) believed that the possibilities for competition were sufficiently large that the rationale for regulation was gone. Second, as the public rationale for regulation eroded, the regulatory process itself became increasingly interested in protecting the interests of the industry rather than the consumers. And many analysts came to believe that industry regulation had begun to do more harm than the monopoly power it was supposed to control.

This was a battle that free marketers won easily. Extensive deregulation of the oil, airline, and trucking industries began under Jimmy Carter. Most economists count these deregulations as a success, even though it turned out that the airline industry still had many more of the aspects of a natural monopoly than anyone had realized.

Some of the same arguments used to justify deregulation of transportation were also used to justify deregulation of financial institutions like banks and savings and loans. This is, however, a quite different story, which we will hold until Chapter 6.

The point for now is that the force of the critique of misguided government regulation of competition—a critique that was shared by economists across a wide band of the ideological spectrum—helped lend credibility to a quite different kind of critique of regulation: the claim that growing impositions on business were becoming a major drag on economic growth.

REGULATION AS A CULPRIT IN THE PRODUCTIVITY SLOWDOWN

In 1979 an economist named Murray Weidenbaum published a book entitled *The Future of Business Regulation,* which made a startling claim: that regulatory costs imposed on U.S. business were costing the economy more than $100 billion annually, and could in fact explain a major part of the productivity slowdown. That claim helped win Weidenbaum a position as Ronald Reagan's first chairman of the Council of Economic Advisers.

The calculations underlying Weidenbaum's estimates relied on a lot of sheer guesswork, and even most conservative economists thought that they were probably too high (just as many liberals more or less privately thought that the high rates of return to infrastructure investment later assumed by Bill Clinton in his economic plans were probably far too optimistic). Nonetheless, there was widespread agreement among economists, even those left of center, that the 1970s had seen a sharp rise in the regulatory burden on business.

The source of this increased burden was not the traditional regulations on competition in trucking, airlines, and banking. It was the new regulations imposed to protect worker health, consumer safety, and the environment. Without question the Occupational Safety and Health Administration, the Environmental Protection Agency, and the Consumer Product Safety Commission — all established by Richard Nixon—imposed significant new costs of doing business.

Although extreme conservatives tended to speak of the new regulations as if they were pure cost, imposed out of some mindless hostility to the business world, they were of course meant to serve valid purposes. Pollution is the classic economic example of a negative "externality," a cost that polluters impose on society but have little incentive to avoid since very little of the cost falls on them. Occupational safety is a slightly more problematic issue. A diehard free marketer would say that workplace safety should be left up to the market, that firms that provide a safe and healthy environment would be able to attract workers at lower wages, and that the market would therefore automatically provide for the optimal degree of safety. In practice, however, workers can't be expected to do the necessary work of policing—the workers who died in the 1992 fire in a North Carolina chicken plant found out that the fire doors were padlocked only after the fire had broken out. So moderate conservatives are willing to support some degree of government regulation of worker health and safety as well.

Two things were, however, pretty clear. First, the costs of the new regulations were quite large in at least some industries. For example, productivity in the U.S. coal-mining industry actually went down steadily during the 1970s, probably largely due to tougher safety regulations in a notoriously dangerous business.

Second, in many cases the costs of regulation were higher than necessary. This was particularly true when it came to controlling pollution. Economists pleaded for some use of the market mechanism—for taxes on pollution, or for auctioning off the rights to release pollutants. Instead, U.S. environmental regulations imposed detailed and inflexible rules, giving no incentive for firms that could cheaply have reduced pollution further to do so, offering no incentive for innovative ways to reduce it, and offering no recourse for firms for whom the costs of pollution reduction were prohibitive.

None of this amounted to a case against health and environmental regulation. The case was only for regulation that was perhaps a little less strict and certainly a lot smarter. In that way the sensible conservative critique of regulation closely resembled its critique of taxation, which called for taxes to be perhaps a bit lower on average but definitely a lot smarter, eliminating the huge tax rates on certain kinds of activities.

The Situation in 1980

By 1980 conservative economists had made a strong case that high rates of taxation on certain things, notably capital formation, had become a significant drag on the economy's growth. They had made a somewhat less strong but still fairly convincing case that rigid regulation was acting as a further brake on growth. In no case did the numbers they came up with suggest that policy changes could produce a really dramatic turnaround in the economy; but the idea that the government should worry more about the incentive effects of its taxation and regulation seemed pretty sensible.

What one might have expected was a modest, less than revolutionary shift in policy. Indeed, such a shift had already begun under President Jimmy Carter: it was Carter who deregulated airlines, trucking, and oil, and there were even some modest cuts in taxes on the very well-off during the Carter years. In January

1980, one might reasonably have predicted a mild trend in the same direction, whoever won the election.

That wasn't how it turned out, because the persuasive, reasonable conservatives who made the case for lower taxes didn't end up defining the Republican policy. Instead, it was a very different group: the supply-siders.

CHAPTER 3

The Supply-Siders

Michael Lewis, the author of *Liar's Poker,* has noted that around 1980 there was a fundamental cultural change in the world of finance. Cautious men who seemed to have been born in gray suits were replaced by ambitious, often rebellious younger men and women who might easily have been—indeed, in some cases actually had been—campus radicals in an earlier era. Prudence was out; aggressive dealmaking, even if it meant abandoning old traditions and risking the reputation of the dealmaker's firm, was in. Lewis attributes this shift to the opportunities brought about by changing technology and deregulation, which created a favorable environment for those who embodied the new "money culture." Yet a wider view suggests that even deeper forces were at work. After all, strange cultural reversals were happening in other walks of life as well. In the 1960s, for example, rebellious young academics who dismissed tradition were invariably leftists. By the 1980s, the universities were full of young conservative economists who were enthusiastic intellectual radicals, brashly dismissing conventional wisdom, while their elders and a few young fogies like myself weakly tried to remind them of hard-won traditional insights.

Perhaps the most important cultural reversal of all, however, was happening in journalism. There was a time when the editorial pages of conservative newspapers tended to be rather dull. They could be counted on to advocate fiscal prudence and to oppose new government initiatives, to be relentlessly, boringly sensible.

During the 1970s, all of that changed. By 1980 it was the traditional liberal press that was dull and sensible,[1] while the conservative press had become brash and aggressive. Above all, the editorial pages of *The Wall Street Journal*—a name almost synonomous with financial probity—had become a hotbed of radical right-wing economics.

This change was due in large part to one man: Robert Bartley, who has run the editorial page of *The Wall Street Journal* since 1972. From the beginning of his tenure, Bartley made it clear that the *Journal* would henceforth be neither cautious nor evenhanded on economic issues. Instead, it would campaign aggressively for what Bartley believed in. And Bartley is a self-confident man, calmly sure that he is right even when nearly everyone around him thinks he has lost his head.

Many of Bartley's enthusiasms have been ignored by the world beyond his own coterie. For much of the 1980s, for example, the *Journal* campaigned vociferously for a return to the gold standard; aside from providing an excuse for a few ludicrously lavish conferences, this campaign was treated by the larger world with bemused indifference. But Bartley did accomplish one remarkable thing: during the 1970s he managed to promote the ideas of a handful of iconoclastic economists into the major ideology that came to be known as "supply-side" economics.

Most people who think about supply-side economics at all

---

[1] In 1980, a *Boston Globe* typesetter forgot to change the working title for a favorable editorial on a recent Carter speech, so a large number of papers went out with an editorial entitled "Mush from the Wimp."

probably imagine that it is simply a strong form of conservative economics, basically Milton Friedman carried a step or two further. But the story of supply-side economics is much stranger than that. There are many conservative economists; indeed, as we saw in the last two chapters, a conservative intellectual agenda dominated academic work on macroeconomics and public finance for much of the 1970s and 1980s. But these academic conservatives are not supply-siders, nor have the supply-siders been drawn from their ranks. Instead, supply-side economics was and remains a movement of outsiders, of a small group that has never found respectability even within mainstream conservatism, exiles in their own intellectual country. Yet this group came to control first the world's most powerful business newspaper, then the economic policies of the world's most powerful nation.

Who were the supply-siders? What, exactly, were their ideas? And how did they come to have so much influence? These questions go to the heart of the political triumphs and economic failures of conservatism in America.

Who Were the Supply-Siders?

During 1992 a reporter for a national newspaper called to ask me to help her on a story about the state of economics education in the United States. She requested an assessment of which economics departments I thought were most influential, an easy enough task. Then she asked me to classify them by their ideological bent: which were Keynesian, which monetarist, which supply-side?

The question revealed some excusable ignorance about the current state of academic economics. The old categories of "Keynesian" and "monetarist" are no longer a very good guide to the lines of cleavage within macroeconomics. (The preferred jargon among the economists now divides departments into "saltwater," vaguely interventionist places like MIT and Harvard, and "fresh-water," sternly free-market schools like Rochester, Carnegie-Mellon, and Minnesota. The University of Chicago, by the way, once the center of the fresh-water world, has gone slightly brackish in recent years.) Nor are economics departments necessarily ideologically uniform: rational expectations is taught at MIT and Harvard, new Keynesian economics at Chicago. But the reporter seemed most surprised by my answer about supply-side economics: not only is there no major department that is supply-side in orientation; there is no economist whom one might call a supply-sider at any major department.

Again, this is not because of some liberal political bias. Economists at key "fresh-water" departments like Chicago, Rochester, Carnegie-Mellon, and Minnesota are extremely conservative, vehemently opposed to any government activism. But they are not now and never have been supply-siders in the sense that they are comfortable with Bartley's view of the world.

Where, then, did the supply-siders come from? The answer is that they came from the fringes of economics: from journalism, from congressional staff positions, from consulting firms; nowadays most of them are employed by conservative think tanks.[2] They promoted their ideas not through papers in academic journals but in op-ed pieces and articles in semi-popular magazines like *The Public Interest*. Above all, the cutting edge of the supply-side movement consisted of the group that Robert Bartley assembled to preach on the editorial page of *The Wall Street Journal*.

The core of Bartley's group was composed of men whose background was entirely in journalism. Bartley himself began work as a reporter at the age of twenty-two, and has worked for *The Wall Street Journal* since he was twenty-five. His right-hand man during the early years of supply-side economics was Jude Wanniski, who came from the *National Observer* to the *Journal*. Somewhat off to the side, but playing a critical role in providing a platform for longer pieces by supply-siders, was Irving Kristol, the neoconser-

---

[2]One supply-sider, Martin Anderson of the Hoover Institution, has written a book denouncing the world of academic economics for its insularity, by which he apparently means above all its unwillingness to adopt supply-side views or hire supply-side economists. He asserts that all of the good economics now being done comes from—surprise!— the world of (conservative) think tanks.

vative editor of *The Public Interest;* like Bartley, he began working in journalism in his twenties, at *Commentary.*

Now, there is nothing wrong with journalists (some of my best friends . . .). As most of them will admit, however, they are usually better at reporting facts than at generating concepts. The whole drive of journalism is toward short, snappy stories, toward presenting ideas in a way that is accessible to readers who have no previous knowledge of an issue and no desire to spend a lot of time on background information or abstract analysis. That is why it is so hard to find qualified science reporters: those who know enough science to get it right can rarely present stories in a way that holds readers' attention. The press more or less manages to report on developments in physics and biology, but nobody would expect a major innovation in, say, cosmology or the theory of evolution to come from the editor of *Omni* magazine.

In the 1970s, however, Bartley and Wanniski managed to convince themselves and a significant number of politicians that they had discovered some fundamental truths about economics that the mainstream, including conservatives like Milton Friedman and Robert Lucas, had failed to discern.

They did not, of course, come to their conclusions without any help from credentialled economists—above all, the supply-side group included two famous economics professors, Arthur Laffer and Robert Mundell. But these economists were also, in a fundamental way, outsiders.

Arthur Laffer has a Ph.D. from the University of Chicago and a full professorship at the University of Southern California, but he has never tried to break into the world of conventional academic research, and has always had a penchant for playing to the crowds. When still in his twenties he went to work for Richard Nixon's Office of Management and Budget (OMB). While there he gained considerable notoriety by claiming that a simple equation of his own devising could accurately forecast the nation's output, and by making a massively overoptimistic forecast on that basis.[3]

---

[3]Some years later, revised figures for 1971 places the dollar value of national output quite close to Laffer's old forecast, something Laffer's defenders have claimed as a vindication.

He went from OMB to academic life after a fashion, but was anything but a quiet scholar: he published few papers in professional
journals, spreading his ideas instead through newspaper articles
and lectures. Laffer came to the attention of Bartley through his
attacks on the 1971–73 devaluation of the dollar, then became a
household word with his famous "Laffer curve." In 1992 he once
again took a surprising turn by endorsing Bill Clinton over
George Bush.

The one figure in the supply-side group who does not at first
blush fit the outsider image is Robert Mundell, who is surely the
movement's intellectual luminary. Mundell teaches at Columbia
University, a respectable address. More to the point, Mundell is a
name to reckon with in the serious study of international economics. His academic reputation rests largely on a series of papers he
wrote in the early 1960s, as his native Canada wrestled with the
question of whether to peg its currency to the U.S. dollar. His
classic analysis of the criteria for an "optimum currency area" is
still must reading for discussion of such issues as the formation of
a European monetary union.[4] And his analysis of how the choice
between fixed and floating exchange rates affects the workings of
monetary and fiscal policy, the so-called Mundell-Fleming model,
remains a staple of almost every international economics textbook.

So one might think of Mundell as a consummate insider in the
economics profession. But one can have blue-chip credentials and
still have an outsider's mind-set. Mundell's career has never been
quite what you might have expected, given his undoubted brilliance. He taught for some years at the University of Chicago,
where he trained some of the leading international economists of

---

But it isn't. What Laffer was trying to forecast was not the dollar value of output but its
growth rate; the revisions that raised the estimate for 1971 also raised the number for
1970, leaving Laffer's growth forecast as far off as before. Also, what Laffer was selling was
not a single forecast but a forecasting equation; that equation can be run with the revised
data, and is still way off.

[4]Somewhat ironically, given the enthusiasm of supply-siders for fixed exchange rates and
even a return to the gold standard, Mundell's optimum currency area analysis is widely
cited by *opponents* of a single European currency.

the next generation, people like Rudiger Dornbusch of MIT, and Michael Mussa, chief economist of the International Monetary Fund. But in 1971 he left Chicago for the obscurity of Canada's University of Waterloo. He eventually returned to the United States to take up his position at Columbia, but he has remained largely isolated from students and colleagues.

The fact is that around 1970 Mundell veered off from conventionality in a number of ways. Some of these were superficial: he began to wear his hair long and to speak in a slow mumble. Some were more significant: Mundell dropped out of the usual academic round of conferences and seminars, and began holding his own conferences in a crumbling, half-habitable villa he owned near Siena. Most important, Mundell completely abandoned his former academic intellectual style; since 1970 he has written little, and what he has written tends to be marked by extravagant rhetoric, accusing his fellow economists of "sheer quackery" in espousing ideas that he himself had held when younger.

It was this new, post-1970 Mundell who was in effect adopted by the supply-siders as their intellectual mascot. First Laffer, then Wanniski, undertook a sustained campaign both to glorify Mundell's ideas and to associate themselves with that glory. This effort led to the widespread impression that Mundell invented supply-side economics—an impression that Mundell has not tried to discourage. Indeed, he welcomes his association with the movement. Yet Mundell himself played relatively little role in the emergence of the distinctive set of ideas that came to characterize the supply-siders, and as we will see, it is questionable given some of his views whether he himself can really be called a supply-sider.

Is this it? Surely a movement as powerful as supply-side economics must have had a far broader intellectual base than two journalists and two eccentric economists? Well, there were some others, notably a group of congressional staffers led by Paul Craig Roberts, a former economics professor who had become an aide to former football player–turned–Congressman Jack Kemp. There were also some independent journalistic voices—above all George Gilder, whose 1980 book *Wealth and Poverty* was must reading for Reagan officials. (Gilder's work shows some of the odd undercurrents beneath supply-side economics. Two of his previous books were *Sexual Suicide* and *Naked Nomads*, both essentially concerned with the emasculation of men by women's liberation. And *Wealth and Poverty* actually blames America's economic woes on working women as well as excessive taxation.)

But that's about it. In 1992, as in its early days, supply-side economics remained a tiny sect, whose ideas commanded the allegiance of only a handful of economists, most of the Republican Party, and the President of the United States.

The Supply-Side Idea

Every economist worries about the supply side of the economy. Even the most unrepentant Keynesian will admit that there are limits to the economy's capacity, and that expanding the economy's capacity is the only way to achieve sustained improvements in living standards. Every economist will also agree that high marginal tax rates reduce incentives, and a heavy majority will agree that the 90 percent marginal tax rates once levied on high-income Americans were far too high to serve any useful purpose.

Most economists believe as well that economic performance depends on the demand side—that there can be Keynesian shortfalls of demand, and that it is such shortfalls of demand that create recessions. But, as we have seen, an influential group of mainstream economists either does not agree that the demand side matters, or argues that governments are best advised to avoid trying to control demand.

There are, then, many mainstream economists who believe that taxes have an important effect on the supply side of the economy, and who are skeptical about the usefulness of any demand-side policy. But these views are not enough to make one a supply-sider.

If one had to define the essential ideas of supply-side economics, they would be these: First, demand-side policies, especially monetary policies, are completely ineffective.[5] Second, the incentive effects of reduced taxation are very large, so that lowering taxes will dramatically increase economic activity, perhaps to such an extent that tax revenue rises instead of falling.

As described, these ideas sound like a souped-up combination of the rational expectations school of macroeconomics and the conservative school of public finance. And there is no question that supply-side economics was helped to flourish by the intellectual environment of the 1970s, in which Keynesians were on the defensive and criticism of the distortions imposed by taxes was widespread. But a supply-sider like Jude Wanniski is not simply an economist who disagrees with the majority assessment of statistical evidence on tax incentive effects. Supply-siders do not fundamentally rely on empirical evidence to back their view; they believe that their ideas are necessarily, logically, right, and that the academic majority is wrong not only about parameters but about principles.

Or, to put it another way, the supply-siders are cranks.

I do not mean by this that they are wrong and my friends are right (although they *are* wrong and my friends *are* right). What I refer to instead is a particular intellectual style, a style identified and labeled as that of a "crank" in Martin Gardner's lovely book on pseudoscience, *In the Name of Science*.

A crank, in Gardner's definition, is someone who challenges scientific orthodoxy—but not in a sensible, well-informed way. Instead, he is an outsider who fails to understand what the orthodoxy is about, and/or is determined to refute the current wisdom for personal or political rather than scientific reasons. "Creation scientists" who deny evolution and "Gaia" enthusiasts who insist that the Earth is literally alive would be prominent among modern cranks. Now of course economics is not as full-fledged a science as biology, and Robert Bartley is not quite a full-fledged

---

[5]Although there is a curious inconsistency in the writings of supply-siders like Paul Craig Roberts. They do not believe that expansionary monetary policy should be given any credit for economic recoveries, but are quite willing to blame tight money for recessions.

crank. But much of Gardner's description applies remarkably well to the supply-siders.

Gardner identifies two defining features of the crank. First, a crank is isolated from the usual channels of discussion. "He does not send his findings to the recognized journals. . . . He speaks before organizations he himself has founded, contributes to journals he himself may edit. . . ."[6] Robert Bartley, in his self-congratulatory book *The Seven Fat Years,* describes the genesis of supply-side economics as taking place over a series of dinners at Michael 1, a Wall Street area restaurant. There it was that he and Laffer discovered that Keynesian economics was logically inconsistent—an insight that had eluded Paul Samuelson and a few thousand other people over the course of hundreds of academic conferences. They also discovered that Milton Friedman was wrong in believing that monetary policy could have important effects on the economy—an insight that had similarly eluded Friedman, Lucas, and the faculty of the University of Chicago over a generation of the notoriously brutal Chicago seminars. And the results of these deep thoughts over dinner were for the most part published—surprise—on the editorial page of *The Wall Street Journal,* or in Kristol's *Public Interest.*

The other characteristic of a crank, in Gardner's discussion, is the belief that failure of the establishment to accept his ideas necessarily represents stupidity, dishonesty, or both. Paul Craig Roberts argued in 1978 that a reduction in profit taxation *must* increase investment; he accused sophisticated economists like Congressional Budget Office director Alice Rivlin of making elementary logical errors in questioning his claim. Bartley's book, in summing up what he sees as the lessons of the Reagan years, calls his chapter "What You Learned If You Were Awake." Martin Anderson, a former Reagan aide, has published *Impostors in the Temple,* an attack on academia whose central message is that the failure of major universities to hire any supply-siders is the result of a deep political and intellectual corruption.

We could belabor this point, but what is important to realize is

[6]Martin Gardner, *In the Name of Science* (New York: Putnam, 1952), p. 11.

that the supply-siders represented a very different element in the debate from the characters we saw in the last two chapters. Milton Friedman has strong views, and has often clashed with majority opinion in economics; I think that he has often been wrong, and that he is sometimes willing to cut corners to win an argument. But nobody could call him a crank. Still less could one use the term to describe Robert Lucas or Martin Feldstein. So the group that Bartley assembled and promoted was something stranger and wilder than a mere collection of conservative economists; more like a cult or a sect than a simple school of thought.

Let us, then, examine a little more closely the views of this sect. What did they believe, and what did they advocate?

First, of course, the supply-siders did not believe that demand-side issues could matter. Bartley reports that Laffer educated him on the importance of Say's Law, an eighteenth-century dictum that says that supply creates its own demand—that is, since people have to spend their income on *something*, there is no possibility of a general failure of demand. This was a rejection of Keynesian (and for that matter monetarist) economics on principle. Unfortunately, the principle is wrong: try telling the unhappy members of the baby-sitting co-op described in Chapter 1 that a general failure in demand is impossible. What happened there was that the members of the co-op tried to spend part of their receipts of scrip, not on goods and services (baby-sitting), but on accumulating more scrip (money), which was impossible in the aggregate, and therefore precipitated a miniature recession. But the Michael 1 diners thought that they had neatly disposed of the whole topic of aggregate demand.

Second, the supply-siders dismissed the real-world importance of the money supply in general. Bartley tells of Laffer drawing a large box to represent the overall stock of credit in the economy, and a tiny box to represent that part of the stock corresponding to the money supply. " 'Do you really think,' he asked, 'this little black box controls all the others?' "[7] Again, economists from

[7]Robert Bartley, *The Seven Fat Years* (New York: Free Press, 1992), p. 50.

Keynes to Lucas had spent a lot of time trying to explain just why it is that the monetary instruments controlled by the Federal Reserve exert a profound influence on the economy; but over dinner this work was found to be obviously wrong.

If recessions are not the result of inadequate demand, and if money in particular doesn't have real effects, how then are we to explain booms and slumps, prosperity and depression? As we will see in Chapter 8, the academic critics of Keynes eventually took refuge in the concept of "real business cycles": a recession is a rational response to a bad technological draw. The supply-siders were not so fatalistic; they saw booms and slumps as driven by the incentives and disincentives of tax policy.

Why, for example, did the Great Depression happen? Both Keynesians and monetarists see it as largely a monetary phenomenon—leaving aside the question of whether the Federal Reserve's sins were ones of omission or commission, the slump is seen as a giant version of the baby-sitting co-op's problem, in which the collective attempt to hoard cash led to a breakdown of economic coordination. But the supply-siders did not believe this; indeed, they believed that this explanation could not be right, on logical grounds. So what could they turn to instead? A tax increase: specifically, the Smoot-Hawley tariff, imposed by the U.S. Congress in 1930.

The supply-siders have never been entirely clear about the mechanism by which Smoot-Hawley is supposed to have created the Depression, but in general it seems to go as follows: By increasing the cost of imported goods, Smoot-Hawley made the returns to work and investment less; it was the resulting reduction in investment and work effort that we call the Great Depression.

A non-supply-sider might note that this story implies an extraordinary response of work effort to incentives. The Smoot-Hawley tariff raised the average tax on imports by about 40 percent, but before the tariff imports were only about 6 percent of gross national product. In other words, the effective tax increase was only about 2.5 percent. Yet employment dropped by one third from 1929 to 1933. Conventional economists find a response this large incredible. But the supply-siders have no doubts about the correctness of their diagnosis—after all, what else could it have been?

It is worth noting that on this key historical episode Robert Mundell has never adhered to the supply-side position. Mundell believes that the Great Depression was a monetary event, albeit one driven largely by international rather than domestic monetary problems. This is a pretty big difference of opinion—after all, the diners at Michael 1 are supposed to have concluded that money cannot possibly be that important. One is led to the conclusion that the intellectual father of supply side is not exactly a supply-sider himself.

But back to the supply-side doctrine. If small increases in taxes can have huge negative effects on the economy, tax reductions can correspondingly have huge positive effects. The supply-siders looked at the long expansion of the U.S. economy during the 1960s and attributed it to Kennedy's tax cut at the decade's start— but not for the conventional reasons. Keynesian economists have always pointed to the Kennedy experience as evidence for the usefulness of policies to stimulate demand. Demand had nothing to do with it, said the supply-siders; it was all supply. And it could be done again.

And so we come to the fundamental supply-side policy proposition: The U.S. economy would benefit from a tax cut, period. No Keynesian qualifications about tax cuts being a desirable tool only if the economy was at less than full employment, and for that matter only if the Federal Reserve could not expand the economy simply through monetary policy. No traditional conservative concerns about making offsetting expenditure cuts, either. On tax cutting, the supply-siders urged, just do it.

What did they think would happen? They believed that a tax cut would lead to a large increase in both labor supply and investment, and hence to a large expansion in output. To those who worried about the impact of such tax cuts on the budget deficit, they offered two lines of defense.

First was the argument that tax cuts might not actually increase the deficit. It's a familiar proposition that if you raise a tax too high, revenue actually falls, because people make such extraordinary efforts to avoid it. In one of the famous scenes of supply-side economics, Arthur Laffer is supposed to have summarized this point with a curve sketched on a dinner napkin, the famous "Laffer curve." Nobody questions that something like the Laffer curve exists; but even the supply-siders are skeptical about whether the U.S. economy is really in the "backward-sloping" section.

But that didn't worry them, because they argued that even if the deficit did increase, the concurrent rise in private savings would easily finance that deficit and still allow an increase in investment.

To a conventional economist, or even to an old-fashioned conservative, the whole thing sounds extremely irresponsible. In the Republican primaries of 1980, candidate George Bush memorably described the supply-side prescription as "voodoo economics." Few respectable people thought that such an idea, proposed by a group of people who not only were cranks in Gardner's sense but were perceived as such, could have any chance of adoption by a great and sophisticated nation.

They were wrong. But before we try to find out why, we need to stop briefly to review one somewhat different doctrine of Bartley's group: their distinctive views on international economics.

International Economics

In 1973 Arthur Laffer was known to the public, if at all, only as the brash young economist who had made such a bad prediction. His reappearance as an influential figure began in that year, with a series of articles in *The Wall Street Journal*. Given what happened later, you might have expected those articles to have been about taxes. But they weren't: they were about the devaluation of the U.S. dollar.

Why were Laffer and Bartley talking about the dollar? Several big things happened in 1973. First, it was the year of the first great rise in the price of oil, as Arab nations imposed an embargo on the West after the Yom Kippur War. Second, it was a year of rises in the prices of many other raw materials, for a variety of reasons: Soviet purchases drove up the price of wheat, animal feed prices rose because of the temporary disappearance of Peru's anchovies, other commodities rose on speculation or because of short-lived attempts to establish OPEC-style cartels. Third, it was a year in which the world's advanced nations gave up on trying to hold exchange rates fixed, and in which the dollar was allowed to drop sharply in value against the German mark, the Japanese yen, and other major currencies. Finally, it was a year of unprecedented inflation in the United States: in 1973–74, for the first time since the Korean War, consumer prices in the United States rose at a double-digit rate.

Most economists thought that the surge in inflation was the result of a mixture of factors, including all of the events mentioned above plus the effects of an overheated domestic economy. But Laffer argued that only one factor really mattered: the fall in the dollar.

How did Laffer arrive at this conclusion? By taking seriously a theoretical simplification widely used in international monetary economics, and in particular by Robert Mundell. It is common for international economists, when trying to think about some financial issues, to envisage a simplified world in which all countries produce the same good, and in which arbitrage—the activities of entrepreneurs who will ship goods from places where they are cheap to places where they are expensive—forces the price of that good to be equal everywhere. (The proposition that arbitrage will eliminate international price differences is sometimes referred to as the "Law of One Price"; like most economic "laws," it is not really true.) International economists like to think about "one-good" models for the same reason that physicists like to talk about the trajectories that cannonballs would follow in a vacuum: the hypothetical world helps you focus on some important issues, in this case the undoubted tendency of international arbitrage to force the prices of internationally traded goods to converge, while temporarily putting on one side others, like the fact that most services and many goods are not internationally traded, and that arbitrage tends to be limited even for those goods and services that are traded.

What Laffer claimed, however, was that the one-good model was not only a useful intellectual exercise but a roughly correct description of the way the world actually works.

If this were true, it would have very important implications. Take the exchange rate between the U.S. dollar and the German mark. In 1985, $1 exchanged for about 3 marks; at the time of writing, the rate was only about 1.5 marks per dollar. In a one-good world, the price indexes of Germany and the United States would have to remain equal *when measured in the same currency,* so the ratio of the U.S. price index in dollars to the German index in marks would have to double. For example, if German prices were stable, U.S. prices would have to double.

In the light of experience, of course, it is clear that nothing like this is true in fact. Since 1980 the dollar-mark exchange rate has engaged in a spectacular roller-coaster ride that was hardly reflected at all in consumer prices. In reality, the one-good model is as misleading for studying the effects of changes in exchange rates as assuming that we live in a perfect vacuum would be for studying aerodynamics. In 1973, however, Laffer claimed that the rise in U.S. inflation after the dollar's fall demonstrated that the one-good model was actually a good approximation to reality—a view that he attributed to Mundell, and that became an article of faith for Bartley and *The Wall Street Journal.* And he also claimed that because the falling dollar had led to nothing but inflation, the decision to allow the dollar to fall was a disastrous mistake.

Why should supply-siders have been infatuated with the Law of One Price? I have to admit that even after reading Bartley's explanation of how it all fits together, I do not fully understand what the Law of One Price and supply-side economics have to do with each other. But the one-good model seems to have appealed to several aspects of the supply-side mind-set. For one thing, it was a poke in the eye of Keynesian conventional wisdom, a satisfying thing in itself for the supply-siders. More important, perhaps, is that it is difficult to reconcile a demand-side view of booms and slumps with a one-good view of the world. After all, if all goods and services are traded on a single world market, there is no way that changes in national demand can drive domestic output and employment; hence it must be the supply side, not the demand side, that accounts for booms and slumps.

In the United States, the international side of supply-side dogma never had much impact. Although the editors of *The Wall Street Journal* were to protest bitterly about the decline in the dollar after 1985, they were ignored by then Treasury Secretary James Baker. Between his role as tax cutter and his later incarnation as welfare reformer, Jack Kemp spent an unlikely period as the apostle of a return to the gold standard, but few took him seriously. The main impact of supply-side international economics in the United States was personal: it was international monetary doctrines that brought Bartley, Laffer, and Mundell together.

Elsewhere, however, the drumbeat of propaganda on behalf of the proposition that devaluing your currency does nothing but feed inflation had a powerful effect. In Europe, in particular, the importance of stable currencies became an item of faith among many conservatives—a faith that did much to create the monetary debacles described in Chapter 7.

The Crisis of Conventional Economics

During the formative years of supply-side economics, few mainstream economists or politicians took it seriously. It got much more exposure than most eccentric economic doctrines, thanks to the magnificent platform of *The Wall Street Journal*, but otherwise it seemed mostly a kind of curiosity—a doctrine not even worth arguing against. The important debates, or so the establishment thought, were about monetary policy, about rational expectations versus Keynesianism, about the appropriate role of the Federal Reserve.

The establishment was wrong: supply-side economics was about to stage a spectacular coup, seizing power not only from the moderate Keynesians of the Carter administration but even from ordinary conservatives.

How did this happen? To some extent it was a matter of a triple coincidence of timing. Supply-side economics happened to capture the mind of a consummate politician running for President; it did so at a time when bad luck and bad management had produced an economic crisis; and all of this took place just when the intellectual battles described in Chapter 1 had produced a crisis of confidence in the economic mainstream. And yet perhaps the triumph of the supply-siders was more than an accident.

THE ECONOMIC CRISIS OF THE LATE 1970S

Robert Bartley, in his *Seven Fat Years,* regards 1978 as the year in which "it all started to come true." That was the year that a bill introduced by Jack Kemp and William Roth, calling for a 30 percent cut in income taxes over three years, actually passed both houses of Congress before dying in conference committee. By the middle of the next year staffer Martin Anderson would put together Ronald Reagan's famous Campaign Policy Memorandum Number 1, essentially endorsing Kemp-Roth. And to the astonishment not only of liberals but even of the conservative establishment, supply-side policies were soon actually put into effect.

Why did things turn in 1978? At least one major part of the reason was that the economic situation was deteriorating in ways that made some kind of radical policy initiative seem increasingly urgent.

With the benefit of hindsight, we now know that the Good Years really ended in 1973, and that their end was essentially due to one factor and one factor only: the slowdown in productivity growth. In the 1970s, however, matters were not so clear. In 1974–75 the economy had slid into a deep recession, with the unemployment rate rising at its peak to 9 percent, a postwar high. The recovery from that slump created a temporary mood of optimism, as the U.S. economy spent three years expanding at a 4.6 percent annual rate. But by 1978 the recovery seemed to be hitting a wall. Although the unemployment rate was still above 6 percent, inflation started to surge. Consumer prices rose 4.9 percent during 1976, 6.7 percent during 1977, and an alarming 9 percent during 1978. (In 1979, with some help from the Ayatollah Khomeini, it soared above 13 percent.)

There is still a little bit of a mystery why inflation accelerated as much as it did in 1978 and 1979. Rising oil and food prices were part of the story, as was a slide in the value of the dollar on international markets. Although the unemployment rate was not very low by historical standards, the changing composition of the U.S. labor force—swollen by baby boomers and large numbers of women—meant that labor markets were tighter than they appeared.[8] And it may be that frustration over the stagnation of real wages, at a time before workers had really adjusted to the end of the Good Years, led to unrealistic wage demands.

Whatever the reasons for the acceleration of inflation, the public was angry and dismayed; and politicians were looking for answers.

THE DISARRAY OF THE ECONOMISTS

In sheer quantitative terms, the economic crisis of the late 1970s was not really that severe. In particular, unemployment was actually fairly low: the 1979 rate would not be attained again until 1987. While people complained about inflation, the actual economic hardships they were suffering at the point when supply-siders began their climb to power were mild compared with those inflicted during the recession of 1982 or even that of 1990–92. What made the crisis seem so bad was the sense that things were out of control, that the establishment had no answers.

[8]White males over twenty have traditionally had much lower unemployment rates than other demographic groups (although in the 1980s the male-female gap disappeared). The unemployment rate among white men over twenty was only 3.6 percent in 1979; it has never fallen that low since then, even at the peak of the Reagan expansion.

After all, what was a conventional economist to propose at that juncture? Conventional theory offered only one surefire way to reduce inflation: put the economy through a prolonged period of high unemployment, so as to wring the inflationary expectations out of the system. This was not pleasant medicine, and economists hesitated to prescribe it—indeed, it was widely believed to be politically impossible to follow such a policy. This belief turned out to be wrong: the Federal Reserve was eventually to bring inflation under control precisely in the conventional way, by imposing on the U.S. economy a slump deeper and longer than anyone in 1978 would have dared to suggest. But in 1978 few people were prepared to face up to the necessity for measures that drastic.

The result was that conventional economists found themselves proposing a variety of weak and unconvincing palliatives such as tax schemes that would reward price restraint and subsidies aimed at mopping up unemployment among relatively high-unemployment demographic groups. Robert Lucas commented caustically on one "report by a distinguished panel"—the convening of such panels being a normal response to intellectual confusion—that it combined a tone of "sad resignation" with "undisciplined eclecticism."

The sense that the usual experts had nothing useful to contribute was reinforced by the obvious internal dissension within academic economics. Policy-oriented economists were still offering essentially Keynesian diagnoses of the economy's problems, but many of their colleagues back in the university were confidently pronouncing Keynesianism to be useless nonsense.

Meanwhile, the supply-siders offered a seductive alternative, one which proposed to cure the country's inflation problem without any economic pain. To control inflation, impose a tight monetary policy—since they did not believe that money had anything to do with the business cycle, they did not believe this would cause a recession. And meanwhile expand the economy by cutting taxes; no need to worry very much about finding matching spending cuts.

Much of the U.S. Congress was willing to try this plan. Still, it is hard to imagine that it would have happened had it not been for one man.

WAS RONALD REAGAN NECESSARY?

I am in no position to add anything useful to the thousands of pages that have been written about Ronald Reagan, his personality, and his style of decision making. Clearly it was far easier for Reagan than it would have been for some other candidate to decide to base his economic program on the advice of a group whom the mainstream found hard to take seriously. After all, the same people found it hard to take Reagan himself seriously. Reagan had an outsider's mentality; his own success at moving from acting to politics, and at overcoming the initial sense of the ridiculous created by that move, predisposed him to be willing to disregard orthodoxy in all areas. For example, his faith in "Star Wars" if anything flew even more in the face of expert advice and analysis than his faith in supply-side economics.

The interesting question is whether supply-side economics would have managed to seize power without Ronald Reagan. It is easy to argue the contrary. As we'll see in Chapter 4, Reagan's political success owed much to good luck with the business cycle. It's easy to imagine an alternative history in which Jimmy Carter or George Bush emerged as President in 1980; suffered the punishing recession of 1982 just like Reagan; but was, like Reagan, in a position to claim unjustified credit for the recovery that followed. Could Walter Mondale have proclaimed "morning in America"?

My guess, though, is that the strength of the supply-siders rested on more than the affection of one man. They were selling something that conservative politicians needed, something that mainstream conservative economists could not supply. They had already achieved remarkable influence before Reagan's election. Without Reagan, they might have had to wait a bit longer, but they probably would have found their way to power eventually. As we'll see in Chapter 10, their counterpart policy entrepreneurs on the left, the strategic traders, faced a much harder time gaining acceptance; they wandered in the political wilderness for more than a decade, yet eventually found their way to the Promised Land. In troubled economic times, politicians need something that is better than the truth.

In any case, Ronald Reagan did exist, and he made supply-side economics the law of the land. How well did it work?

PART II

CONSERVATIVES IN POWER

CHAPTER 4

Growth

The core of the conservative economic promise can be summed up in one word: growth. Extreme supply-siders like Jude Wanniski and Arthur Laffer claimed that lower tax rates would lead to such an explosion of growth that everything—even tax revenue— would rise. More moderate conservative economists, like Murray Weidenbaum or Michael Boskin, did not go so far, but they did argue that the burden of taxation and regulation was one of the main explanations of slowing U.S. growth in the 1970s, and implied that getting government out of the way would yield big rewards. Even many liberals believed that deregulation and some reform of the tax system could raise the U.S. growth rate.

Once conservatives were in power, the word "growth" became a kind of mantra, used to pacify anyone worried about the way the U.S. economy was going. Was the spectacle of supposedly tight-fisted conservatives running unprecedented deficits dismaying? Don't worry, we'll grow our way out of the deficit. Did the widening disparity between rich and poor seem like a problem? Don't worry, growth will benefit everyone.

So, how well did conservatism in power deliver on its promise of growth?

At first glance, the answer seems to depend on who you talk to. The supply-side faithful claim that the record of Ronald Reagan shows that cutting taxes really does produce spectacular growth, and blame the poor growth record of the Bush years on George Bush's failure to continue supply-side policies. Democrats, on the other hand, warned at least as early as Walter Mondale's campaign that supply-side policies would have disastrous effects on long-term growth, and in 1992 they were able to convince a plurality of voters that chickens had finally come home to roost. Who is right?

The answer is, of course, neither. The conservative claim to have found the secret of growth is entirely false—there was *no* sign of an acceleration of long-term growth rates at any point during the twelve years of conservative rule, except, ironically, at the very end. The insistence of supply-siders on claiming glorious success was at first an infuriating piece of intellectual dishonesty, although in the aftermath of Bush's defeat it seems less infuriating than pitiful. On the other hand, there was no noticeable deceleration of growth either; claims that Reaganomics was a disaster for overall economic growth are as unfounded as claims that it was a brilliant success.

The truth is that nothing much happened to U.S. economic growth under conservative rule. But if that's the case, how were conservatives able to argue, in a way that temporarily convinced much of the American public, that they had done something wonderful? That's an interesting story, which tells us a lot about the U.S. economy, and even more about the way that economic debate is carried on in this country.

How to Lie with Statistics

If you knew very little about economics, you might think that assessing the economic performance of an administration is easy. Just ask how fast the economy grew while that particular president was in office. The numbers tell the story, don't they?

Well, suppose that you compare the growth rates of real GDP under the last five administrations: Nixon/Ford, Carter, Reagan I, Reagan II, and Bush. These numbers seem to tell a very clear story: Ronald Reagan was a very good economic leader, who improved with age, while George Bush was a disaster. It's easy, looking at these numbers, to understand the feeling of betrayal among many conservatives: If only George Bush had stuck with Reaganite policies, wouldn't the growth have continued?

But even someone innocent of economics must feel a little queasy about the idea of assigning all of the credit or blame for growth over a four-year period to the person who happens to occupy the White House during those years. At the most basic level, it is or should be obvious that not everything that happens in the economy is under the control of the President. (We'll see later that in fact hardly any of the levers that control short-term economic performance are in the administration's hands.) Furthermore, even to the extent that a president's policies do matter, their effects can't be instantaneous. Unemployment rates were quite high for much of Reagan's first term; but Reagan came to power during a recession that began under Jimmy Carter. Should we attribute everything that happened after January 1981 to Reagan, or should we blame at least some of the high unemployment of the early Reagan years on his predecessor? Conversely, the recession that destroyed George Bush's presidency began only eighteen months after Reagan left office; was the Reagan Revolution really so fragile that it could be shattered by a year and a half of more moderate conservatism, or should at least some of Bush's problems be regarded as Reagan's legacy? Finally, Bill Clinton entered office during a recovery that officially began in 1991, and accelerated dramatically during the second half of 1992; how much credit can he claim for any good things that happened early in his term?

These dating issues sound like pesky little details, but they aren't, for one basic reason: growth in the U.S. economy is highly variable over time. Look at Figure 4, which shows annual growth rates of real GDP in the United States since 1973. On average, the economy grew at 2.5 percent per year, but individual years showed growth as high as 6.8 and as low as − 2.2 percent. When growth rates vary this much from year to year, the average growth rate over four, eight, or even twelve years depends crucially on exactly which years you choose to include. As a result, by choosing your years carefully and talking a good game, you can seem to prove whatever conclusion you like.

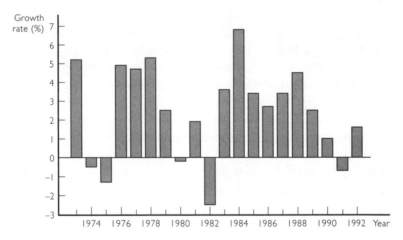

Figure 4. The growth rate of the U.S. economy fluctuates a good deal from year to year, so your assessment of an administration's performance depends a lot on how you pick your dates.

For example, suppose that you want to show that Reaganomics was a marvelous success. Then you do the following: You blame Jimmy Carter not only for whatever bad things happened on his watch, but also for the recession of 1981–82, which you attribute to the inflation that Reagan inherited. So your baseline—the "Carter years"—is the average growth rate of the U.S. economy from 1976 to 1982, 1.8 percent. Then you give Reagan credit for the long recovery that followed: the "Reagan years" (the source for Robert Bartley's title *The Seven Fat Years*) run from 1982 to 1990, an era of 3.6 percent growth.[1] And there it is—incontrovertible evidence! Supply-side economics took an economy that was growing at less than 2 percent a year and turned it into an economy that grew at almost 4 percent per year.

Suppose, on the other hand, that you want to make the case for conservative failure. Then you might do this calculation: Compare the 2.1 percent growth rate over the whole period of Republican rule, from the end of 1980 to the end of 1992, with the 3.4 percent rate of growth over the "good years" of the postwar period from 1947 to 1973. And there it is again—incontrovertible proof! Reaganomics failed to restore good growth. In fact, growth was unacceptably slow, clearly because Republican policies failed to put people first. (If you want to make an even stronger anti-conservative case, you focus not on overall growth but on median family income and real wages, in effect emphasizing the widening inequality of income distribution in the United States; but we'll reserve that discussion for Chapter 5.)

What do we learn from these two ways of looking at the same numbers? We learn that a clever propagandist, right or left, can almost always find a way to present the data on economic growth that seems to support her case. And we therefore also learn to take any statistical analysis from a strongly political source with handfuls of salt. Someone once said about partisan analysts that they use economic data the way a drunkard uses a lamppost: for support rather than illumination. Or as Disraeli put it, there are three kinds of lies: lies, damn lies, and statistics.

Should we therefore conclude that nobody knows; that it's all in

---

[1]In the spring of 1992 I found myself on TV, debating with Alan Reynolds, a supply-sider at the Hudson Institute. In rolling out his pro-Reagan statistics, Reynolds self-righteously declared: "I don't believe in all this playing around with dates, so let's just look at what happened over the whole decade of the 1980s—from 1982 to 1990."

the prejudiced eye of the beholder? No: there is actually a very clear answer to what *really* happened to U.S. growth in the era of conservative rule—namely, nothing. But this is an answer that requires that we step back to think about what it is we are trying to measure.

Thinking About Growth

Any attempt to get a picture of the performance of the U.S. economy has to start with a few concepts. Practical people tend to be impatient with concepts—they want to get to the facts. For different reasons, political polemicists also get impatient with concepts—they get in the way of their efforts to argue their case. As the great Victorian economist Alfred Marshall once noted, however, "the most reckless and dangerous theorist is the man who claims to let the facts speak for themselves." Only after we think a little bit about how to look at the record can we interpret the facts sensibly.

Luckily, to sort out the growth record of conservatism in power we only need to understand one basic concept and one basic principle. The concept is the distinction between the business cycle on one side and growth in the economy's capacity on the other, between the short-term fluctuations that we call recessions and recoveries, and the long-term upward trend. The principle is that the success of the conservative agenda is to be measured by an acceleration of the long-term trend, not by the short-term ups and downs.

Why do we need to complicate the story this way? Why can't we just look at the facts? We've already seen why: because the rate of economic growth fluctuates so much from year to year that playing a little bit with who gets responsibility for which years can dramatically change your assessment of how well conservatives have done. So looking at the raw facts on growth, especially over short periods, tells you very little about the success of long-term economic policies.

Let's reinforce the point with one more example. In 1983, the U.S. economy grew at a torrid 7 percent. In 1986, it grew only 3 percent. Now Ronald Reagan was President in both years. Did the slowdown of growth reflect a deterioration in the quality of his leadership, or a change in his policies? Could 7 percent growth have continued if only his advisers had let Reagan be Reagan? Of course not. In 1983, the United States was recovering from a deep recession; it could grow rapidly by putting unemployed resources—factories as well as people—back to work. By 1986, most of the workers and machines that had been idled by the great slump of 1979–82 were back on the job; it was inevitable that growth would slow.

The example does more than make the point that it is silly to dwell too much on short-term growth; it also tells us why we need to distinguish between two sources of economic growth. On one side, there is growth in our underlying productive capacity, determined by the number and skill of our workers, the size and quality of our capital stock, and the level of our technology. On the other side, there are changes in the degree to which we utilize that capacity, determined by fluctuations in the money supply and in business confidence. Clearly short-term growth rates can easily fluctuate a lot due to changes in capacity utilization, even if the rate of capacity growth is quite steady. If a recession has left millions of workers unemployed and thousands of factories idle, the economy can experience a spurt of growth as these unemployed resources are put back to work. Conversely, the economy's output can grow slowly or even shrink despite rapidly growing capacity if capacity utilization is falling.

It turns out that short-term fluctuations in economic growth are, in fact, overwhelmingly the result of changes in capacity utilization; the capacity of the economy grows relatively steadily through booms and slumps alike.

One way to see this is to compare the growth rate of the economy with *changes* in the unemployment rate. If the economy is growing fast by bringing unemployed workers back to work, then unemployment should fall; if it is growing fast because the number of willing workers or their productivity is rising exceptionally fast, then growth might actually be accompanied by rising unemployment. In fact, not only does unemployment tend to fall when the economy is growing fast (and rise when it is growing slowly or actually shrinking), the relationship is remarkably exact. Figure 5 shows a plot of real growth versus changes in unemployment from 1973 to 1991 (the choice of dates is not an accident; more on that later). By the standards of the inexact science of economics, this is a startlingly tight fit. Indeed, the relationship between growth and unemployment is one of the few quantitative relationships reliable enough for economists to call it a "law" (Okun's Law, after Arthur Okun, an economic adviser to John F. Kennedy) without embarrassment. The line suggests the size of the tradeoff: an extra percentage point of economic growth is associated with about a 0.5 percentage point fall in the unemployment rate; equivalently, a 1-point fall in unemployment is associated with about 2 percentage points of economic growth.

Now, unless the economy is emerging from a terrible slump, you can only cut the unemployment rate by a limited amount. From the fourth quarter of 1982 to the fourth quarter of 1989, the unemployment rate fell from 10.7 to 5.2 percent, a fall of 5.5

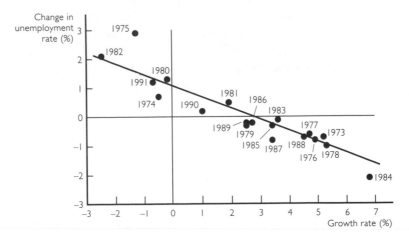

Figure 5. There is a pretty tight relationship between growth and the change in the unemployment rate.

percentage points. Could this have continued? If it had gone on for another seven years, the unemployment rate would have become negative. That's even more impossible than it sounds: the sheer frictions of a constantly changing labor market ensure that the unemployment rate cannot drop much below 3 percent. In practice, the U.S. economy probably cannot go below 5 percent unemployment without overheating and developing a bad case of accelerating inflation.

So, long-term economic growth cannot be achieved by bringing down the unemployment rate; it can only be achieved by accelerating the rate of growth that the economy can achieve at a *given* unemployment rate. This long-term rate of growth is generally referred to as the rate of growth of "potential" output; it is, in effect, the rate of growth of the economy's productive capacity.

In years when the unemployment rate is more or less constant, the U.S. economy has grown by about 2.5 percent. More generally, you can take the relationship between unemployment and growth implied by the line in Figure 5 to estimate how much the U.S. economy would have grown in any given year if unemployment had remained constant—its "potential" growth in that year. We have already seen, in Figure 1, what you get.

What do we learn from this exercise? First, we learn that potential growth does not fluctuate nearly as much as actual growth. Second, we learn that nothing much happened to potential growth in the 1980s. Since the resignation of Richard Nixon, actual economic growth was most rapid under Jimmy Carter and Ronald Reagan, slower under Gerald Ford, slowest under George Bush. Potential growth was about the same under all four.

The Conservative Growth Record

So far I have said nothing at all about the success or failure of conservative economic policies, although alert readers will already have picked up some of the implications. But we are now prepared to make a preliminary assessment.

Let's begin with two basic assertions.

First, supply-side economics was supposed to raise potential output, not simply increase the utilization of capacity. For one thing, supply-side economics was formulated in the relatively low unemployment era of the late 1970s; creating jobs was not high on the list of priorities. Anyway, the supply-siders wanted and promised a fundamental, large increase in the growth rate, something that no mere business cycle recovery could produce. And in any case, fluctuations in unemployment are driven primarily by changes in demand—and supply-siders were contemptuous of the Keynesian preoccupation with maintaining demand.

Second, business cycle fluctuations have very little to do with the economic policies of the administration in power—any administration. The management of the business cycle is left largely in the hands of the Federal Reserve, the non-partisan, quasi-independent agency that manages the nation's money. The Fed tries, with considerable honesty and varying competence, to achieve as high and stable a level of employment as it can while maintaining stable prices. We'll take a look at the Fed's role soon; the important point is that the business cycle is essentially the Fed's domain, not the administration's.

Since conservative economic policies were not aimed at the business cycle, and since the short-term fluctuations of the U.S. economy since 1980 have had little to do with administration policies, it seems obvious that to assess the success of conservative policies at promoting growth, we should focus on the growth in potential output. We can do this in two ways. The more elaborate way is to try to calculate the growth in potential output year by year. The alternative, which is easier and useful for some other comparisons, is to look at pairs of years that were at more or less comparable positions in the business cycle. The natural calculation for assessing U.S. performance is to compare growth between major business cycle peaks: growth from 1979 to 1990 versus growth from either 1969 or 1973 to 1979.

We already saw that calculating potential output year by year shows a slowing of that growth after about 1973, and no acceleration in the 1980s. Comparing business cycle peaks gives you the same result: from 1979 to 1990, the U.S. economy grew at an annual rate of 2.3 percent, versus 2.4 percent from 1973 to 1979, and 2.8 percent from 1969 to 1979. Growth in the 1980s was slower than in the 1970s as a whole, about the same as growth in the period after 1973. By no stretch can the growth performance in the 1980s be called exceptional, or even satisfactory.

That is the simple fact. A dozen years of conservative economic policies were not disastrous for growth. But there is absolutely no sign that these policies did anything to produce faster growth.

The Conservative Answer

There are many conservatives who accept the conclusion that the policies followed under Reagan and Bush did little to accelerate U.S. economic growth. Indeed, the 1992 *Economic Report of the President* contained a revealing chart on productivity growth, which classed the whole period from 1973 to 1990 into a single era—that is, George Bush's own economic advisers implicitly agreed that the era of disappointing economic growth continued through the years of conservative rule. Such conservatives blame the failure to raise America's growth rate on factors beyond their control, or on the incompleteness with which the conservative agenda was applied. This is a position that an honest and reasonable person could hold, although later we'll get to the reasons why I think it is wrong.

The true believer supply-siders, people like Alan Reynolds of the Hudson Institute or Paul Craig Roberts, take a different line. They claim that the supply-side program was a rousing success.

How can they do this? Part of the answer is that they move the goalposts closer. Alan Reynolds, for example, has described the 11 percent rise in median family income from 1980 to 1989 as a "huge increase," constituting an "unprecedented middle-class boom"; he seems unaware, or expects his readers to be unaware, of the much faster rate of rise of median income during the Good Years (for example, median income rose 17 percent just in the six years from 1967 to 1973).

Mostly, however, the conservatives award themselves a prize by denying the distinction between the business cycle and long-run growth—and by blaming all bad business cycle developments on liberals, while taking credit for all the good outcomes. We've already seen how to do this: the now-standard conservative line is to blame everything that happened to the U.S. economy until 1982 on the current and lagged effects of Jimmy Carter, then give Ronald Reagan complete credit for the economic recovery from 1982 until 1990. As for the economic slump after 1990, this was due to George Bush's apostasy; if Reagan were still in office, the 1982–90 expansion could have continued indefinitely.

But this is nonsense.

Recessions and Recoveries, 1979–93

In terms of its core economic promise, that of increasing the rate of growth of the economy's potential output, supply-side economics was neither a success nor a disaster, but simply ineffectual. In fact, potential output grew just about as fast under both Reagan and Bush as it did under Ford and Carter. But one could hardly say that the economy was placid over the era of conservative rule. On the contrary, a severe recession helped catapult conservatism into power; a strong recovery from that recession turned Reagan's presidency into a triumph; and a final stubborn recession hurled George Bush and the conservative movement out of the White House. What was all of that about?

The answer is deeply ironic: The economic tides that determined political fortunes over the course of the 1980s had very little to do with administration policy. The story of recessions and recoveries from 1979 to 1993 is essentially one of monetary policy, made by the non-partisan and more or less independent Federal Reserve Board.

This assertion requires some background explanation of what the Federal Reserve is and why it has so much power.

The Power of the Central Bank

The Federal Reserve is America's central bank—the counterpart of Germany's Bundesbank, the Bank of England, and similar institutions around the world. What central banks do is control the supply of "monetary base": cash in circulation, plus the reserves of private banks, which they may convert into cash to pay off their depositors. The Federal Reserve can add to the monetary base at will, essentially by simply printing more money and using it to buy bonds; no other institution can do this.[2]

This is a tremendous source of economic power, because the monetary base plays a special strategic role in the economy. Although our financial markets are huge and sophisticated, nearly every transaction requires that somebody hold a small but crucial amount of cash or bank reserves. If I plan to pay my plumber cash (best not to ask why he prefers not to receive checks), I personally need to hold a certain amount of monetary base in my wallet. If I pay my mortgage by check, I need to have the money in my bank account—and banks are required to hold reserves of monetary base equal to a fraction of their deposits. If I buy a stereo with a credit card, I will need money in my bank account to settle the credit card bill, and this bank account will be backed by monetary base . . . well, you get the idea. The whole financial structure, huge and complex though it is, is in effect a sort of inverted pyramid resting on the monetary base that the Federal Reserve supplies.

Because of the strategic role of monetary base, the actions of the Federal Reserve can have a profound effect on the economy. If the Fed irresponsibly increases monetary base by 20 percent, it can set off a huge inflationary surge. If for some reason it chooses to cut the monetary base by 10 percent, it can plunge the economy into a punishing recession.

What makes the Fed's role in recessions and recoveries so decisive, however, is not simply how profound its influence is but the speed and ease with which it can make drastic changes in

---

[2]The Fed can also reduce the monetary base by selling some bonds and withdrawing the cash it receives from circulation.

policy. The monetary base at the end of 1992 was only $348 billion, in an economy in which the daily volume of financial transactions is measured in trillions of dollars. This means that the Federal Reserve can easily alter the monetary base sharply in a very short time. Suppose, for example, that Fed policy were somehow to fall under the control of a maniac, who chose to increase the monetary base by 10 percent on Monday and reverse that decision on Tuesday. Could he do it? No problem. In each case it would take only a few phone calls to the usual banks, and the policy would be accomplished.

All of this is in sharp contrast to the sluggishness with which other kinds of economic policy usually take effect. An administration may, as the Clinton administration did in 1993, decide that the economy needs a boost, and try to offer tax incentives for investment and/or start a number of public works projects. But even if the party in the White House also controls Congress, it takes time to put such measures into legislation and time to work out the details; if government money is to be spent, it will also be necessary to call for bids, award contracts, and so on. In other words, where monetary policy can spin on a dime, other government policy makes very wide turns.

I just said "other government policy." But that's a bit misleading, because there is one final point about the Federal Reserve: it is not exactly part of the government.

Now, it's not exactly not part of the government either—it's sort of in between. The British have a lovely term for neither-fish-nor-fowl entities like the Fed: they call them "quangos," short for "quasi-non-governmental." The Federal Reserve System, legally at least, is an association of private member banks, given the privilege of controlling monetary base by a 1914 law. Its Board of Governors is a hybrid, with some members (including the chairman) appointed by the President, while others are chosen by the member banks. Even the presidential appointments are, however, for fourteen-year terms designed to ensure immunity to political pressures. (The chairman's term, though, is only for four years; it's not a completely insulated institution.) Moreover, the Fed has a powerful culture of independence. It jealously guards its right to make decisions as it sees fit, and above all not to be bullied to make monetary policy in the interests of the governing party.

It is worth noting that the same is not always true for comparable institutions in other countries. Germany's Bundesbank is even more independent than the Fed, but Britain's Bank of England has no autonomy at all—it is simply an arm of Her Majesty's Treasury. Given the poor track record of the Bank of England, however, even politicians who are critical of the Fed are reluctant to threaten its autonomy.

The important point is that the institution whose decisions have the greatest impact on the short-run performance of the economy, a short run that may easily extend the length of a presidential term, is a non-partisan body controlled by more or less apolitical technocrats.

THE FED AND THE ECONOMY

Now that we understand that it is the Federal Reserve, not the administration, that calls the shots on recessions and recoveries, we can tell the story of what happened during the era of conservative rule.

As in the introduction, I find a play metaphor useful. Think of it as a story in three acts.

Act I actually began in 1979. By the fall of 1979 it was clear to everyone that the U.S. economy had a dangerous problem of inflation, the result of a combination of outside shocks like the explosion in world oil prices and a history of mistakes in domestic monetary policy. In November of that year Paul Volcker was appointed Chairman of the Federal Reserve's Board of Governors. Volcker, with bipartisan support, began fighting inflation the only reliable way we know: by tightening up on monetary policy. If the conservative critique of Keynes that we described in Chapter 1 had been right, Volcker's highly credible commitment to disinflation need not have led to a severe recession; but in fact it did. Indeed, by the summer of 1982, while inflation had fallen sharply, the real economy appeared on the verge of a tailspin. So the Fed abruptly shifted policy, as only the Fed can do, and began trying to expand the economy.

Act II is the "Reagan" expansion from 1982 to 1990. In fact, it should be called the Volcker expansion, since it had its roots in that reversal of monetary policy in the summer of 1982. Monetary policy worked: the economy's engine roared to life in November of that year. And as we've already seen, it was possible for the boom to run fast and long, precisely because there were so many unemployed resources available as a result of the previous recession.

The durability of the expansion was also at least partly due to good judgment on the part of Volcker and his successor, Alan Greenspan. By 1984, when the recovery was well established, the Fed began trying to rein the economy in, so as not to squander the earlier gains against inflation; it was successful in this effort, and thereby helped allow a slower expansion to continue. In 1987, the spectacular crash of the stock market threatened a new recession: the Fed, by now under Greenspan's leadership, responded with a quick expansion in monetary base, and managed to avoid any slump.

Act III, by contrast, is a tale of fumbles by the Fed. By 1989, the U.S. unemployment rate had dropped below the levels of the inflationary late 1970s. While there was no dramatic takeoff in inflation, Federal Reserve officials believed that a gradual acceleration of underlying inflation was visible in wage settlements and price changes. At the same time, some conservative members of congress were pressing for a policy of zero inflation within five years. The Fed was therefore more worried about inflation than about keeping the expansion going. In fact, one Fed staffer remarked around that time that "We can't go out and create a recession to control inflation, but we can try to take advantage of any little recessions that happen to come our way."

This mind-set left the Fed unprepared for the big recession that actually came along. In fairness, there is still considerable controversy about why the U.S. economy was so weak in 1990–92. Consumers, whose savings rates had been falling throughout the

1980s, suddenly became much more cautious: was this because they had run up so much debt in the past, or because they had finally come to realize the hollowness of conservative claims that it was morning in America? Credit contracted throughout the economy: was this because misregulation during the 1980s had left banks overextended? (We'll discuss financial markets in Chapter 6.) It is possible to make the case that the weakness of the economy after 1990 was at least in part due to the legacies of Reaganomics.

Still, the most important fact about the recession was that the Fed failed to prevent it, essentially through a series of misjudgments. First, the Fed overestimated the danger of inflation and underestimated the risks of recession; then, although monetary policy was steadily eased, the Fed consistently did too little too late. Before condemning the Fed too much for this, one should bear in mind that nearly all forecasters were consistently overoptimistic from the summer of 1990 to that of 1992.

And in the end, the Fed's policies did work. In the second half of 1992 the economy's growth rate suddenly picked up to more than 4 percent. Job creation was disappointing at first—more on that below—but the recession was clearly over.

THE INJUSTICE OF IT ALL

Voters, understandably, judge presidents by the performance of the economy during their terms in office. In fact, however, growth rates over four-year intervals are dominated by the ups and downs of the business cycle—and these are mostly the responsibility of the Fed rather than the administration. The injustice of the situation is made even worse by the documented tendency of voters to have short memories, and to vote on the basis of the growth rate of the economy, not even over a full presidential term, but only over the few quarters preceding an election.

One therefore cannot help feeling a bit sorry for Jimmy Carter and George Bush, both booted from office largely because of short-term economic woes that had little to do with their policies.

Back to the Long Term

Let's take it as a settled fact that the United States did not see any acceleration of its underlying, potential rate of growth during the era of conservative rule. Could we or should we have done better?

At the most basic level, the rate at which an economy's potential grows is the sum of two terms: the rate at which the number of able and willing workers expands, and the rate at which the productivity of the average worker rises.

Over the past twenty years, the United States has actually had an exceptionally rapid growth in its supply of labor. Indeed, the rate of employment growth was a lot higher in the disappointing 1970s and 1980s than in the boom 1950s and 1960s. There is no mystery about why. Employment could grow rapidly because of a huge increase in the supply of labor. Baby boomers grew up; women entered the labor market in large numbers.

This growth in employment is one of the great successes of the American economy; this chapter will not deny that some things have gone right. It is not a forgone conclusion that a rapid increase in the number of people who want to work will necessarily be matched by an increase in the number of jobs. Indeed, in Western Europe employment stagnated during the 1970s and much of the 1980s, leading to a persistent rise in unemployment. It turned out that the United States had a sufficiently flexible and, yes, free labor market to match demand to supply, and to absorb a vast increase in the number of people who wanted to work with hardly any rise in unemployment.

Of course, the way that a freely functioning labor market ensures that almost everyone who wants a job gets one is by allowing wage rates to fall, if necessary, to match demand to supply—and as we will see in Chapter 5, wages fell a lot for many American workers. But still, the American experience with employment is one of our great plus marks. U.S. employment growth has dwarfed that in the rest of the industrial world.

But if we were putting so many people to work, why weren't we growing rapidly? The answer is that we were not doing much to raise our productivity.

Consider two different measures of U.S. economic growth in the 1970s and 1980s. The first is the growth of real GDP per capita. By this measure, the U.S. experience looks pretty impressive: 18 percent growth in the seventies, another 18 percent in the eighties, for a total of 39 percent. The main basis of this growth was, however, the rapid growth in the employed fraction of the population. The second measure is the growth of output *per employee;* in 1979–89 this was only 10 percent, or 0.8 percent per year. This compares with a 2.8 percent rate of growth over the twenty-five years following World War II.

So mediocre overall growth in the 1980s was the sum of rapid labor force growth and slow productivity growth. It's hard to give the Republicans much credit for the rapid growth in the labor force; should they take the blame for the slow growth in productivity?

The answer is maybe a little bit. Despite the rhetoric of growth, the policies followed during the Reagan and Bush years actually had a bias against productivity growth. On the other hand, it is unfair to assign those policies more than a fraction of the responsibility for disappointing performance.

POLICY AND PRODUCTIVITY

There are three main things that an economy can do to raise the productivity of its workers. It can raise the quantity and quality of its business capital; it can improve the public capital that supports the private economy; and it can improve the quality of its work force, what is sometimes called human capital.

No reasonable economist can claim that we have any accurate accounting of the value of each of these three sources of growth. Most estimates of the effects of both business and human capital on growth are based on their market return; yet it is a well-understood point that the returns to society from an investment may be either much less or much more than their payoff to the private investor. When it comes to public investment, the situation is even worse, since there isn't any market return to use as a benchmark.

So we can't really say what rate of productivity growth the United States is "earning" by its investments, or how much better our productivity growth would be if we did everything right. What we can say is that during the years of conservative rule, the United States did not act like a country that was determined to achieve faster productivity growth. Indeed, we pretty much did everything wrong.

Let's start with business investment.

It is an accounting identity—something that is true by definition—that private investment equals the sum of three sources of saving: private saving, government saving (that is, budget surpluses), and net inflows of capital from other countries. If you want to increase private investment, you must have a plan that will increase one of these three sources of savings.

Supply-siders and even some more moderate conservatives may have hoped that Reagan's tax cuts would provide an incentive for higher private saving. If they did, the incentive was swamped by other factors: the private saving rate in the United States crashed during the 1980s, from 9.1 percent of disposable income in 1980 to 5.1 percent in 1987. And at the same time, the Reagan administration presided over a massive increase in budget deficits: public "dissaving" soon began to offset much of whatever private saving was taking place. The overall rate of national saving, public plus private, had averaged 7.7 percent in the 1970s, but was only 3 percent from 1988 to 1990.

If the United States had been been alone in the world, this collapse of national saving would have required an equal fall in private investment. Essentially, the borrowing needs of the government would have driven interest rates up to the point that they "crowded out" just enough investment to match supply and demand for funds. Interest rates did indeed rise: the real interest rate in the United States had averaged only 0.5 percent from 1960 to

1980, but averaged 4.9 percent in the 1980s. But they didn't rise as much as they might have, because high rates attracted an inflow of foreign capital that made up part of the savings shortfall.

It is another accounting identity that net inflows of foreign capital are equal to the U.S. trade deficit (or more precisely, the U.S. deficit on current account). So the collapse of U.S. national savings, due in part to the surge in the budget deficit, was indirectly responsible for the emergence of large trade deficits in the 1980s. This relationship became famous under the name of the "twin deficits"; but it is not a subject I want to dwell on here. For current purposes, the only point we need to make is that the net effect of Republican policies was to *discourage* private investment. And indeed, private investment in the period 1980–92 was only 17.4 percent of GDP, compared with 18.6 percent in the 1970s.

What about public investment? The high-water mark of public investment in the United States was during the 1950s and 1960s, when outlays for vast infrastructure projects like the Interstate Highway System brought the capital spending of governments at all levels to 3 percent of GDP. Since then there has been a steady slide in the share, down to about 1 percent of GDP. The Reagan and Bush administrations didn't start this slide, but their policies reinforced it; not only did a deficit-hobbled federal government prefer to put off long-term spending in order to make the short-term numbers look better, but the virtual elimination of federal financial aid to state and local governments helped enforce similar constraints at lower levels.

Finally, we come to human capital. This means, above all, the education—in the broad sense—of the nation's children. Education is primarily a state and local responsibility in the United States, and in some ways these local governments actually tried harder; in spite of the emergence of a number of "distressed" school districts unable to buy textbooks or furniture, overall measures such as classroom size improved. Such financial efforts, however, were surely swamped by the growing problem of child poverty and its associated social consequences. Even at the end of the Reagan expansion, poverty in the United States was higher than it had been under Jimmy Carter; and poverty among children maintained a rapid upward trend. This growth in child poverty was largely tied to the growing inequality of income. For the most part, the conservatives in power did not cause that inequality, but they did nothing to limit it or contain its consequences.

If one goes down the checklist, then, one sees that the policies of the Reagan and Bush administrations were if anything biased against long-term growth. But how much difference would better policies have made? Should Reagan and Bush be blamed for the continuation of the productivity slowdown?

Probably not. Budget deficits did reduce the funds available for investment and lead to a runup of U.S. foreign debt, but if you try to put numbers to their impact they turn out fairly modest. For example, a comprehensive study by the Federal Reserve Bank of New York estimated that had there been no budget deficits in the 1980s, real income in 1990 would have been only 3 percent higher. (We'll explain the basis of this calculation in Chapter 6.)

The effects of low spending on infrastructure are more controversial. A widely quoted study by David Aschauer of Bates College claimed that reduced infrastructure spending was the major cause of the productivity slowdown, a theme eagerly picked up by candidate Bill Clinton. Most economists, however, regarded Aschauer's statistical analysis as shaky, more a matter of correlation than causation. Meanwhile, experts on the details of infrastructure spending were skeptical about the potential payoff of much higher levels. There were a few high-priority issues like repairing bridges that could easily absorb some $10 billion a year of money well spent. Beyond that it was hard to come up with projects that would have had much impact on growth.

Arguably the ultimate problem was that of taking care of the nation's children. One might have hoped that a government less wedded to conservative ideology might have done better—but what, exactly? Also, by definition education has only a very long term effect on productivity, since it can't matter until the children become workers. So, whatever wages America will pay for conservative sins of neglect will not come due until late in the 1990s or early next century.

In a way, the worst sin of the conservatives was that of hypocrisy. They proclaimed growth as their objective, offered it as the answer to all problems, all while following policies that actually inhibited that growth at least a bit. At the end of the day, however, the most striking fact is how *little* happened to U.S. long-term growth, good or bad, on their watch.

Except, maybe, at the very end.

THE *1992* REVOLUTION

A funny thing happened to the U.S. economy on the way to George Bush's 1992 defeat. Productivity in 1992 grew by 2.8 percent—its best performance since 1972.

There is usually a spurt in productivity during the early stages of a business cycle recovery, because during a slump firms are reluctant to fire everyone who is not immediately needed; when demand recovers, they can use their "hoarded" workers to expand output without much new hiring. But the 1992 spurt didn't fit the pattern. Instead of the mix of job and productivity growth usually associated with recovery, this was all productivity and no jobs. Furthermore, this productivity surge during a slow recovery was larger than the productivity growth during the roaring recovery year of 1984.

What was happening? It was too soon to be sure, but a few observers suspected that something profound was taking place—a fundamental acceleration of productivity growth associated with new technologies applied in unexpected places.

We'll come back to the implications of this sudden and unanticipated development, and simply close this chapter by suggesting that the story of growth in the United States may have been marked not only by political injustice but by political irony: just as the American people, fed up with the failed promises of conservatism, looked for a change, the economy may spontaneously have begun to heal itself.

CHAPTER 5

Income Distribution

The big story of the era of conservative rule was not the growth of income but its distribution. Once you correct for the ups and downs of the business cycle, the growth path of the economy was virtually the same before and after Ronald Reagan took office. But the conservative era was marked by a huge fanning out of the spread of incomes, with the rich becoming far richer, the poor a lot poorer, and the middle class going nowhere in particular.

The important questions about the rise in income inequality are, of course, why it happened and whether anything can or should be done about it. But before we can get to those questions, we need to spend a little while getting the facts straight. For the most remarkable thing about the debate over growing inequality in the United States has been the reluctance of many conservatives to admit that it happened at all.

Some Basic Facts

FROM PICKET FENCE TO STAIRCASE

Figure 6 shows a picture that ought to be part of the consciousness of anyone who thinks about trends in the U.S. economy since the 1970s. The figure shows the rate of growth of income at selected points in the income distribution over several different periods.

The points at which the income distribution is measured are percentiles. For example, the first set of bars shows the rate of growth of income of the family 20 percent of the way up the income distribution, the second set the rate of growth 40 percent of the way up, and so on. The choice of percentiles ranging from 20 to 95 means excluding the real extremes—changes in income for those in the bottom fifth, on one side, and changes within the top 5 percent, on the other. As we will see in a moment, some very important developments are missed by these exclusions, espe-

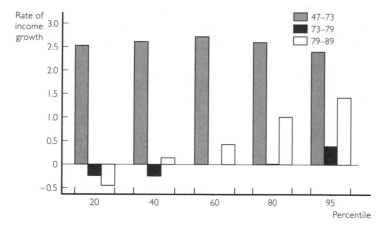

Figure 6. The change in the pattern of growth, from picket fence to staircase, signaled growing inequality of family incomes.

cially at the top. But this picture still gives us a useful baseline.

The three periods chosen are 1947–73, 1973–79, and 1979–89. The first period represents the period we already recognize as the Good Years—the great postwar boom generation. The remaining two periods show the "seventies"—the period from the business cycle peak of 1973 to that of 1979—and the "eighties"—from the 1979 peak to the 1989 peak. The decision to measure from peak to peak of the business cycle is sensible given our discussion of growth in Chapter 4, but also controversial; we will turn to that controversy below.

What do we see in the figure? First, the 1947–73 numbers show what real, broad-based prosperity looks like. Over that period, incomes of all groups rose at roughly the same rapid clip, more than 2.5 percent annually. That is, the Good Years were about equally good for everyone. Between 1973 and 1979, as the economy was battered by slow productivity growth and oil shocks, income growth become both much slower and more uneven. Finally, after 1979, a new pattern emerged: generally slower income growth, but in particular a strong tilt in the growth pattern, with incomes rising much faster at the top end of the distribution than in the middle, and actually declining at the bottom.

Some apologists for the 1980s have attempted to claim that what was happening during that period represented a normal process, that there was nothing unusual or distressing about the rise in inequality. As the discussion gets a bit complicated, it will be useful to retain the basic image of Figure 6: "good" growth looks like an all-American picket fence, but growth in the 1980s looked like a staircase, with the well-off on the top step.

THE SERIOUSLY RICH

The numbers shown in Figure 6 come from the U.S. Bureau of the Census, specifically from a questionnaire called the Current Population Survey. They tell a pretty clear story. Nonetheless, the story is incomplete, because it fails to give a full picture of gains among families with very high incomes.

Census numbers are of little use in studying high-income families, for two reasons, one major, one minor.

The main problem is the arcane technical issue of "top-coding." The questionnaires on which the Current Population Survey is based do not ask for precise incomes; instead, families are asked to place their income within a series of categories, of which the highest is "over X," where X is currently $250,000. This means, of course, that the Census data give no information about changes in the fortunes of families with incomes high enough to be above that top number.

The minor problem is that Census data do not count one important source of income for high-income families: capital gains when an asset is sold for a higher price than you paid for it. High-income people get much of their income from returns on investments rather than in the form of salaries. Most of this income is in the form of things like interest or dividends on stocks, but some of it also comes from successful investment in growth stocks or real estate whose value goes up sharply.

It is precisely because Census data are weak when it comes to very high incomes that those who use that data usually look no higher than the 95th percentile, i.e., the bottom of the top 5 percent.

Over the period 1947–73, when everyone's income went up at about the same rate, the weakness of Census data at the top end didn't matter much. But it became obvious during the 1980s that the very highest incomes were rising even faster than those at the 95th percentile.

One might have guessed this simply from Figure 6: since the available data show that the higher you go in the income distribution, the bigger the gains, one might reasonably suppose that the same is true for the unavailable data. Indeed, data on changes in U.S. income distribution during the 1980s have a "fractal" quality: one sees the pattern of growing inequality among the population as a whole replicated within any subgroup of that population, so one might well expect to find that inequality *within* the top 5 percent has risen, implying larger gains at, say, the 99th percentile than at the 95th.

One could also guess that income was growing especially rapidly at the top from less formal evidence. For example, Graef Crystal, a consultant on management compensation, reports that from the mid-1970s to 1990 the ratio of CEO compensation to the wages of ordinary workers tripled, and virtually every social observer noted an apparent explosion of affluence at the top. (Not everyone thinks that Tom Wolfe's *Bonfire of the Vanities* was a great novel, but it was certainly brilliant as a piece of reporting.) So something was happening here, and what it was was pretty clear; all that was lacking was hard statistical evidence.

Work by the Congressional Budget Office (CBO) filled the gap. The CBO is charged by the House Ways and Means Committee with the task of estimating the incidence of changes in federal taxation, in order to provide the supporting appendices for that committee's mammoth annual publication, the *Green Book*. To do this, the CBO has developed a model that pools Census data with data supplied by the Internal Revenue Service. This model allows the CBO to bypass the problem of top-coding, and also allows incorporation of taxable capital gains.

Figure 7 shows the CBO estimates for the gains in income at different parts of the income distribution over the period 1977–89. (Ideally, we would use 1979–89. Unfortunately, for reasons having to do with its original mandate to focus on tax incidence, the CBO did not do an estimate for 1979. Again, we will need to look at the timing issue later.) The data are presented a little differently from those in Figure 6. We are shown changes in, say, average income for families lying in the bottom quintile, rather than for the individual family at the top of that quintile, and the numbers show the percentage change over the period as a whole, rather than annual rates of change. But the picture is clear: there were truly huge income gains at the very top. In particular, the top 1 percent of families saw their incomes roughly double over a twelve-year period. That's a 6 percent rate of growth, which means that for the very well-off the 1980s really were a very good decade—not only compared with the slow growth lower down in the distribution, but even compared with the postwar boom years.

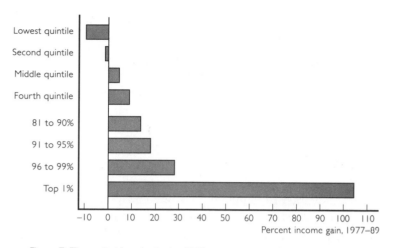

Figure 7. The really big gains in the 1980s went to very high income families.

There is one other important point to be learned from the CBO numbers: just how well off the well-off actually are.

The usual picture—one still offered by conservatives—is that the so-called rich are not really all that rich. Conservatives often point out that according to Census numbers, in 1989 it required an income of only $59,550 to put a family in the top quintile, an income of only $98,963 to put it in the top 5 percent. The implication is that we are essentially a middle-class society, with only an insignificant handful of people rich enough to excite any concern about ill-gotten gains.

But the CBO numbers paint a different picture, partly because they show higher incomes at the top, mostly because they let us look higher up the scale. According to the CBO, to be classified in the top 1 percent a family of four needed a pre-tax income (in 1993 dollars) of at least $330,000.[1] The *average* income of four-person families in the top 1 percent was about $800,000. We are no longer talking about the middle class.

[1] The CBO model ranks families not by their raw income but by their income as a multiple of the poverty line; thus a family of four needs more income to be counted in the top 1 percent than a childless couple. Correspondingly, the CBO prefers to measure income not in absolute terms but in units of "adjusted family income," i.e., multiples of the poverty line.

WHY THE RICH MATTER

It is a remarkable fact that incomes have soared so much at the top of the U.S. income distribution. But is it important? Until recently, most economists would have told you that it wasn't; growing poverty might be an important social issue, but the fact that some people are very rich was only a social curiosity. But during the 1980s the rising incomes of the rich were an essential part of the economic picture.

Let's start with a puzzling fact: By most measures, the income of the typical worker or family in the United States grew very slowly during the 1980s. For example, even if one uses a revised consumer price index that shows lower inflation than the standard index, one finds that median family income—the income of the family at the midpoint of the income distribution—in 1989 was only 4.2 percent higher than in 1979. That is, median family income rose at only about a 0.4 percent annual rate. And many measures of real wages for typical workers show a decline during the 1980s.

Now, one would have expected American incomes to grow more slowly than in the good years before 1973, because of the productivity slowdown. Productivity growth in the U.S. economy fell from about 3 percent annually during the postwar boom to about 1 percent annually after 1973; and there is ordinarily a more or less one-to-one relationship between productivity growth and real income.

But although productivity growth is slow, it is not negligible. We are a substantially more productive country now than we were in 1979. So why isn't the typical family significantly better off? Where did the productivity growth go? The answer hinges on the distinction between *average* and *median* income.

Average family income is the easier measure to understand: it is the total income of all families, divided by the number of families. It doesn't depend on how the income is distributed.

Median income, by contrast, is a measure that is supposed to tell us how the typical family lives. It is calculated in effect by lining up all families in order of their incomes, and then taking the income of the family in the middle of the lineup.

Now suppose that there is a rise in income, but that almost all of the increase goes to very well-off families. What will happen? The answer is that *average* income will rise, but that *median* income won't.

For example, suppose that over the next five years the income of families making more than $300,000 per year were to double, while everyone else's income stayed the same. Average family income would rise substantially—actually about 12 percent. But that family in the middle wouldn't see any gain, and so median income wouldn't rise at all.

It turns out that from 1979 to 1989, average family income rose 11 percent, just about exactly what one would have expected given 1 percent productivity growth. The reason why median income rose only 4 percent was that the reality looked something like our example: growth in average income was heavily concentrated in a few well-off families.[2]

When we talk about "well-off" families, however, who are we talking about? Are we talking about two married schoolteachers, whose $65,000 income is enough to put them into the top quintile? Or are we talking about CEOs of major corporations, whose incomes averaged more than $3 million in 1992?

The answer is that we are *not* talking about those schoolteachers: the really big income gains were not near the bottom of the top quintile, but at its top. Indeed, according to the CBO's numbers, the share of after-tax income going to the ninth decile—

---

[2]In principle, an increase in inequality need not depress median income: a shift of income toward high-income families could be offset by a shift of income away from low-income families, leaving the incomes of families in the middle unchanged. In reality, this never happens, because the initial incomes of families at the top are so much higher. In 1980, for example, the average income of families in the top quintile was about 8 times that of families in the bottom quintile. Thus to leave incomes in the middle unchanged, a 1 percent rise in income in the high-income group would have to be matched by an 8 percent fall in the low-income group. In practice, an increase in income inequality always lowers median income relative to average, and a fall in median relative to average always signals an overall increase in inequality.

families between the 81st and 90th percentiles—actually fell slightly between 1977 and 1989. So all of the siphoning went to families in the top 5 or 10 percent. And the bulk went to the top 1 percent.

To get a sense of the concentration of the gains, imagine two villages, each composed of one hundred families representing the percentiles of the family income distribution in a given year—in particular, a 1977 village and a 1989 village. According to the CBO numbers, the total income of the 1989 village is about 10 percent higher than that of the 1977 village; but it is not true that the whole distribution is shifted up by 10 percent. Instead, the richest family in the 1989 village has twice the income of its counterpart in the 1977 village, while the bottom forty 1989 families actually have lower incomes than their 1977 counterparts.

Now ask: How much of the difference in the incomes of the two villages is accounted for by the difference in the incomes of the richest family? Equivalently, looking at the real numbers, how much of the rise in average family income went to the top 1 percent of families? By looking at this measure we get a sense of who it was that was "siphoning off" the growth in average incomes, accounting for the fact that median income went up so little.

The answer is quite startling: 70 percent of the rise in average family income went to the top 1 percent.

What does this tell us? Since the 1970s, median income has failed to keep up with average income—or, to put it differently, the typical American family has seen little gain in spite of rising productivity. We already knew that this was because of rising inequality, which meant that high-income brackets received the bulk of the gains. What we have learned is that when we speak of "high-income" families, we mean *really* high income: not garden-variety yuppies, but Tom Wolfe's Masters of the Universe.

POLITICAL IMPLICATIONS

Rising inequality need not have any policy implications. Even if you would prefer to have a flatter distribution, other things being equal (and not everyone even shares that goal), what do you propose to do about it? Few people in America would currently support a policy of wage and salary controls that attempted to meddle with the pre-tax distribution of income. One might use growing inequality as an argument for restoring some of the progressivity of the tax system; but most of the growth in inequality has come from changes in pre-tax income, not from regressive tax policies. An honest conservative like Herbert Stein of the American Enterprise Institute is willing to say, "Yes, inequality has increased, but I don't think that calls for any policy response."

Nonetheless, many conservatives were infuriated when income distribution emerged as a political issue in the early 1990s. Above all, the emergence of income distribution as an issue made the editors of *The Wall Street Journal* and the Bush administration see red.

The reason was pretty clear. Supply-siders like Robert Bartley believed that their ideology was justified by what they perceived as the huge economic successes of the Reagan years. The suggestion that these years were not very successful for most people, that most of the gains went to a few well-off families, was a political body blow. And indeed the belated attention to inequality during the spring of 1992 clearly helped the Clinton campaign find a new focus and a new target for public anger: instead of blaming their woes on welfare queens in their Cadillacs—and on the do-gooder bureaucrats who wanted to help the poor—middle-class voters could be urged to blame insider traders in their limousines—and the conservatives who wanted to cut their taxes.

So the dismay and anger of conservatives was understandable. The response from the Bush administration, the *Journal,* and other conservative voices was to try to deny that the apparent increase in inequality was real.

Conservative Denials

Conservative denial of the reality of the growth in inequality in the United States has taken three main forms. The first is to question the numbers; the second is to dismiss the distributional question as irrelevant in the face of a supposed growth triumph; the third is to argue that income distribution is irrelevant in a society with high social mobility.

QUESTIONING THE DATA

Although some of the less scrupulous conservative commentators have tried to suggest that the whole issue of increasing inequality is some kind of liberal fraud, the fact of growing inequality is not really questionable. In particular, the picture shown in Figure 6—the picket fence changing into a staircase—is based upon Census data that nobody has challenged.

What is a bit more open to question is whether the very well-off have really done as well as they seem to have in the numbers shown in Figure 7. Recall that one of the reasons the CBO had to do special estimates for the very well-off was the importance of capital gains in their income. Many conservative commentators have argued that these gains should not have been included in the CBO estimates. They charge that this inclusion overstates the income of the rich in several ways: it includes one-time sales as if they were persistent income; it counts capital gains on assets held by the rich, but ignores the non-taxable gains of middle-class families on their houses; it counts as income the inflation component of capital gains. And all of these commentators have claimed that the CBO's capital gains estimates are the basis of the conclusion that the rich have done better than you or me.

There are answers to each of these criticisms: asset sales must take place sometime; capital gains on houses are much smaller than the critics imagine; the inflation component has fallen with the rate of inflation, so that if anything the rate of growth of income at the top is understated. The main point, however, is that excluding capital gains from the CBO numbers makes very little difference. With capital gains included, the CBO shows the share of income accruing to the top 1 percent rising from 7 to 12 percent between 1977 and 1989. Without capital gains, the shift is from 6 to 10 percent.

In other words, however you measure it there was a radical increase in income inequality. You can quarrel with the details, but the overall picture won't change.

EMPHASIZING GROWTH

The second line of conservative defense has become a familiar one: to claim that the growth record of the Reagan years shows that supply-side policies produced gains for everyone, and that it is destructive to worry about or even to notice the distribution of income.

If you are willing to play the right kinds of games with dates, this sounds correct. From the recession year of 1982 to the business cycle peak in 1989, median income rose substantially (12.5 percent, versus 16.8 percent for average income). If you use these years as the basis of comparison, the lag of median behind average income doesn't look very important. The question is whether these are really the right years to compare.

But of course they aren't. Rapid growth from 1982 to 1989 was possible because the economy was recovering from a deep recession—and even that recovery had little to do with the administration in power. Meanwhile, the long-term rate of growth hadn't changed at all. And the income distribution issue is or ought to be about how the benefits of long-term growth are shared.

INCOME MOBILITY

We've saved the best conservative response for last: the fact that the income distribution at any point in time may be a misleading picture.

America is not a static society. People who have high incomes one year may have lower incomes the next, and vice versa. In the two hypothetical villages that I described earlier, one would not necessarily suppose that the same people (or their children) occupied the same positions in 1977 and 1989. And economic welfare depends more on the average income you earn over a long period than on your income in any given year. So there are some risks in drawing too many conclusions about the distribution of economic welfare from statistics on the distribution of income in any one year.

There are two ways in which income mobility—the shuffling of the economic deck that takes place as families move up or down the income ranking—could offset the proposition that inequality has increased sharply.

First, if income mobility were very high, the degree of inequality in any given year would be unimportant, because the distribution of lifetime income would be very even. I think of this as the blender model: whatever the current position of the bubbles in your Mixmaster, over the course of a few minutes each bubble will on average be halfway up.

Second, if income mobility had increased over time, this could offset the increased inequality at each point in time. An increase in income mobility tends to make the distribution of lifetime income more equal, since those who are rich have nowhere to go but down, while those who are poor have nowhere to go but up.

Unfortunately, neither of these possibilities actually characterizes the U.S. economy.

There is considerable income mobility in the United States, but by no means enough to make the distribution of income irrelevant. For example, Census data show that 81.6 percent of those families who were in the bottom quintile of the income distribution in 1985 were still in that bottom quintile the next year; for the top quintile, the fraction was 76.3 percent. Over longer time periods, there is more mixing, but still not that much. Studies by the Urban Institute and the U.S. Treasury have both found that about half of the families who start in either the top or the bottom quintile of the income distribution are still there after a decade, and that only 3–6 percent rise from bottom to top or fall from top to bottom.

Even this overstates income mobility, since (i) those who slip out of the top quintile (say) are typically at the bottom of that category, and (ii) much of the movement up and down represents fluctuations around a fairly fixed long-term distribution. Joel Slemrod of the University of Michigan has provided a useful indicator that suggests how persistent high incomes tend to be: the average income of families whose income exceeded $100,000 in 1983 was $176,000, in that year; their average income over the seven-year period ending in 1985 was $153,000.

Nor is there any indication that income mobility increased significantly during the 1980s. Greg Duncan, also of the University of Michigan, calculated transitions over a five-year period into and out of a somewhat arbitrary but reasonable definition of the "middle class." This middle-class category shrank in the 1980s, so that middle-class families became more likely both to rise and to fall; but correspondingly fewer poor families moved up or rich families down into the middle class. (Vanishingly few poor families became rich, or vice versa.) The overall picture suggests little change in mobility.

Income mobility might in principle be an important offset to the growth in inequality, but in practice it turns out that it isn't. That did not stop conservatives from trying to use it as a debating point.

It's not worth tracking all of the ins and outs of this debate, but there is one calculation that is worth mentioning, because it is such a classic example of how to use statistics in a misleading way.

Let's give the fact first: Families who start out with high income on average have low or negative income growth over the next decade, while families who start out with low income on average see their incomes rise rapidly. Families who were in the bottom quintile in 1977 saw their income rise 77 percent by 1986, while families in the top quintile saw their income rise only 5 percent.

This calculation seems striking; but it is completely consistent with the conclusion that the United States has rapidly growing inequality. It shows only that there is indeed some income mobility—but nobody denied that. And it is no more a sign that supply-side policies helped the poor than the fact that very few people win the lottery several years in a row.

Unfortunately, it is hard to explain this without a numerical example; so with apologies, here we go.

Imagine an economy in which in any given year half of the families earn $100,000 and the other half $200,000. And imagine also that this economy fits the blender model, so that a family that starts in the bottom half has a 50 percent chance of being in the top half ten years later, and conversely.

Now do the calculation. Families that start in the bottom half begin with $100,000; ten years later, on average they have $150,000, so they gain 50 percent. Families that start in the top half begin with $200,000; ten years later, on average they also have $150,000, so they *lose* 33 percent.

But has the distribution of income gotten more equal? No: it is unchanged. All that we see is the familiar statistical phenomenon of "regression toward the mean." Essentially, the initially rich have nowhere to go but down, the initially poor nowhere to go but up. So, if the income distribution were stable, income mobility would inevitably produce the result we see; and it is not surprising that we still get it even when income inequality is rising.

If income mobility were as high as in this example, of course, the income distribution at a point in time wouldn't matter very much. But as we have already seen, income mobility isn't that high: most poor or rich people stay that way. So we have enough income mobility to make this kind of calculation seem right, but not enough to change the real story that inequality is rising.

If you want a more concrete image, think of it this way. In any given year, some of the people with low incomes are just having a bad year. They are workers on temporary layoff, small businessmen taking writeoffs, farmers hit by bad weather. These people will be doing much better in a few years, so that the average income of people who are currently low income will rise a lot looking forward. But that does not mean that people who have *persistently* low income are doing well: they aren't.

Perhaps the most revealing way to show what is wrong with the calculation is to do it in reverse, as Isabel Sawhill of the Urban Institute did. In her data,[3] families who were in the top quintile in 1977 had experienced an 11 percent fall in income by 1986. But when she instead looked at families who were in the top quintile *in 1986,* she found that they had experienced a 65 percent gain![4] Which is the right measure of how well-off families did over that decade? Clearly neither one.

Conservatives like to emphasize income mobility, because they can evoke the historical image of America as a land of opportunity, an image that has always been partially if not completely true. But when all is said and done, the facts on mobility make hardly any difference to the overwhelming picture of growing inequality.

The Reason Why

It is a clear and overwhelming fact that income inequality in the United States increased sharply during the Reagan and Bush years; and it is a sad commentary on conservatives that so many of them tried so hard to deny it. But should they be blamed for the fact of the rise as well as their failure to acknowledge it?

As in the case of the lackluster record on growth, the answer is yes, but only a little bit. Reagan's tax cuts mostly benefited very high income families, while sharp real cuts in social spending on everything except health care disproportionately hurt the poor. Still, most of the increase in income inequality was accounted for by increased inequality in pre-tax earnings, and it is hard to blame that increase on any deliberate government policy.

So, what did cause the increase in inequality in the United States? On one side, there is a popular view, which makes sense,

[3]These numbers differ slightly from those cited above because of differences in coverage.
[4]Consider the numerical example again. Families in the top half at the decade's end would have gone from an average $150,000 to $200,000, a 33 percent gain, while those in the bottom half would have suffered a 33 percent loss.

sounds reasonable, and happens to be wrong on the facts. On the other, there are some speculations which have not yet had a chance to be refuted.

The Popular View: Globalization

The most common explanation given for increased income inequality in the United States is that it is due to the increased integration of the United States into the global economy. The argument runs like this: The United States is a country with a highly educated and skilled work force. As long as foreign trade was a minor factor in its economy, the abundance of educated and skilled workers, in good economic fashion, kept their earnings relatively low and the wages of less skilled workers relatively high. But increasingly the United States is part of a global economy. In that global economy unskilled labor is much more abundant and highly educated labor correspondingly scarcer. So the globalization of the U.S. economy has meant declining real wages for the less skilled, big gains for the highly educated.

It's a nice, clear story. In fact, it is a standard story from the academic theory of international trade, introduced by MIT's Paul Samuelson in the 1940s in a series of elegant papers on "factor price equalization." A version of this story was the core of Robert Reich's *The Work of Nations* in 1991, and business publications like *BusinessWeek* often state it as a fact rather than a theory.

Unfortunately, when you look close up at the facts, and particularly when you try to put the numbers together, the story doesn't seem to work very well.

The first problem you run into is one of timing. The United States had a generally constant or even equalizing distribution of income until the mid-1970s; after 1980, inequality began rising at a rapid rate. Was this because of a sudden increase in the importance of international trade? Figure 8 shows the importance of international trade, as measured by the average of imports and exports as a share of U.S. GDP from 1960 to 1991. There was indeed a large increase in trade over that period, but it took place during the 1960s and the 1970s, not the 1980s. (It is in fact startling, given the rhetoric of globalization that now pervades economic discussion, to notice that trade was barely higher as a share of GDP at the beginning of the Clinton administration than it was when Jimmy Carter left office.)

Even if one fudges the timing, the numbers don't look big enough. Increased trade in effect makes unskilled labor in the United States more abundant, because there is unskilled labor "embodied" in the goods we import, while it makes skilled labor scarcer, because we effectively send some of that labor overseas embodied in our exports. But if you make a calculation of the changes in "effective" skilled and unskilled labor supplies due to increased trade since, say, 1970, they just aren't very large.

How can this be true? The main reason is that the image of a U.S. economy flooded with imports from countries that pay very low wages just isn't right. While the United States does some trade with low-wage, Third World nations, the great bulk of its trade is with countries that are more or less as advanced as it is, and that pay wages close to or even exceeding its own. A recent calculation by Robert Lawrence of Harvard's Kennedy School makes this point clearly. If you take the average of the wage rates paid by all

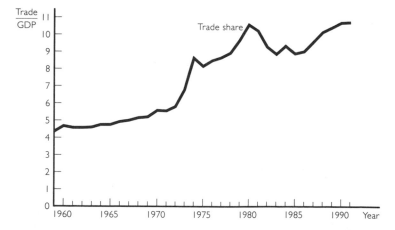

Figure 8. The big increase in the importance of trade to the U.S. economy took place in the 1960s and 1970s, not the 1980s.

the countries the United States trades with, weighted by the amount of trade we do with each country, you find that workers in the "typical" U.S. trading partner are paid almost 90 percent of the U.S. wage rate.[5]

Also, if increased trade were the main explanation of increased inequality in the United States, the opposite should be happening abroad. For example, Mexico ships low-skill goods to the United States and imports high-skill goods in return. If trade were the main driving force behind increased inequality, Mexico should be experiencing greater *equality*, as the premium on skill there falls. In fact, it has not; inequality seems to be on the rise just about everywhere.

Finally, remember that we have noted that the growth in inequality in the United States is "fractal": one sees that growth not just between groups but within groups. For example, lawyers have seen their earnings rise compared with factory workers; but the best-paid lawyers have also outperformed the average lawyer, by a substantial amount. Trade could, in principle, explain why the value of a college degree has risen, but how can it explain why among those of comparable education the premium paid for hotshots has increased so much? Or to put it another way, what does globalization have to do with Michael Eisner and his $50 million paycheck?

OTHER EXPLANATIONS

If trade doesn't explain the rise in inequality, we are left primarily with the all-purpose explanation known as "technology."

A simple explanation of rising inequality would be that the

---

[5]It's also worth pointing out that while the United States is now importing more than it used to from low-wage suppliers like China, some of our more traditional trading partners now pay much higher wages than in the past. Twenty years ago Japanese wages were only one third of those in the United States; today they are a little bit higher than our own. Another striking calculation by Lawrence shows that imports from low-wage countries, defined as those paying less than half the U.S. wage rate, have hardly increased over time: they were 2 percent of GDP in 1960, 2.7 percent in 1990.

increasing sophistication of our technology puts a growing premium on those who are trained to make use of it. And there is certainly something to this: the emergence of a computer hacker, Bill Gates of Microsoft, as America's first nerd billionaire is certainly a sign of the times. Yet more broadly the biggest gains in income do not seem to have gone to the most technological professions. Lawyers, doctors, and corporate executives outperformed engineers and programmers.[6]

Sherwin Rosen, a labor economist at the University of Chicago, has proposed an alternative theory, the "superstar" model. He points out that today a few entertainers make huge incomes, but that the large numbers of comedians, singers, and so on who used to make a living providing live entertainment has shrunk to a small contingent. The reason is, of course, modern media, which allow the best entertainers (in the judgment of the market) to appear to large numbers of people dispersed over space and time. Rosen suggests that the same is true for other professions: the reach and span of control of top lawyers, business executives, and so on is extended by modern telecommunications, allowing a larger number of people to bid for the services of the perceived best. The effect is to turn labor market competition into a kind of tournament in which a few winners get huge payoffs and the rest get little. Or in other words, Lee Iacocca and Madonna are, in economic terms, basically the same.

I would add yet a third technological story: some of the growth in inequality may represent temporary skill shortages created by the incomplete application of modern technology. The parallel here is with the early part of the Industrial Revolution in Britain. Mechanization of some operations, like spinning, created temporary shortages and very high wages for certain skilled professions, like weaving. These wages, of course, crashed a little bit later, as the new technology was more widely applied. I think there is a

---

[6]A cartoon on my secretary's door shows an engineer (identifiable by the plastic pen protector in his pocket) declaring the power of computer knowledge: "Someday the world will be divided into those who know how to use computers and those who don't. And there will a word for those who do. . . ." Another character fills it in: "Secretaries."

potential parallel story today involving white-collar workers, such as investment bankers—but we'll get back to that story in Chapter 10.

The bottom line of all of this is that while we can make some interesting speculations, we really don't know very well why inequality has increased. That doesn't mean that nothing can be done about it—but let's hold off on that discussion until the story of the liberal revival has been told.

CHAPTER 6

███████

The Budget Deficit

Once upon a time, it was liberals who were soft on budget deficits. Keynesian macroeconomics suggested that sometimes a budget deficit could be helpful to the economy; anyway, liberals always wanted to spend more on social programs, and had trouble finding ways to pay for them. Conservatives, on the other hand, were tight-fisted types who constantly warned about the menace of government borrowing.

The supply-siders changed all of that. As we saw in Chapter 3, they took a relaxed attitude toward the possible effects of tax cuts on the deficit. With a little luck, they thought, lower taxes might actually increase revenue; even if the deficit did increase, the economic benefits would outweigh any petty budgetary concerns. Once supply-siders had come to power, there was an almost comic role reversal: liberals became the stern prophets of fiscal doom, while George Bush adopted Bobby McFerrin's "Don't worry, be happy" as his unofficial theme song.

Who was right? There is a simplistic version of the

story that goes like this: Ronald Reagan cut taxes for the rich and increased military spending, without managing to cut very much spending elsewhere. He promised that the economy would grow so much that the deficit wouldn't increase, but he was wrong. The result was that he burdened America with a huge federal debt, which is crippling our economy.

Guess what: the simplistic story is basically right, except for the last few words. Reagan increased the budget deficit pretty much as described. But the debt he left us is a modest drag on our economy, not a crippling burden.

The Sources of the Deficit

At first glance, you might think that the U.S. deficit problem began long before Ronald Reagan. The federal government has run a surplus in only one year out of the past thirty. Why blame Reagan for continuing the trend?

The answer is that until the Reagan years, budget deficits were small and economically more or less irrelevant. A simple indicator of that irrelevance is the ratio of federal debt to GDP, a measure of the size of debt compared with the size of the economy. As Figure 9 shows, during the 1960s that ratio was generally falling, and even during the 1970s it was basically flat. The reason was that the deficits were small enough to be outpaced by the combined effects of inflation and growth. Inflation eroded the real value of the debt outstanding; meanwhile the real economy grew. So, even though the dollar value of debt grew, the ratio of that debt to national income actually fell. In terms of the size of its debt relative to the size of its tax base, the U.S. government was in noticeably worse shape when John F. Kennedy took office than it was when Jimmy Carter left it.

After 1980, however, the gradual downward trend became a steep climb. The era of deficits had begun.

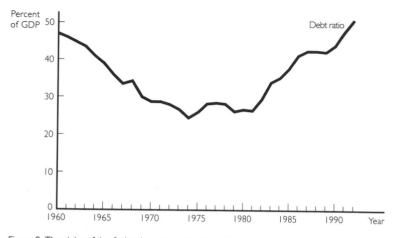

Figure 9. The debt of the federal government generally grew more slowly than the tax base until Ronald Reagan became President.

TAXING AND SPENDING

You can get a pretty good idea of the reasons why the United States has a persistent deficit by looking at Table 1, which compares some of the main elements of federal revenues and expenditures in fiscal 1981, the last pre-Reagan budget year, and fiscal 1992. (All of the items are measured as percentages of GDP.) In both years the economy was in a recession, which made the deficit worse than usual—during a recession, tax revenues fall while some government costs, like unemployment insurance, rise. But the unemployment rate was about the same in the two years, so they serve as a reasonable basis for comparison.

Table 1

	1981	1992
RECEIPTS: TOTAL	20.2	18.6
Personal income tax	9.6	8.2
Corporate income tax	2.1	1.7
Social insurance	6.2	7.0
OUTLAYS: TOTAL	22.9	23.5
Defense	5.3	5.1
Health + Medicare	2.2	3.5
Social Security	4.7	4.9
Interest	2.3	3.4

In 1981, the federal government ran a deficit of 2.7 percent of GDP; in 1992, the number was 4.9 percent. With some caveats we can say that the difference between those two numbers, 2.2 percent of GDP, represents the deficit problem that Ronald Reagan created.

Where did the increase come from? Mostly from a reduction in tax income: a fall in the share of GDP collected as government revenue accounted for more than 70 percent of the rise in the deficit. The rest was due to an actual slight rise in expenditures as a share of GDP. One might be tempted to summarize this by saying that the conservatives succeeded in cutting taxes, but failed to reduce the size of the government. But that's not quite right. By 1992 the federal government was paying interest on a debt that was twice as large a share of GDP as in 1981, so even though the interest rate was lower, interest payments were much higher; expenditure other than interest had in fact fallen as a share of output.

The impact of conservative policies, and the reasons for the persistent deficit, become clearer when we look at how the government spent its money. The federal budget can usefully be thought of as consisting of five roughly comparable pieces: interest on the debt; health care (including Medicare); defense; Social Security; and everything else.

When people think of wasteful government expenditures, they usually do not have the first four of these items in mind. Yet it was with these items that the problem lay. Interest on the debt rose with the debt itself. Health care expenditures shot up, driven by soaring medical costs. By 1992, with the end of the Cold War, defense expenditures were back to their 1981 level—but the much higher expenditures of the mid-1980s had contributed to the buildup of debt. And while Social Security payments had not risen as a share of GDP, they were almost certain to start rising as soon as the population aged. Meanwhile, the "everything else" category, which contains all of the expenses of running the government plus programs targeted at humanitarian causes such as poverty and the environment, was in fact cut considerably.

So in fact the Reagan and Bush administrations did cut a lot of government spending—and not always wisely, as we'll see below. But they couldn't find enough spending cuts to make up for their tax cuts and the inexorable rise of health care costs.

WINNERS AND LOSERS

The Reagan Revolution didn't lower all taxes equally. As the first part of Table 1 shows, income taxes fell considerably, while "social insurance contributions" such as Social Security and Medicare payments actually rose. This was not simply a matter of taking away with one hand what was given with the other. The income tax is progressive; that is, the rate you pay increases with your income. Social insurance payments, by contrast, are usually levied only up to a certain income—$40,000 in the case of Social Security—so that they are actually a smaller share of the income of the well-off. Any shift from income taxes to social insurance payments tends to raise the taxes of low- and middle-income families while lowering those of the rich. Furthermore, the main cuts in income taxes were on higher brackets. The key objective of the supply-side tax reduction was to lower marginal rates, that is, the rates that people pay on any additional income they make. That makes economic sense: marginal rather than average rates determine the incentive to work and invest. By cutting marginal rates, however, the government also disproportionately lowered the tax rates of high-income families.

The net result of the mix of tax changes was that only very well-off families got any significant reduction in taxes. The Congressional Budget Office has calculated the impact of all tax changes after 1980 on families at different levels of income. It finds that a family in the middle of the income distribution was actually paying a higher share of its income in taxes in 1989 than it was in 1980: the increase in social insurance payments was more than twice as large as the fall in income tax. By contrast, a family in the top 1 percent of the distribution[1] got a lot of tax

---

[1] Strictly speaking, the calculation is for a family whose real income would have put it in the top 1 percent in 1989.

relief: the fall in its income tax was twenty times as large as the increase in its social insurance payments. The overall tax rate on these high-income families fell from 36.5 percent in 1980 to 26.7 percent in 1989.

Meanwhile, what happened to the poor? Families below the poverty line in the United States have relatively little taxable income, so that they are not much affected by changes in the tax system. During the Reagan years, however, the effort to reduce spending led to a sharp reduction in the generosity of programs that help the poor, such as food stamps. The number of people who were below the poverty line after taking into account the value of these benefits rose by 7 million between 1979 and 1989; about 3 million of these new poor were made so by cuts in benefits.

Supply-siders get furious at what they see as the simplistic claim that Reaganomics involved cutting taxes on the rich, raising them on the middle class, and punishing the poor. In fact, however, that seems to be just about what happened.

The Burden of the Deficit

The budget deficit emerged just the way the popular story has it: Ronald Reagan cut taxes on the rich, and even though he was willing to be nasty to the poor, he couldn't find enough spending cuts to balance the budget. But why should we care about the deficit? Does the deficit do any harm?

There are two stock positions on this subject. One is what we might call the H. Ross Perot viewpoint: The deficit is a terrible monster which threatens our whole way of life. After all, just look at the numbers: in 1981 the federal debt was $994 billion, but by the end of fiscal 1992 it was more than $4 *trillion*. Isn't it obvious that we are on a road to disaster?

The opposite position is what we might call the Robert Bartley position: The deficit is an unimportant byproduct of a hugely successful policy. Reagan's tax cuts brought a moribund economy back to life; who cares if some accountant's number has grown?

Both positions are, of course, wrong. The deficit is a real problem. It is not, however, quite the monster that Perot and others seem to think.

THE SUPPLY-SIDE APOLOGY

Let's start with the supply-side claim that the deficit does not represent a problem, or a failure of their ideology.

In the really strong form of supply-side ideology, as expressed by the Laffer curve, Reagan's tax cuts should not have increased the deficit at all. People should have responded by working harder and investing more to such an extent that revenues should actually have increased. Obviously that didn't happen.

Even before the reality of the deficit became apparent, however—and to an even greater extent afterward—many supply-siders had a fall-back position. They argued that tax cuts might increase the deficit, but that they would generate so much growth in the economy and therefore in savings that the increase in the deficit would not be at the expense of private investment. In making allowances for the deficit after the fact, they claim that that is just what happened.

We've already dealt with part of this argument; in Chapter 4 we reviewed the record of growth in the 1980s and saw that the conservative claims of triumph have no basis in reality. It only remains to look at the record of saving and investment. Did private saving rise so much that actual investment rose?

The answer is a resounding no. The facts are, indeed, almost too bad to be true: by any measure, over any time period, investment fell.

The most favorable number one can look at for the conservative era is the ratio of gross investment—that is, all money spent on building factories, shopping malls, and so on—to GDP. Surely one would expect that lower taxes on corporations, lower taxes on high-income individuals, and a general pro-business climate would have led to higher investment. But in reality, the ratio went down. Gross investment averaged 18.8 percent of GDP from 1974 to 1980, a period that contained two major recessions and during which many business leaders warned of an impending capital shortage. From 1981 to 1991, the number was only 17 percent. Even if one looks only at Robert Bartley's Fat Years from 1983 to 1989, the average investment ratio was only 18 percent. However you measure it, investment in the conservative era was low, not high, by comparison with previous experience.

Moreover, looking at domestic investment alone gives too favorable a picture. The United States has traditionally invested abroad as well as at home, using part of its savings to finance at least a small amount of net investment overseas. During the 1980s that traditional position was reversed, with the U.S. economy becoming a major importer of capital, and correspondingly becoming a net debtor to the rest of the world. If one deducts these capital imports from the gross investment number, one gets "gross national saving"; this fell from 19.2 percent of GDP in 1980 to 15.6 percent in 1989 and only 14.4 percent in 1990.

Finally, one gets a truly dismal picture if the depreciation of the capital stock is deducted, yielding *net* national saving. Net saving was 8 percent of GDP in the 1970s. It averaged only 3.4 percent in the 1980s.

In sum, there is absolutely nothing in the record to justify the cheery supply-side view of the deficit. Growth did not accelerate, investment fell instead of rising.

But if the deficit was not a good thing, how bad was it?

THE COSTS OF DEFICITS

There are many countries in which budget deficits are not an abstract threat, where the actual solvency of the government is on the line. When a government is unable to borrow, either because it is not viewed as trustworthy or because it is already impossibly in debt, a budget deficit leaves it unable to pay its bills—or obliged to pay them simply by printing money, thereby embarking on the road to hyperinflation. The United States is not, however, in anything like that situation. Even though a book entitled *Bankruptcy 1995* rode high on the best-seller lists for months in 1993, financial markets are quite happy to lend to the U.S. Treasury. The debt of the U.S. government is immense, but so is the tax base, namely, the U.S. economy. Federal debt as a share of GDP, while it has been rising, is less than half of its level at the end of World War II. The U.S. government is not in any kind of financial crisis.

The federal budget deficit, then, is a problem only to the extent that we think that it indirectly hurts the U.S. economy. There is nothing mysterious about the channel through which this harm comes: when the government borrows money, it is taking savings that could otherwise have been used to finance real investment, which would have raised our productivity. To a first approximation, we can think of the debt run up since 1980 as having taken the place of an equivalent amount of productive investment in machinery, computers, factory buildings, and so on. (Or to the extent that we financed investment by relying on foreign capital, some of the debt has its counterpart in bonds, stocks, and companies sold to Japanese and European investors.)

Suppose that the U.S. government had balanced its budget from 1980 until the present. At the end of fiscal 1981, federal debt was $994 billion, while by the end of fiscal 1992, it was $4.004 trillion. So if the budget had been balanced, the federal government would have borrowed about $3 trillion less than it did. That $3 trillion, which amounts to half of one year's output, could have been productively invested, and that productive investment would have made us richer.

But how much richer? The answer is a bit disappointing: about 3 percent. That is, the whole effect of the dread deficits of the 1980s was to leave the United States only about 3 percent poorer than it would have been had it balanced its budget all along. That's not a negligible amount, but it hardly lives up to the heated rhetoric of many critics of the deficit.

Where does this surprisingly low number come from? You can estimate the effect of the deficits a number of ways, but they all come out more or less the same. The simplest is to assume that the real rate of return on the funds that would have been released if the U.S. government had not been borrowing would have been the same as the average rate of return on all private assets. This average real rate of return is about 6 percent. Since the total buildup of debt was equal to half of one year's output, the returns on that debt would have been 6 percent times ½, or 3 percent of GDP.

It's possible to argue that even the 3 percent number is a bit high, for at least two reasons. First, it may be unreasonable to compare the actual deficits of the 1981–92 period with a benchmark of completely balanced budgets. After all, the United States hasn't run a literally balanced budget for decades. A more natural comparison may be with the level of deficits that the country ran during the 1970s, which were small enough to keep the ratio of debt to GDP constant. That ratio rose by only 35 percentage points between 1981 and 1992, suggesting a net cost of less than 2 percent.

Second, the United States did succeed in financing much of the deficit with imports of foreign capital, largely in the form of foreign purchases of U.S. bonds (either government or corporate). The rate of return on bonds is generally lower than the rate of return on other, riskier assets; so the cost to the country of running up a foreign debt is actually less than the cost of cutting back domestic investment by the same amount.

A dispassionate accounting of the deficit's effect on the U.S. economy, then, produces a fairly mild result. By running unprecedented deficits for a decade, we reduced our income by at most 3 percent, and probably less.

It's worth pointing out that the conclusion that the deficits of the 1980s had only modest negative effects on growth fits with the evidence presented in Chapter 4. There we looked for the effects of Reagan and Bush administrations on long-term growth and found nothing—neither a positive nor a negative shift in the trend. If the deficits had done the economy grievous harm, one would have expected to see some visible impact on growth. The absence of such a visible impact does not confirm but is consistent with the idea that deficits were a bad but not a terrible thing.

Nonetheless, many people find this conclusion hard to swallow. Partly this is because they want economics to read like a morality play: either Ronald Reagan was a good leader or a bad leader. If he was a good leader, his policies must have been successful. If he was a bad leader, they must have been immensely destructive. The conclusion that his policies were not successful, but that they did only limited damage, just doesn't make for a good story line.

A more legitimate concern is whether this purely financial accounting captures the full extent of what happened during the 1980s. Can we make the case that the fiscal deficit was only the tip of the iceberg, that there were "hidden deficits" during the 1980s that did more harm than the buildup of federal debt?

Hidden Deficits

One can make a case for the existence of three "hidden deficits" that hurt the long-term prospects of the U.S. economy during the 1980s. First, misregulation of financial institutions like savings and loan associations, banks, and pension funds set the stage for future costs to taxpayers even though there was no immediate increase in the measured budget deficit. Second, there may have been too little public investment in infrastructure, public services, and so on. Finally, the federal government may have been making too little provision for a future in which a smaller number of workers will have to support a larger number of retired people.

HIDDEN FINANCIAL LIABILITIES

In 1989, the public was startled to learn that the federal government had an unexpected obligation: it was going to have to spend well in excess of $100 billion to pay off the depositors of bankrupt savings and loans. At first Congress and the administration tried some elaborate accounting gimmicks to keep the cost of the S&L

bailout from appearing in the budget, but eventually reality was acknowledged. The costs of the bailout were one of the reasons that the budget deficit, which had been declining as a share of income during the later 1980s, suddenly shot up again after 1990. In economic terms, however, the costs of the S&L affair really occurred during the 1980s, and should be viewed as a hidden part of that decade's deficits.

By now the story of the savings and loan fiasco should be familiar. An S&L or thrift is a special kind of bank that flourished during the days of highly regulated financial markets. Like any bank, a thrift accepts deposits from the public and lends the money out, normally at a higher interest rate. The depositors in thrifts, as in other banks, were protected by a national insurance system, the Federal Savings and Loan Insurance Corporation (FSLIC), which guaranteed the value of deposits if the bank should fail.

It has long been known that insuring the deposits of a bank presents dangerous temptations to its owners. Suppose that you own a bank, and that the government insures anyone who deposits money in your bank against loss. Then you have a wonderful opportunity to gamble with taxpayers' money. You simply attract as much money in deposits as you can, which you can do by offering interest rates a little bit higher than what other banks are offering. (The depositors don't worry about whether you can really afford to pay that high interest rate, because they know that their money is protected in any case.) You then lend out the money to risky borrowers, individuals or firms who are willing to borrow at high interest rates but who may well be unable to repay their loans. If it turns out that they are able to pay, you will have made a lot of money on the spread between what you pay your depositors and the interest on the loans. If, on the other hand, your loan customers can't pay, you can simply walk away from the bank and let the government pay off your depositors. It's heads you win, tails the taxpayers lose.

This kind of temptation has a quaint but evocative name: "moral hazard." Banking experts have long been aware that the

American system of banks with deposit insurance poses potential problems of moral hazard, but until the 1980s these problems didn't get out of hand, largely because of tight regulation of the banking system. This regulation had three effects. First, banks were not allowed to make loans that the regulators thought were too risky; in the case of S&Ls, this meant that they were largely restricted to home mortgages. Second, the owners of banks were subject to so-called capital requirements, essentially rules that forced them to put a substantial part of their own money at risk, making gambling with depositors' money less attractive. Finally, rules that prevented banks from raising the interest rates they offered depositors and that made it hard for new banks to enter the business made banking a very profitable business; bankers didn't want to take risks that might endanger their profitable "franchises."

The inflation and high interest rates of the 1970s brought this workable if not very efficient system to an end. In order to attract deposits in a world of double-digit interest rates, thrifts had to be allowed to pay high interest rates themselves. Many of them had, however, tied up much of their money in long-term mortgages during a time of much lower interest rates. So they found themselves paying higher interest rates on deposits than they were receiving on their loans. By 1980 many S&Ls were effectively bankrupt.

What the federal government was supposed to do at this point was close down the bankrupt thrifts and pay off the depositors. What it did instead was deregulate them: allow thrifts to make riskier loans in the hope that they could grow their way out of bankruptcy. This policy had the predictable result: an epidemic of moral hazard, as S&Ls made very risky and for the most part unsuccessful investments in such assets as junk bonds and loans to real estate speculators. The nature and magnitude of the problem were apparent to many experts by around 1986, but it was conveniently ignored until after the 1988 election.

From 1980 to 1989 the quietly growing S&L scandal represented a significant hidden federal deficit. In effect, there was a growing taxpayer liability that didn't appear on the books. At this point, however, the costs of the S&L cleanup have already been largely budgeted. The interesting question now is whether there are other hidden elements in the budget deficit, elements that have not yet appeared in that $3 trillion debt accumulation since 1980.

The answer is surely yes. The S&L story is only the most extreme case of a broader phenomenon.

Start with the rest of the banking system, and in particular the commercial banks—firms like Citibank or Chase Manhattan that specialize in lending to businesses. These banks were subject to many of the same forces that led to the S&L debacle. Their profitability was eroded during the 1970s by inflation and deregulation; since they were no longer highly profitable, they were tempted to make risky loans; and the federal government encouraged them to do so by relaxing restrictions on their investment. The result was a lot of questionable lending, especially of two kinds: financing for financial schemes like leveraged buyouts,[2] and financing for speculative real estate deals. By 1991 a number of reasonable people were warning that there might have to be a commercial bank rescue similar to the S&L bailout, with a price tag of $50–$100 billion.

At the time of writing, this crisis had been postponed if not necessarily avoided—but only through sheer luck. The attempts of the Federal Reserve to pull the U.S. economy out of a stubborn recession had led to very low short-term interest rates. Since these rates determine the interest rates that banks have to pay on deposits, the paradoxical result was a surge in bank profitability. Still, this windfall gain doesn't contradict the conclusion that misregu-

---

[2]Commercial banks do not buy junk bonds, but they do participate in deals that involve junk bonds. When a group of investors took a firm private during the 1980s, it would typically do so with financing that looked something like this: 10 percent of the money came from the new owners, 30 percent from junk bonds, and 60 percent from bank loans. In principle, the banks had first claim on any profits, so that they were not supposed to be taking much risk. In practice, the debt created was often so large that full payment on the bank loans was by no means a sure thing.

lation was doing some peculiar things to bank lending during the 1980s.

There are also a number of other, fairly obscure government policies that produce hidden future liabilities. For example, there is an institution called the Pension Benefit Guarantee Corporation (PBGC), which guarantees corporate pension plans in much the same way that FSLIC guaranteed thrift deposits. It turns out that there are incentives for companies to set aside insufficient money for their pension plans, then dump the problem in PBGC's lap; the Federal Office of Management and Budget has estimated that there may be a hidden federal liability of $30 billion to $45 billion.

This sounds like a lot of money. Compared with the $3 trillion of additional federal debt run up during the 1980s, however, it is not that impressive. As Everett Dirksen once said about the federal budget, a billion here, a billion there, and soon you're talking about real money. The same surely applies here. If we are trying to assess the impact of deficits on the growth of a $6 trillion economy, however, it seems unlikely that any of the hidden financial liabilities of the U.S. government will change the basic picture of real but modest costs.

Public Investment

If a family finds its income reduced for some reason, it may respond in several ways. One way is to lower its standard of living. Another is to take out a loan. A third way, however, is to postpone some long-term spending. For example, the family may put off repairing the roof or replacing the furnace. This kind of postponement of long-term spending is in effect a hidden form of borrowing from the future.

Governments do the same thing. When a legislature is faced with a deficit and is under pressure to keep its borrowing down, it is likely to postpone spending on projects that will only have long-term payoffs. It is easier to hold off on replacing an aging bridge than to lay off schoolteachers.

To at least some extent the financial deficits of the conservative era were accompanied by a hidden deficit in long-term spending, an investment deficit. The question is how big that deficit was, and whether the investment deficit was a bigger drag on growth than the financial deficit. The short answer is that there is a range of reasonable views.

The strong case on the investment deficit runs as follows: If you go back to the 1950s and 1960s, when the U.S. economy was achieving rapid productivity growth, governments on all levels (federal, state, and local) were spending about 3 percent of GDP on infrastructure: roads, bridges, sewage and water systems, and so on. In the 1980s, the number was only about 1 percent. If you think that infrastructure spending at the rates of the 1950s should have continued, that means that over the course of a decade the cumulative investment deficit was about 20 percent of GDP—a sizable fraction of the accumulation of debt itself. If you also believe that there is a high rate of return to infrastructure investment, you can end up concluding that this hidden deficit may be as important as the visible deficit.

The problem with this argument comes when one tries to get specific about how the additional money might have been spent. It is true that roads and bridges have not been adequately repaired; estimates suggest that something like $100 billion more could usefully have been spent on repair and replacement over the course of the 1980s. It is also true that the country is suffering from increasing traffic congestion, and that more and better roads could be useful (although many economists would prefer to start with the use of road-pricing schemes, such as higher rush-hour tolls, to encourage better use of the highway network we already have). Beyond that, however, one gets into more questionable ideas. For example, would federally funded high-speed trains be worth building? Such trains are prestige items in Japan and France, but they also lose a great deal of money, and there is no strong evidence for high social payoffs. The Clinton administration is interested in futuristic infrastructure projects, such as a national "data highway" to link computers around the country; whether or not such projects are justified, it is hard to argue that they should have been pursued during the 1980s.

There is another kind of public "investment" that one may argue was neglected during the 1980s: spending on child care and education. The Head Start program for poor pre-school children is generally regarded as a success, yet throughout the conservative era it did not have enough money to serve all eligible children. Child care advocates argue that money could be productively spent on a variety of other causes, including early intervention programs to help poor mothers and very young children and aid to financially distressed school districts. More questionably, some liberals think that the United States should be spending more on adult education, for example, to retrain workers displaced by new technologies or shifts in the world market.

It is certainly true that all such "human capital" spending was held to a minimum during the conservative era. This was partly because conservatives were skeptical about its effectiveness, but it was also partly because of the way that the budget deficit put pressure on Congress to keep all spending down.

There was, then, a second deficit: in addition to the money the federal government borrowed, there was the money it should have spent but didn't. But how important was this second deficit? It is hard to argue that it changes our conclusion that the deficit was only a moderate drag on U.S. economic growth.

The trust fund

The federal government in principle has more than one budget. Social Security, Medicare, and unemployment insurance have their own trust funds, financed by specially earmarked taxes. As a result, official statistics divide federal receipts and outlays into "on-budget" and "off-budget," where the latter refers to the trust funds.

A funny thing happened during the 1980s. The federal budget proper moved deeply into deficit. This plunge was partly offset, however, by a rising off-budget surplus. Indeed, between 1983 and the end of 1991 the cumulative off-budget surplus amounted to $287 billion.

The reason for this surplus was that Congress had increased

Social Security taxes. Why? Because there is a completely predictable surge in Social Security spending scheduled to begin in the
year 2007, when the first baby boomers reach retirement age.
From that point on, the number of retired Americans will grow
much more rapidly than the number of Americans of working age.

The implication for the Social Security system is obvious. If it
were to run on a pay-as-you-go basis until 2007, at that point it
would become necessary either to cut benefits sharply or to institute a huge increase in Social Security taxes. To avoid that crunch,
the system must run a surplus now, building up a reserve that can
be used to pay part of the bills later. Refreshingly, Congress chose
to act responsibly and make provision for the future.

But if it is necessary for the Social Security system to run a
surplus now to meet predictable future demands, then it doesn't
seem like a good idea to count that temporary surplus as an offset
to the deficit run by the rest of the government. The additions to
the Social Security trust fund since 1983 now exceed $300 billion.
Shouldn't this, together with additions to the Medicare trust fund,
be counted as part of the deficit?

Yes, it should, and the deficit numbers you usually hear under-
state the true deficit. But that doesn't change our estimate of the
costs of the deficit, which bypasses the problem. The trust funds
hold their reserves in the form of federal debt, and the number
shown in Figure 9 is the total federal debt, including that part of it
held by the Social Security and Medicare trust funds. The $3 tril-
lion increase in that debt includes the increased assets of the
Social Security system.

So it is true that the deficits of the conservative era were worse
than they appeared, because the U.S. government should have
been running a surplus to prepare for the aging of our population
early next century. Taking this into account does not, however,
change our conclusion that a more responsible policy would have
left national income at most 3 percent higher at the end of the
conservative era than it actually was.

The Verdict

In the court of conventional wisdom, Ronald Reagan stands accused of inflicting a huge burden of debt upon his country. He cut taxes on the rich, increased military spending, and failed to cut enough spending elsewhere to pay for his largesse. The result was a string of unprecedented peacetime deficits, and a debt that will be a drag on the national standard of living for decades to come.

Reagan is guilty as charged. The supply-side apologists' claim that some extraordinary economic success vindicates Reaganomics in spite of the deficits just doesn't hold up in the face of the evidence. The question, however, is whether the crime was a felony or a misdemeanor.

The answer proposed here will not satisfy those with a taste for drama. Reagan created a deficit, and it hurt American economic growth. But even if the effects of the visible deficit are supplemented with appeals to several alleged hidden deficits of the 1980s, the cost was not catastrophic. The deficit is not nearly the monster some people imagine.

CHAPTER 7

■

Conservatives Abroad

It is fashionable in the 1990s for Americans to berate themselves for failing to appreciate the extent to which we are now integrated with a wider world. Our habits of thought are outdated, we tell ourselves—we are preoccupied with domestic affairs, when what really matters are the winds of change sweeping through the global economy.

In fact, this is nonsense. As a nation, we *are* inexperienced with and naive about the world economy, but our ignorance rarely leads us to underrate the importance of international linkages. On the contrary, it usually leads us to glamorize and thus overrate them. The shock of finding that we are no longer the world's dominant economic power leads us to treat international economic affairs with a kind of naive awe. The adjective "global" applied to a topic lends it cachet; it seems far more sophisticated to pontificate about global competition or global financial markets than to talk about merely domestic antitrust or bank regulation.

Our excessive fascination with the mystique of the international can sometimes have serious consequences. In the early and mid-1980s, economists and politicians swarmed over the sexy issue of Third World debt, an issue that turned out to have only minimal repercussions on the U.S. economy. Meanwhile, few people wanted to get involved with boring domestic questions like the regulation of savings and loan associations; malign neglect allowed what should have been a manageable problem to grow into the financial scandal of the century. In the 1990s, the glamorization of the international has led to widespread acceptance of the fundamentally wrong idea that U.S. economic difficulties are largely the result of a failure to compete on global (that magic word again) markets; we'll come back to that fallacy in Chapter 10.

But there is one sense in which we do pay too little attention to the world economy. While the American public is all too ready to blame its troubles on foreigners, and even would-be sophisticates tend to overstress the international side of our domestic problems, as a nation we are often unwilling to learn from foreign experience. (In this, even the educated public is not that different from the American teen-aged movie audience, which likes its villains to have accents but refuses to watch foreign films.) Conservatives who revere Ronald Reagan and liberals who revile him usually know little about the record of Margaret Thatcher; and yet Thatcher's story contains vital lessons for that debate. Supply-siders and revived Keynesians argue about the roots of recession and recovery in the United States, while paying little attention to the abundant lessons of European business cycles.

Without doubt, this book commits the same sin. The debates and evidence it covers are overwhelmingly domestic. But at least in this chapter it will tell some stories from the outside world.

In particular, let's focus on two crucial adventures of conservative economic ideology in Europe: the remarkable experiment known as Thatcherism, and the sad story of European money.

Thatcherism

There are some strong parallels between the story of Thatcherism in the United Kingdom and Reaganism in the United States. In both cases, a leader with strong ideological views and an out- sider's mentality challenged the moderate conservative establish- ment as well as the left. In both cases, the new leader took power during a period of severe inflation and general malaise. In both cases, the new regime began with a period of severe economic distress, followed by a recovery that was claimed as a triumph of the new policies. And in both cases, the regime was followed by a successor government that found itself in deep economic diffi- culties, difficulties that led to popular disillusionment with the movement that bears the leader's name.

Differences in history and political systems, however, make the histories of Margaret Thatcher and Ronald Reagan quite different in detail, so that the British tale serves up a different perspective on the achievements and failures of conservatism in power.

Let's take a look at two interesting stories: the roller-coaster ride of Britain through inflation and deflation, recession and re- covery; and the unique and in the end disastrous story of privati- zation.

Money, Inflation, and Unemployment

Margaret Thatcher's Conservative Party came to power in 1979. Like America's Republicans a year later, the Conservatives were elected in an atmosphere of deep concern over inflation. In Brit- ain's case, however, the situation was even scarier. Britain had already seen inflation spiral out of control in the first half of the 1970s. In 1976, the country had been forced to accept loans and advice from the International Monetary Fund—a humiliation usu- ally reserved for Third World nations. The reemergence of dou- ble-digit inflation so soon created a sense of panic, of fear that the country was slipping over the brink. And the storm surge of inflation reached much higher in Britain than in the United States, with consumer prices rising more than 18 percent during 1980.

In the United Kingdom as in the United States, the orthodox answer to inflation was to wring it out of the system with a recession; and in both countries, that was in the end what monetary policy did. We've already seen, however, that the Federal Reserve was able to carry out this brutal if effective policy by calling it something else. The rhetoric of monetarism cast an obscurantist cloak over the harsh reality: we were "targeting monetary aggregates," not throwing people out of work so that those still holding jobs would reduce their wage demands. The same rhetoric was used to justify the same policy in the United Kingdom.

The difference was that the people deciding British monetary policy believed their own rhetoric.

Part of the reason for that difference was that the Bank of England, unlike the Federal Reserve, is not an autonomous institution. It is simply an arm of Her Majesty's Treasury, and as such must answer to the ruling party. This leads to an odd role reversal. Traditionally, the United States is governed by inexperienced political appointees, while Britain is ruled largely by professional civil servants (referred to by the British themselves as "mandarins," reflecting both respect for their competence and an uneasy sense that they are an unelected governing class). When it comes to monetary policy, however, our decisions are made by the mandarins of the Fed, theirs by the politicians of the Prime Minister's inner circle. Now, the professionals at the Federal Reserve were always skeptical of monetarism; if they briefly made a show of obeying monetarist prescriptions in 1979–82, it was largely because they found it a useful way to mask the harshness of their actual policy. Margaret Thatcher, however, was surrounded by men who had really been convinced by Milton Friedman. Their monetarist leanings were not a convenient cloak, to be thrown aside as soon as events required a change in policy. Even when they were forced by events to abandon Friedman-type monetary rules, they continued to search for some way to make monetary policy without trying actively to manage the economy. That search was eventually to have disastrous results.

For a period of almost seven years, British monetary policy was in principle run on Friedmanesque lines. The Bank of England did not announce goals for output, unemployment, or inflation; it simply announced targets for a broad monetary aggregate, M3.

If the conservative macroeconomic doctrines we described in Chapter 1 had been right, this decision to adopt a monetary rule should have had two desirable effects. First, it should have led to a reasonably stable rate of growth in the economy as a whole. Second, it should have led to a relatively low cost reduction in inflation, because the visible commitment of the government to its monetary targets should have had an immediate favorable effect on inflationary expectations. Unfortunately, neither of these desired results actually materialized.

The M3 rule did not produce a stable economy. From 1979 to 1983, the British economy plunged into a terrifyingly steep recession; the unemployment rate soared from 5.4 to 11.8 percent. This slump was so much deeper than expected that the Bank of England violated its own M3 targets, engaging in exactly the type of discretionary monetary expansion that was supposed to be unnecessary. British monetarists attempted to explain this deviation away by pointing to special events such as changes in the structure of the banking industry and of financial markets; they pointed out that base money had been growing more slowly than M3. And the Bank of England continued to set M3 targets. Again and again, however, erratic swoops and dives in the real economy placed Britain's monetary authorities under irresistible pressure to deviate from their targets. Finally, in 1986, the Bank of England gave up announcing monetary targets altogether.

This is an important lesson, one that has not reached the consciousness of even the informed public in this country. In the United States, it is possible to argue that monetarism was never really tried, that the Fed was insincere in its pretended conversion. In Britain, however, real monetarists tried with great earnestness to run an economy on monetarist principles, and failed completely. So much for Milton Friedman I.

What about the other side of conservative macroeconomics, the claim that a visible commitment not to accommodate price increases with monetary expansion would bring inflation down quickly and easily? Here, too, the results of the Thatcher experiment were disappointing. Inflation did come down, from that scary 18 percent peak in 1980 to less than 4 percent in 1986, but only at the cost of a huge rise in unemployment. As Figure 10 shows, the British unemployment rate, which had averaged less than 3 percent in the 1960s and was still only 5.4 percent when Thatcher took office, remained above 10 percent eight years later.

Indeed, the emergence of massive long-term unemployment is the most distinctive feature of Britain under Conservative rule. It is unfair to blame the Conservatives for causing the problem: since the mid-1970s persistent high unemployment has been endemic throughout Europe, with the ultimate explanation still something of a mystery. The point is, however, that Thatcherism did nothing to cure it.

If you recall the story of U.S. growth in the 1980s, you will remember that there was a dramatic recovery in output and employment after the slump of the early 1980s; by blaming Jimmy Carter for the early slump and taking credit for the subsequent

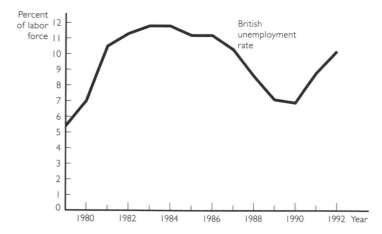

Figure 10. Conservatives were unable to achieve a sustained reduction in the British rate of unemployment.

recovery, the Reagan administration was for a time able to advertise itself as a great success. The UK story bears some resemblance to that in the United States, but with some important differences.

As in the United States, there was a resumption of growth after 1982. In contrast to the U.S. experience, however, this growth at first made little dent in unemployment. From 1983 on, the unemployment rate stabilized; but in 1987 it was still more than 10 percent. Eight years into the Thatcher experiment, conservatism in Britain could not deny that it had presided over a sharp rise in unemployment.

The inevitable claims of economic triumph were therefore based on a different indicator: productivity. Britain has had productivity problems for a long time. Sometime in the late nineteenth century British productivity fell far behind that of the United States; at the end of World War II, it was only about half the U.S. level. The same was true of other European nations, but from 1950 to 1980 France and Germany closed much of the gap. Britain did not; by 1980, it was the least productive major country in Europe. From 1973 to 1979, British productivity rose only 1.3 percent annually, less than half the rate in the rest of the European Community.

From 1981 to 1987, however, productivity growth was an impressive 2.8 percent. The United Kingdom moved up the league tables, from 80 percent of German output per worker in 1981 to 88 percent in 1987. Thatcher's supporters proclaimed the end of British decline: a newly invigorated Britain would now be able to hold up its head again.

The productivity surge did not last, or at least if it did, its effects have been obscured by subsequent business cycles. Still, it must be admitted that even looking back from 1993, amid the shambles of the Thatcher experiment, the 1980s seem to have brought some improvement in Britain's relative productivity performance. Whether it was Margaret Thatcher's doing, or just one of those things that happen, is unclear. Still, productivity did improve.

Nonetheless, high unemployment remained a sore point for Thatcher's government. The Thatcherites felt that their conservative virtue ought to have been rewarded with a lower overall unemployment rate; and this feeling that things should be going better contributed to a disastrous policy misjudgment after 1987.

THE 1987–89 DEBACLE

In 1987, the British unemployment rate began dropping rapidly. Within two years it was down to less than half its 1986 peak, although still higher than it had been when Thatcher took office. Some Conservatives heralded the boom as the final demonstration of the success of their policies. Yet the employment surge quickly proved unsustainable, and within another two years unemployment was back in double digits.

What happened? There should have been several clues that the rapid employment growth of the late 1980s was not a sign of economic health. The surge in demand was partly due to a collapse of personal savings, which fell from 4 percent of disposable income in 1986 to zero in 1988. Growing demand translated into rapid employment growth partly because the productivity surge of the mid-1980s came to an abrupt end. Most important, the fall in unemployment quickly began to be reflected in rising inflation.

The mystery is why the Bank of England remained passive, allowing an inflationary boom to develop rather than trying to rein the economy in. There seem to be two main explanations.

First, Margaret Thatcher's advisers had never given up their longing for a way to make monetary policy without making judgments about the economy. M3 targeting hadn't worked, but they were still eager to find a simple, mechanical rule to follow. What they chose was to target the exchange rate.

This wasn't an explicit policy: for political reasons, Thatcher was fiercely opposed to British membership in the European Monetary System (EMS). But looking for a monetary anchor, the Bank of England chose to "shadow" the German mark rather than try to manage the British economy.

The passivity associated with this policy was reinforced by wishful thinking. Thatcherites wanted to believe that their policies had been highly successful, yet those policies had conspicuously failed to reduce unemployment. It was therefore extremely tempting to see the decline in unemployment as a long-delayed reward for virtue, rather than the dangerous overheating of the economy that it proved to be.

And so British policymakers basically stood aside while inflation soared back into double digits.

At that point they suddenly slammed on the brakes. Interest rates were raised to levels not seen since the early 1980s. The boom turned into a severe slump, driving unemployment quickly back into double digits. Inflation came down again, but the brief euphoria of 1987–89 turned into howls of distress. In 1990, Margaret Thatcher was forced from office by her own party, to be replaced by John Major, who tried to repair the damage by doing what she would not: take Britain into the European Monetary System.

That turned out to be another disaster, but one we'll need to view in the broader European context, later in this chapter.

PRIVATIZATION

One major aspect of Thatcherism has no parallel in U.S. experience: the move to privatize previously state-owned sectors of the economy.

When Margaret Thatcher came to power, the British government controlled a substantial range of businesses whose U.S. counterparts are privately owned. The most important of these were utilities: telephone, gas, and electricity. Less important were a variety of businesses ranging from hotels owned by the national rail company to the country's coal mines.

Liberal and conservative economists alike had little trouble agreeing that the British government had no reason to operate businesses like hotels that effectively duplicate the activities of private firms. The important state-run enterprises, however, were very different, because they were and are "natural monopolies."

One cannot have several power or gas companies competing for customers in a given city; although new technologies have made it possible for several competing companies to offer long-distance service in the United States, there is still room for only one local phone company in each region.

Natural monopolies pose a well-known dilemma for public policy. There are three ways to deal with them; all have problems.

First, they can just be left alone. This is the solution that conservatives tend to prefer. The problem here is that yes, Virginia, unconstrained monopolists *do* use their power to exploit consumers. Conservatives tend to dismiss concern about monopoly power as a liberal myth, but it is simply the truth. (The American public got its own lesson in monopoly power, and a mild taste of the Thatcher experience, when Ronald Reagan deregulated cable TV. Cable companies quickly raised their fees an average of 40 percent in real terms, even while the quality of service from these companies was becoming the butt of innumerable jokes.)

Second, at the other extreme, natural monopolies can be put under public ownership. In an ideal world, they would then be run efficiently in the public interest. But in our not terribly ideal world, it is usually a good idea to avoid creating more government bureaucracies.

An intermediate solution is to leave natural monopolies under private ownership but to regulate prices and quality of service. This is the normal American solution. It has its own problems. Most notably, it can have adverse effects on the incentives facing the regulated firms. For example, suppose that a regulated firm is considering whether to spend money on research today that may lower its costs in the future. If it is tightly regulated, it may not bother, on the grounds that it will be forced to pass the bulk of its cost reductions on to consumers, leaving it with little return on its investment. Again in an ideal world, regulators would set rules of the game that would restrain monopoly abuses without greatly distorting incentives. But a government that smart and honest might as well run the firm directly!

There was a good case in 1980 for doing something about

Britain's public enterprises. Without question they were highly inefficient and poorly managed. One solution would have been simply to try to improve management—and indeed, the Thatcher government was quite successful at raising productivity in state-owned sectors that it did not privatize. Privatization was the other option, and not an unreasonable one, as long as it was carefully thought out.

Instead, first telecommunications, then gas, then electricity and water were privatized with astonishingly little concern for how the natural monopolies thus set free would operate. The Thatcher government seems to have been convinced that private owner-ship would work its productive magic even in monopoly condi-tions. It was also pleased with the idea of financing budget deficits by selling off enterprises rather than by borrowing, even though the net effect on national saving was exactly the same.

Telecommunications went first. The government was delighted with the response of the financial markets, which quickly bid the stock up to 25 percent above the government's asking price (gen-erating some large windfalls for wealthy investors in the process). It soon became clear why investors were so bullish on British Telecom: the firm's monopoly position allowed it to raise prices and degrade the quality of service. By 1987, public complaints about British Telecom's performance had become so insistent that the government grudgingly began tightening regulation on its prices and service. Gas came next. Although there were fewer public complaints, many observers believed that British Gas was seriously overcharging its customers.

The interesting story, however, came when electricity was pri-vatized. The industry was split up both horizontally (into compet-ing producers) and vertically (into upstream and downstream firms). Power-generating plants were divided among three com-panies, one of which was restricted to nuclear facilities. Each re-gional electricity distribution network was also made into an inde-pendent firm. So the typical British consumer would buy power from a local firm that in turn bought its electricity from one of the large generating firms. As a way to increase potential competition, however, regional distribution companies were free to build generating capacity of their own.

In retrospect, what happened was predictable. The distribution companies looked at their suppliers and saw a highly concentrated industry: one of the new firms alone had more than half of the generating capacity. Given the record of very lax control over prices in telecommunications and gas, the distributors had no reason to expect that they would be protected from being squeezed by their suppliers. As soon as they were privatized, they therefore began feverishly investing in their own generating capacity, even though there was no shortage of existing generating capacity in the United Kingdom as a whole. In early 1993 the expansion plans already announced were expected to produce 70 percent excess capacity by 1995.

A side consequence of this rush to build was the destruction of what was left of Britain's once-proud coal industry. Electric power can be generated using a variety of fuels. Coal-fired plants, the traditional source, are expensive to build but fairly cheap to run; gas-fired plants are the reverse. And gas turbines can be installed quickly. So, in their dash for independence, the distribution companies almost exclusively built gas-fired plants; as their purchases of electricity from the generating companies fell, the demand for coal plummeted. In the fall of 1992 the British government stunned the public by announcing plans to close more than half of the remaining coal mines in the country and lay off 70 percent of the miners.

It is easy to say in retrospect that British privatization was deeply mishandled. Unfortunately, the pattern seems likely to continue. At the time of writing, the Major government has declared its intention to privatize British Rail, with an enthusiasm and lack of concern for consequences that suggests little has been learned. Conservatives in Britain apparently have not yet realized that markets are not magical. They can work well when conditions are right, but leaving a natural monopoly free to do its worst is blind ideology.

European Money

Monetarism in Britain was a spectacular failure. It was not, however, immediately followed by a return to a more Keynesian policy. Instead, Britain joined its European neighbors in their own version of conservative orthodoxy misapplied: the road to European Monetary Union (EMU).

The story of Europe's money in the 1980s and the 1990s is a more edifying one than some of the other conservative excursions we have considered. Europe's commitment to fixed exchange rates began as a reasonable economic strategy in difficult times, and the transformation of a modest effort at stabilization into an ambitious effort to create a unified money had both grandeur and some economic logic on its side. Unfortunately, rigid thinking led to rigid policies, and the result was economic crisis and political disaster.

But let's begin at the beginning, with the early success of the European Monetary System.

THE EUROPEAN MONETARY SYSTEM, 1979–89

The economies of the European Community (EC) are far more closely linked than those of other industrial countries. For example, Germany exports about 18 percent of its GDP to other EC nations, whereas the United States exports only 1.5 percent of its output to Japan, only 2 percent to all of Europe. As a result, issues that may have only nuisance status for U.S. business become major preoccupations in Europe. In particular, while fluctuations in the foreign exchange value of the dollar are a matter of serious concern to only a limited range of businesses in the United States, fluctuations in the relative values of European currencies are crucial to virtually all business decisions.

In response to business complaints about the uncertainty created by erratic exchange rate movements, in 1979 the advanced nations of the European continent agreed to a set of rules that they hoped would reduce the instability of exchange rates. This European Monetary System, or EMS, committed each pair of nations to intervene in the markets whenever the exchange rate between their currencies moved outside a narrow "band" around an agreed rate, or "parity."[1] For example, since late 1982 the agreed parity between the French franc and the German mark has been 3.35 francs per mark. If the market rate rises more than 2.25 percent above that level, France must buy up francs and Germany sell marks on the foreign exchange market to keep the franc from falling any further; if the rate falls more than 2.25 percent, they must do the reverse. It is possible for the nations of the EMS to change the agreed parities, a process known as realignment, but this is not a step taken lightly: it is something of a humiliation for the countries whose currencies lose value, while it puts the industry of the countries whose currencies rise at a cost disadvantage.

The decision to create the EMS was not especially a conservative policy. In fact, the question of whether to peg exchange rates or to let them float is an issue that is fairly unique in the way that it cuts across the usual ideological lines. Advocates of fixed exchange rates include both conservatives—who long for a return to something resembling the traditional gold standard—and liberals who are unwilling to leave exchange rates at the whim of speculative markets. Advocates of flexible exchange rates include monetarists who want their countries to follow rigid monetary rules and Keynesians who want them free to pursue full employment. As we have already seen, supply-siders were devoted admirers of Robert Mundell, who denounced currency devaluations, and *The Wall Street Journal* spent much of the 1980s campaigning for a return to gold. Yet the most famous advocate of flexible

[1] Strictly speaking, the European Monetary System was a set of technical agreements; within that agreement was a special one setting up the Exchange Rate Mechanism (ERM). Legally, Britain has always been a member of the EMS; what it entered in 1991 and left in 1992 was the "ERM of the EMS." In practice, everyone takes the EMS to mean the system of narrow exchange rate bands.

exchange rates was none other than Milton Friedman, and the monetarist Thatcher government was a bitter opponent of entry into the EMS.

But both those who applauded an effort to fix exchange rates and those who deplored it gave the EMS little chance of success in its early years. After all, there were huge disparities among the member countries. Germany and a few of the smaller nations, such as the Netherlands, had low inflation rates and a history of being willing to pay whatever price was necessary to keep inflation down (a willingness ultimately rooted in bitter memories of the German hyperinflation of the 1920s). France and Belgium had much weaker records of inflation-fighting, while Italy's inflation had spiraled out of control for much of the 1970s. These disparities were important because it is ordinarily impossible for a country with high inflation to maintain a stable exchange rate against the currency of a country with low inflation: the high-inflation country's prices and costs keep rising, leaving its industry increasingly uncompetitive. Sooner or later, the high-inflation country must either suffer a painful deflation or, much more likely, succumb to the pressures to let its currency drop. Most observers therefore expected that the EMS would be forced into realignments so frequent as to make the system ineffectual.

During the first three years of the EMS, realignments were indeed very frequent. But after 1982 something unexpected occurred: the EMS solidified into a remarkably durable, stable set of exchange rates. From 1979 through 1982 there were five realignments; but from 1982 through 1987 there were only two more; and from 1988 until the debacle of September 1992 there was no realignment at all.

What happened? It turned out that during the 1980s, as European countries struggled to control inflation, the EMS provided a useful psychological anchor. In France and in Italy, in particular, governments felt that it was necessary to bring inflation down even at the expense of prolonged high unemployment. It would have been difficult, however, to announce this policy in so many words. It was far easier to describe the policy as one of maintaining the value of the national currency against other EMS members, especially the mark. In order to keep their currencies within the bands, of course, France and Italy were compelled to maintain tight money policies that matched Germany's, and to accept a period during which the momentum of past inflation carried their industrial costs and prices to uncompetitive levels. The end result was therefore a policy of high unemployment to cure inflation, but cloaked under a less brutal-seeming label.

This should sound familiar. It's essentially the same thing that the Federal Reserve did in the United States from 1979 to 1982. As we saw in Chapter 4, the Fed used the rhetoric of monetarism to justify what was in fact a policy of wringing inflation out of the system with a massive recession. It remains unclear whether the Fed actually believed in that rhetoric, but in the end what mattered was that it served the purpose of packaging a harsh policy under a confusing label.

To be fair, European central bankers also hoped that the highly visible commitment to stable exchange rates would reduce the cost of disinflation. If companies and labor unions setting prices and wages knew that their governments would be very reluctant to devalue, one could hope that this would reduce their expectations of future inflation, and therefore make it possible to bring the inflation rate down with a more modest bulge in unemployment than if the signals had been less clear. In practice, there is no evidence that this "credibility" effect worked, but there is enough uncertainty in such evidence that many European leaders chose to believe that it was really there.

So the EMS was a surprising success, because it provided governments with a useful way to justify the swallowing of unpleasant economic medicine. The refusal of governments to take any measures to reduce high unemployment could be described, not as the harsh choice it was, but as no choice at all: after all, the currency must be defended.

The system depended, of course, on the existence of a country on which it could be anchored. That is, there had to be a country which would follow strong anti-inflationary policies *without* the need to justify them with the mystique of international finance, whose currency could then serve as the benchmark for the other players. That country was, of course, Germany; and a side effect of the EMS was to give Germany a special, seemingly dominant role in European economic affairs.

THE GERMAN HEGEMONY

During the 1980s, many people began to believe that German economic leadership within Europe was inevitable, a matter of sheer raw power. A look at the numbers reveals, however, that German dominance is by no means preordained. West German workers are, of course, as productive as any in Europe; but they are roughly matched by the French, and even the British and Italians lag only 20–30 percent behind. Thus in 1990 the 63 million West Germans produced only about 25 percent more than the 56 million French, and accounted for only 28 percent of the output of the European Community as a whole. That is not exactly overwhelming dominance. By way of comparison, the United States accounts for 35 percent of the output of the advanced nations as a group, yet the days when the United States could effectively dictate the economic policies of the West are long gone.

German reunification has, of course, swelled the Federal Republic's population: at 80 million, it is now markedly larger than that of any other European nation. But the 17 million East Germans have not added to German economic might. They brought to their union with the West a dowry of antiquated factories, environmental disasters, and socialist work habits. For at least the next decade they will be a burden on the West Germans; indeed, there is a real possibility that Germany's East will become a chilly version of Italy's Mezzogiorno, the seemingly permanently backward southern half of an otherwise advanced nation.

In any case, during the 1980s West Germany was a nation that was bigger and richer than any other in Western Europe, but not by an overwhelming margin. So how did this slightly-bigger-than-medium-size economy come to be perceived as an economic superpower?

The answer lies in the way that the European Monetary System evolved. France, Italy, and the smaller nations of continental Europe were looking for a rope to hang on to, some external standard by which to justify their harsh anti-inflation policies. They were able to discipline themselves and pacify or at least confuse the voters by making the defense of their EMS parities a sort of sacred commitment. Since Germany, with its low inflation, normally had the strongest currency in the EMS, this in effect meant that all of continental Europe tied its currencies to the German mark. And since the only way to sustain those parities was to match German monetary policy, in effect the Bundesbank (Germany's central bank) was put in charge of monetary policy for Europe as a whole.

In retrospect, we can see that the success of the EMS was something of a fluke. It worked for a decade because large, rich countries like France and Italy were willing to allow a foreign central bank to dictate their monetary policies. They were willing to do this because controlling inflation was their dominant priority, and the Bundesbank had a reputation for stern opposition to inflation; in effect, like bicycle racers who ride in the leader's slipstream, they were willing to borrow some of Germany's credibility. The EMS's decade of success was possible only because of the coincidence of two factors: European leaders were preoccupied with inflation rather than unemployment; and Europe's biggest economy also happened to have its most anti-inflationary central bank.

Suppose that the latter had not been true—suppose, for example, that Germany had not had a reputation for stable prices. Could the EMS still have worked? Probably not. There are other countries in Europe with a reputation for monetary virtue, like the Netherlands, but a Dutch monetary hegemony would not have been credible. Germany was not big enough that it *had* to be Europe's monetary hegemon, but it was big enough that it *could* be during an epoch in which European nations found it useful to elect one of their number to that role.

That epoch would last, however, only as long as the nations of Europe shared a common monetary goal—that is, as long as fighting inflation took priority over everything else. What would happen if other goals came to the top of the stack, presenting real conflicts over monetary issues? Europe would find out when Germany was reunified; but its ability to respond to that revelation was hampered by the myths that had grown up around the success of the EMS.

THE EMS MYTH AND THE EMU BLUNDER

The reality of the EMS was that it was a useful way for governments to justify hard choices, while obscuring the harshness of the consequences of those choices. The European experience, like that of the United States, was that controlling inflation required a prolonged, extremely painful recession. This may have been a price worth paying—it is difficult to imagine what might have happened if the industrial world had tried to live with double-digit inflation. Still, European governments chose to cloak the reality of their policy in the mystique of international finance rather than admit it openly.

Was this such a bad thing? What's wrong with a fiction that helps a government do what needs to be done? The danger is that the government may come to believe its own rhetoric. And that's what happened: a myth developed about the EMS that was rooted in ideology rather than experience—specifically, in the ideology of conservative macroeconomics.

The myth of the EMS said that the benefits of the EMS came without costs. The loss of independent monetary policy involved in pegging the exchange rate was, according to this myth, no loss at all, because having an independent policy would be of no economic use. Monetary discipline brought lower inflation with no cost in unemployment.

This optimistic view flew in the face of the traditional wisdom, which said that the decision to fix exchange rates always involves a painful tradeoff. Stable exchange rates reduce business uncertainty, and can serve as an anchor against inflationary storms. On the other hand, they leave a country with no recourse if there is a local recession or unanticipated events put the country's production costs out of line with its trading partners. The question, according to this traditional view, was not whether a tradeoff exists, but what international financial arrangement makes the best of it—a discussion carried out under the name of the "optimal currency area" debate.[2]

In the 1980s, however, it became increasingly common in Europe to dismiss the costs of fixed exchange rates and the benefits of allowing rates to change. Why? Because of the influence of conservative macroeconomic ideas closely related to, indeed largely borrowed from, those of the monetarists and rational expectations theorists in the United States.

Recall that the rational expectations view of Robert Lucas and his followers was that unemployment cures itself through the flexibility of wages and prices. Any Keynesian policy of trying to accelerate this natural healing process by printing more money would, according to this view, fail; all that it would do would be to produce inflation.

In the European context, this view of the uselessness of monetary policy became an equivalent view of the uselessness of exchange rate adjustment. Keynesian economists worried that a country might find itself at a cost disadvantage; the European anti-Keynesians argued that markets would solve the problem, through a fall in wages and prices—and the idea that this process would be slow and painful was dismissed as an obsolete Keynesian notion. The idea that one might be able to smooth the adjustment process by devaluing the national currency was also dismissed: devaluation, it was argued, would immediately translate into inflation.

These European ideas were to a considerable extent borrowed

---

[2]Ironically, the concept of optimum currency areas was first suggested in 1961 by Robert Mundell—the same economist who was later to be adopted as intellectual guru by the supply-siders. It was his own previous views, among others, that the later Mundell would dismiss as "sheer quackery."

from American theorists, and as a result they tended to lag behind U.S. trends by several years.

We've already seen how in America the attack on Keynes pushed traditional macroeconomists into a corner during the 1970s. By the late 1980s, however, Keynesianism in America had come out of the corner fighting, and the influence of conservative thinking on macroeconomic policy had faded. In Europe, the story was different: as late as the fall of 1992, a hard-line defense of fixed exchange rates and a laissez-faire approach to unemployment were still standard in the rhetoric of central bankers across the continent.

Indeed, so strong was the belief that the increasingly rigid EMS was cost-free that Europeans believed themselves ready to take the next step, to a single currency.

THE MAASTRICHT TREATY

The details of an agreement to proceed to a single European currency were spelled out in a treaty signed in the Dutch city of Maastricht in 1990. The inability of anyone except the Dutch even to pronounce the treaty's name (roughly, it is "mahs-TREEKHT") may have been an omen of problems to come. But the treaty itself is a fascinating if unreadable document.

Much of the text is taken up with a huge variety of technical issues, ranging from the legal status of holiday homes in Denmark to the diplomatic status of the Pope in trade disputes involving the Vatican. The so-called social charter dealing with such issues as labor law was a significant bone in British throats. But the heart of the treaty was the definition of a set of tests—so-called convergence criteria—that a country would have to meet before it would be allowed to get rid of its own money and adopt the new European currency, the ecu. What was so interesting about these criteria was that taken at face value they made no sense whatsoever.

The first criterion was that a country maintain a stable exchange rate for two years before joining. This in effect tested the skill and resolve of the country at managing its own national currency: only a country that showed that it was very good at living with an independent currency would be allowed to abolish it.

The second criterion was that long-term interest rates should be close to that of the EC's best performers. The principal determinant of those long-term rates would be precisely the bond market's beliefs about European Monetary Union (EMU): if it believed that the lira and the mark would soon both be abolished and merged into the ecu, then German and Italian long-term rates would be about the same. So this criterion was circular: a country would be allowed to join EMU if the markets thought it would.

The third criterion required inflation to be close to that of the EC's best performance. This sounds more plausible, until you recognize that under fixed exchange rates—which were required by the first criterion—a country has no independent monetary policy. So any unusual inflation would represent a natural consequence of voluntary market choices, such as an investment boom, and there was really nothing a country could do about it without violating the first criterion.

Finally, two criteria set limits on budget deficits and the size of government debt. These are reasonable things, but what do they have to do with monetary union? The Federal Reserve does not need to police the budgets of New York and California, because they cannot print money to cover their deficits. The same would be true of national governments after EMU.

In short, a group of highly dignified, serious people, sitting at their baize-covered tables with their bottles of mineral water, created an agreement that sounded good but on closer examination was sheer nonsense. What was going on?

There are two theories about Maastricht. One is the "hazing" theory: that the purpose of the criteria was not really to prepare countries for entry into EMU but simply to test their resolve by making them do unpleasant and difficult things. The other is the "Italian" theory: the list of criteria makes no sense as a list of things needed for EMU, but sounds very much like a set of constraints that Italy's exasperated central bankers would like to impose on that country's corrupt politicians, suggesting that Italian diplomats, who are rumored to have done much of the drafting, were using Maastricht to serve domestic political ends.

In any case, by early 1993 political and economic stresses had made the solemnity of Maastricht seem almost comic. If there is a lesson here, it is that serious and dignified men and women in impressive international meetings may have absolutely no idea what they are talking about.

THE COLLAPSE OF THE EMS

The Maastricht Treaty was negotiated in an atmosphere of high optimism. After all, the European Monetary System had been a stunning success; even the United Kingdom, the last major holdout, was about to join. Since a system of fixed exchange rates had been so successful, a common currency seemed the logical next step.

Three years later, the scene looked very different. Britain and Italy had pulled out of the EMS, while Spain, Portugal, and Ireland had devalued their currencies. The EMS had effectively shrunk to a hard core of Germany, France, and several small neighbors. And France itself looked a bit wobbly.

What went wrong? The short answer was that the fixed rates of the European Monetary System had become untenable in the face of an unexpected shock: the fall of the Berlin Wall. Nobody could have predicted that shock. But it was mishandled badly, because of the inability of European policymakers to see past their convenient myths.

The essence of the problem was obvious to many independent economists from the start. When East Germany emerged from Communist rule, it turned out that the economy was a mess. Productivity was low, factories were antiquated, and there were huge needs for investment in infrastructure and environmental cleanup. It quickly became apparent that the West German economy would need to start running large budget deficits to pay for the rebuilding of the East.

These large budget deficits tended to raise demand in West Germany, which could have been inflationary. In order to offset this inflation risk, the Bundesbank raised interest rates—a sensible policy from Germany's point of view.

The rise in German interest rates, however, caused serious problems for the rest of Europe. In order to stay within the EMS, countries like France or the United Kingdom were obliged to match Germany's tight money without getting the benefits of Germany's fiscal stimulus. The paradoxical result was that the cost of Germany's reunification ended up producing a recession, not in Germany, but in the rest of Europe.

The logical answer should have been a realignment of parities, raising the value of the mark in terms of other European currencies. But European policymakers had convinced themselves that fixed exchange rates were always a good thing, and had committed their own political credibility to maintaining a rigid EMS and moving on to EMU. So they did nothing, allowing their economies to slide into deepening recession while waiting for the situation somehow to solve itself.

Finally the system cracked. As the recession in the United Kingdom deepened, political pressure on that country's government increased. Speculators, guessing that the pound might be devalued, began pulling money out of the United Kingdom, forcing the British government to spend huge sums trying to maintain its currency's value. After spending $30 billion in a few days, the British gave up on September 17, 1992, dropping out of the EMS and allowing the pound to float. Italy did the same, and several other European countries were forced to devalue.

The debacle was political as well as economic. British and German political leaders publicly engaged in mutual recriminations, and European unity seemed further away than it had for years.

Lessons of Europe for the United States

Conservatives in Europe chose somewhat different targets from their U.S. counterparts. They made less effort to dismantle the welfare state; they were more obsessed with monetary than international affairs. Yet their experience, like that of their ideological allies in the United States, was a lesson in disappointment: conservative policies did not work as well as advertised.

The promises of conservatism in Europe were alluring. Thatcherites believed that deregulation and privatization would work a productivity and employment miracle, and that monetarism showed the way to a stable, low-inflation economy. The believers in European Monetary Union thought they had found the way to achieve not only a stable, more productive European economy but a way to make a giant step toward European unity.

The actual record was far less encouraging. What Britain's conservatives delivered was a modest success on the productivity front, a rising trend in unemployment, and instability in both growth and inflation. The grand design of European monetary union led both to recession and to a political debacle as the European Monetary System fractured.

By the early 1990s, then, conservatism had failed to deliver on its promises in Europe as well as in the United States. The public was ready to listen to new ideas. But what sort of ideas would they be?

In the next part of this book, we examine the swing of the pendulum: the revival of liberal ideas in economics—and the strange things that happened to those ideas on the way to power.

PART III

THE
PENDULUM
SWINGS

CHAPTER 8

In the Long Run Keynes Is Still Alive

In 1992 MIT Press published a two-volume set of collected articles, edited by N. Gregory Mankiw and David Romer, entitled *New Keynesian Economics*. In that same year Mankiw, a young professor at Harvard, published a textbook on macroeconomics, whose core was based on "new Keynesian" ideas. In contrast to the disappointing performance of the rational expectations-based text of Mankiw's Harvard colleague Robert Barro, published in 1984, this textbook quickly became an academic best seller.

What was going on here? When we last looked at the story, it seemed that the conservative attack on Keynesian economics had been triumphant. In 1980, Irving Kristol declared with finality that Keynes was dead. Yet here he was, still influential a dozen years later. Indeed, Keynesianism was starting to look like the Energizer Bunny of economics: it just kept on going.

Nor was this just a matter of academic fashion. By 1992, monetarist and rational expectations theorists had lost virtually all influence over actual policy, in the United States and elsewhere. The Federal Reserve had responded to the 1987 stock crash with an aggressive monetary expansion that horrified monetarists, but it was pleased with the results. Efforts to pull the U.S. economy out of the 1990–92 recession were slower to take effect, but there was little talk in Washington of the hands-off attitude that conservatives might once have prescribed. Indeed, in February 1993 the new Democratic President included traditional pump-priming measures like a burst of public works spending and a temporary investment tax credit in his economic package. And in perhaps the biggest climbdown of all, in September 1992 the once-so-monetarist Conservative government of the United Kingdom abandoned the European Monetary System in order to pursue a blatantly Keynesian effort to stimulate the slumping British economy.

The story of the rebirth of Keynesian economics, and of the implosion of conservative macroeconomics, has been oddly ignored by the press. If anything, reporting on macroeconomics often seems locked in a time warp; one can still read the occasional piece describing how upstart economists (many now in their fifties) are challenging Keynesian orthodoxy. I'm not sure why the real story hasn't gotten out—it may be that the ability of conservative governments to hang on to power so long obscured the erosion of a big piece of their ideology, or it may simply be that the revival of Keynesianism has not had the kind of obviously colorful characters that make for entertaining stories.

Still, if you want to understand where our economic policy is going, you need to know that in the long run it seems that Keynes is still alive—and it is his critics who seem to lack staying power.

The Troubles of Conservative Macroeconomics

Ideas in economics usually get into trouble in one of two ways. Some ideas work in theory but not in practice—that is, the reasoning that underlies them seems to be right, but experience in the real world tells you that something is wrong. To take an example that we'll come back to in Chapter 9, there's a perfectly reasonable argument that says that international trade should be mostly between countries that have very different resource bases and thus can supply each other's lacks. Unfortunately, in the real world most trade is between similar countries; so there's something wrong with the argument (and with any policy conclusions based on it).

Other ideas work in practice but not in theory. In the 1960s, all the evidence showed a more or less stable tradeoff between unemployment and inflation. As we saw in Chapter 1, however, Milton Friedman argued on purely logical grounds that this tradeoff was a sort of optical illusion, which would go away if you tried to use it—and he was right.

By the late 1970s, conservative macroeconomists had put together a powerfully compelling theory of the business cycle. This theory had been so persuasive that it had put traditional Keynesian economists deeply on the defensive, and the intellectual triumph of conservative macroeconomics had done much to raise the prestige of economic conservatism in general.

In the next few years, however, this theory ran into deep trouble, as it became clear that it worked neither in theory nor in practice.

Let's start with the failure in theory. As you may recall, Milton Friedman first turned macroeconomics on its ear by proposing that recessions basically amount to periods in which workers and firms are fooled, mistaking a general fall in demand (which would simply lead them to reduce their prices) for a fall in the specific demand for their own product or labor. Robert Lucas then took the argument a step further, by arguing that firms and workers are at least as smart as the government: they are fooled only when the situation is genuinely confusing. Thus no attempt to smooth out the business cycle through an active government policy can succeed. Monetary expansions may in the past have led to output increases, but that was only because they were unexpected and hence added to the confusion. The bottom line was that an active monetary policy is at best irrelevant, at worst a major additional source of instability. What was so intellectually attractive about this argument was that it conceded that monetary policy has *seemed* to matter in the past, even while denying that it can play any useful role in the future.

But by 1980 it was becoming apparent that there was a big problem with this argument. The problem? People have too much information.

Suppose, for example, that the Federal Reserve decides on a whim to cut the money supply (or sharply reduce its rate of growth). Experience tells us—and Lucas would agree—that this would produce a recession rather than simply reducing the price level. In his story, however, the slump occurs precisely because firms setting prices do not realize that it is a general slump, not something peculiar to themselves. Once they become aware of the pervasiveness of the slump, it will cure itself.

The question is whether it is reasonable to suppose that businesses are really confused in that way. Leave aside the fact that in the real world you can read about a recession in *The Wall Street Journal*—maybe you don't believe what you read. (Actually, their news pages are fine; it's only the editorial page you should ignore.) Nonetheless, there are many clues to the state of the economy other than your own direct business experience, like the levels of interest rates and stock prices. Won't the private sector take these into account? And if it does, will the business cycle story still hold together?

In the late 1970s Lucas and his disciples worked feverishly, attempting to produce theoretical models in which firms and households can observe stock prices and interest rates, yet still be subject to the kind of rational confusion needed to create booms and slumps. They failed. The theory underlying a rational expectations business cycle just didn't work out.

At the same time, it was becoming increasingly obvious that the rational expectations story didn't work in practice either. Here the difficulty is easier to explain: *economic slumps last too long.*

Bear in mind that the problem for rational expectations theorists is to explain why, during a slump, prices and wages don't immediately fall enough to restore full employment. The proposed answer is that firms and workers don't realize, or aren't sure, that it really is a general slump. This might make sense if slumps typically lasted only a few months, or even a year. But after the economy has been running high unemployment rates for several years, you would expect people to figure it out.

The experience of the 1980s and early 1990s provided a pretty clear test. The determination of the Federal Reserve to bring inflation under control seems to have produced a double-dip recession that began in 1979. Although the economy began to recover in 1982, the unemployment rate didn't drop back to its 1979 level until 1987. Is it really believable that it took eight years for companies and workers to figure out what was happening? Nor was the experience an aberration: a slump that began in early 1990 was visible enough to the general public to push a once-popular president out of office, yet not until halfway into 1992 did the slump turn into a real recovery. The experience from 1979 to 1993 was almost custom-designed to demonstrate the inadequacy of a theory that tried to explain business cycles as the product of a confused public.

Not everyone saw the theoretical and empirical collapse of rational expectations macroeconomics as clearly as I've put it. After all, quite a few economists had based their careers on a kind of discipleship to the ideas of Lucas and the first wave of his followers; some graduate students had been so indoctrinated in the new theories that they could hardly conceive of an alternative. Yet I think it's safe to say that even by the mid-1980s, when Lucas's business cycle theory was still widely admired, it had few remaining believers. But where were macroeconomists to turn?

The answer is that some turned right, and some left. Those who turned left became the new Keynesians; we'll talk about them shortly. First, however, let's look at those who turned right, and who (to my way of thinking) ended up trapped in an intellectual cul-de-sac.

TRUE BELIEVERS: THE REAL BUSINESS CYCLE

To conservatives, who believe that markets work efficiently, a recession is a hard thing to explain. If markets work so well, how can something like a reduction in the money supply lead to so much waste and hardship?

Milton Friedman proposed a clever answer: It's because erratic monetary policy confuses people. His answer gained immense prestige after his successful prediction of stagflation. But as we've just seen, the idea that people are fooled in a recession just didn't hold up very well once people began seriously kicking its tires. So another answer had to be found. Either markets don't actually work that well, or a recession is something very different from what it seems to be.

The true believers were unwilling to compromise their faith in markets, so they needed to reinterpret recessions. As early as 1982, a new faction had formed within economics. Led by Edward Prescott of Carnegie-Mellon, it denied everything that most economists had believed about recessions. Where most economists, Milton Friedman included, thought that monetary factors had something to do with recessions, this new school claimed that money and the business cycle were completely unrelated.[1] Where

[1]What about times when there is an obvious correlation betwen monetary and real events, like the collapse of the money supply which Milton Friedman claimed caused the Great Depression? The new school argued that the causation actually runs in the other direction: the Great Depression caused the monetary shrinkage. This is an assertion that many economists would accept at least in part—but they would not accept the view that output

most economists—and just about all business managers—think that a recession is a time of inadequate demand, the new school claimed that the business cycle is driven by the economy's supply side. And where most people think that recessions are a bad thing, the new school regarded them as part of the economy's natural and indeed optimal behavior.

The new set of ideas has come to be known as "real business cycle" theory. It is usually expressed in complex mathematical models, and its exponents like to stress the subtleties, yet in its essence it is very simple.

To a real business cycle theorist, economic fluctuations are driven by changes in the economy's productivity. The sources of these changes are left unexplained, but in general one supposes that they are due to a mix of natural factors (harvest fluctuations, cold winters, etc.), political events (tax changes, wars that raise the price of oil), and the randomness of technological progress (like the surprise productivity surge in the United States in 1992). An unusually good year means a boom; a surprisingly bad year means a slump.

This isn't all there is to it, of course. For one thing, most of the year-to-year fluctuation in the economy's output is not because the productivity of each worker-hour changes; it's because of fluctuations in the number of hours worked. Also, productivity rarely actually goes down, while output often falls for several quarters in a row (because the number of hours worked declines faster than productivity rises). So real business cycle theorists needed to have an explanation of why fluctuations in productivity should be amplified by much larger fluctuations in the number of hours worked.

Their answer was simple: People make rational decisions to work more when their productivity is unusually high, to work less when it is unusually low. Consider a farmer facing fluctuating weather. She is likely to put in very long days when the weather is

---

and unemployment would have been exactly the same even if the banking collapse had been avoided.

good, but stay indoors when it is bad. If you were to measure her daily output, you would find that most of the fluctuation is explained in a direct sense by changes in the length of the work day, but nonetheless it is fluctuating weather that is the root cause.

Now comes the kicker: if fluctuations in work effort are rational responses to random real shocks, then they are nothing to worry about. The business cycle is simply part of how a free market responds to a changing world, and since real business cycle theorists believe that markets are efficient, they conclude that the business cycle is actually a good thing.

I think I know how this description must seem to most readers. Is this really serious? Indeed, a number of Keynesians attacked the real business cycle idea in articles with titles like Willem Buiter's "The Economics of Doctor Pangloss" (Voltaire's fictional philosopher who always explained that everything is for the best). If recessions are a rational response to temporary setbacks in productivity, was the Great Depression really just an extended, voluntary holiday?

Nonetheless, this book is at least partly dedicated to the proposition that serious economists need to be taken seriously, and real business cycle theory had a major impact on academic economics during the 1980s. Its basic story may sound deeply implausible, but for those who bought into its premises it provided a framework for hundreds of theoretical papers and for elaborate if often peculiar assessment of statistical data. For some seven or eight years a real business cycle paper could be found in virtually every issue of the leading economics journals, and real business cycle theorists came to dominate a number of university economics departments.

Yet the real business cycle movement, as the heir of conservative macroeconomics, took a very different course from that of monetarism and rational expectations. Those movements steadily broadened their reach. Monetarism was not just an academic doctrine, it was a philosophy about policy, and for at least a little while it actually ruled the monetary policies of several major nations. Rational expectations was a doctrine that even its critics found so important that it very nearly tore down the whole structure of Keynesian orthodoxy.

By contrast, real business cycle theory never got close to the world of policy—not even the most extreme conservative politicians were prepared to tell the American people to welcome recessions as part of the natural and optimal course of events. And instead of spreading its intellectual range, the movement became increasingly ingrown over time. Indeed, one observer described it as becoming like a fringe political movement that successively purges itself of the ideologically impure until only a handful of members are left.

What about the giants of rational expectations? Where did they stand on all of this?

The answer is that they seem to have stepped off to the side. Robert Lucas and his major disciples, notably Robert Barro, never really weighed into the debate when rational expectations macroeconomics began to dissolve and the real business cycle theory was presented as its successor. Instead, they became preoccupied with other issues like long-run growth (see Chapter 9) or with technical matters far from policy.

In other words: by the mid-1980s, indeed by the end of Ronald Reagan's first term, conservative macroeconomic theory had run aground. In the political realm, conservatives were wildly triumphant; at the level of public discussion, many of conservatism's ideas had become virtual dogma. But the Republicans were no longer the party of ideas.

Instead, the new ideas were coming from the left. And at the cutting edge of those new ideas was a sophisticated revival of Keynesianism.

Rationality and Recessions

THE IRRATIONALITY OF PERFECT RATIONALITY

I once heard a composer of folk music described as a man who could create songs that were so compelling that after one hearing it seems as if you must always have known them. There are economists who have the same talent: they manage to have ideas that are so basic, yet so simple, that once you've heard them it's hard to believe you didn't always understand them.

George Akerlof has that talent. His most famous idea, so famous that younger economists sometimes don't realize that it came from somewhere, came in a classic paper entitled "The Market for 'Lemons,' "[2] behind whose flippant title lurked a deep insight into why markets can break down when buyers and sellers do not have access to the same information. The lemons idea (or, to give it the more formal name, the theory of adverse selection) was in the area of microeconomics, and indeed until 1982 Akerlof didn't work as a macroeconomist. But in that year he came up with another idea that was simple, yet so powerful that it had the strength to bring Keynes back from the dead.

The idea had two parts. First, like a few other economists (notably Herbert Simon, who won a Nobel Prize for his work on "bounded rationality"), Akerlof pointed out that it is often rational to be a little bit less than totally rational. Suppose that I am trying to decide how much to spend and how much to save out of my current paycheck. If I really wanted to do it right, I should sit down with every piece of information I can on the state of the economy, including long-term forecasts, best guesses on future taxes, and the likely lifetime earnings profile for people in my profession. Once I've done all of that, I should make a budget plan for the next few decades, and try to figure out from that plan how much to put aside this month.

[2] As in used cars, not citrus fruit.

Of course I don't do that, and I shouldn't. A rough guess will probably lead to an acceptable solution, and the time and expense of trying to improve on that guess is probably not worth it. As the saying goes, the perfect is the enemy of the good.

That sounds obvious, but it prepares the ground for the second part of the idea: "near-rational" people, people who make good guesses but don't try to use every piece of information they could possibly lay their hands on, may behave very differently from the idealized rational individuals of many economic theories. In particular, they may respond very differently to economic policy.

Akerlof's point may perhaps best be explained with a hypothetical example. Imagine a country whose government plans to have a temporary burst of spending for some reason—to fight a war, to build some long-needed public works, to throw an inaugural party, whatever. This government would, however, like to avoid driving up interest rates and crowding out private investment. It is faced with the following choice: Should it sharply raise taxes now to pay for the project, and cut them later; or should it issue bonds to raise money for the project and pay off these bonds only gradually with a slightly higher tax rate?

This is actually a familiar question in economics—Robert Barro, the rational expectations macroeconomist, made much of his reputation with a 1981 paper on the subject. As he pointed out, there is a very clear answer to this question when individuals are perfectly rational: Buy now, pay later. Here's the argument. Why would the government want to raise taxes to pay for the project on a current basis? The only reason is to try to produce a rise in national savings large enough to finance the project without cutting into private investment. Since national savings are the difference between national income and national consumption, the purpose of the tax increase is therefore to induce people to consume less. But if people are fully rational, they will realize that they have to pay for the project in higher taxes sooner or later—if not in a much higher tax rate for a short time, then in a slightly higher rate for a very long time as the government services its bonds. So rational and fully informed taxpayers would cut their consumption just as much if the government borrows to pay for the project as if it taxes them right away. Therefore, there is no advantage in a sharp tax increase. And there are disadvantages to any bulge in taxes—as we saw in Chapter 2, the indirect costs of taxes in distorted incentives tend to be more than proportional to the amount of taxes collected, so that a period of unusually high taxes will produce a lot of hidden costs. In other words, the government should not worry about the current level of the deficit.

Does this argument sound convincing? It did (and still does) to many economists. Akerlof pointed out, however, that it depends crucially on the assumption that people do something that they are unlikely to do in real life: take account of the implications of current government spending for their future tax liabilities. That is, the claim that deficits don't matter implicitly assumes that ordinary families sit around the dinner table and say, "I read in the paper that President Clinton plans to spend $150 billion on infrastructure over the next five years; he's going to have to raise taxes to pay for that, even though he says he won't, so we're going to have to reduce our monthly budget by $12.36."

Why does this sound silly? Not because the average family is stupid or uninformed; the truth is that even the families of brilliant conservative economists don't have conversations like this. No, the point is that the effort isn't worth it. If a family has arrived at a sensible rule of thumb for deciding how much to spend, trying to improve on that rule by making sophisticated predictions about the future implications of government spending will improve the family's decisions so little that it isn't worth the investment of time and attention.

Each individual family, then, does almost as well with a good rule of thumb as it would with perfect rationality—close enough to make perfect rationality an irrational goal. But now comes Akerlof's big insight: *"near-rational" behavior and perfectly rational behavior have very different implications for policy.*

In this particular example, a population of near-rational households will probably *not* cut their consumption very much in response to the news of a government spending boom. Maybe they should ideally understand that current spending means future taxes, but in practice they are much more likely to wait to see an actual tax increase before they really respond. And what that means is that deficits do matter, after all.

But what does all this have to do with recessions?

Remember the puzzle of a recession: How can it be that a market economy, which we like to imagine is an efficient way of organizing economic activity, sometimes leads to such a seemingly irrational outcome? Milton Friedman thought he knew the answer: It's because people, though behaving rationally, are confused—and what the government should do is stop adding to their confusion. As we've seen, however, that argument broke down in the 1980s. George Akerlof and others now proposed an alternative story: Recessions can happen because people, though sensible, are not perfectly rational. And that alternative story leads us right back to Keynes.

THE NEW KEYNESIAN IDEA

From 1980 to 1987, the economy of Massachusetts boomed. The state's specialties—notably minicomputers and high-technology weapons—flourished during the Reagan years, in spite of the state's Democratic leanings. After about 1984, the growth in these base industries was supplemented by an increasingly feverish real estate boom that led to a surge in construction employment. In 1987, the state's unemployment rate was an astonishingly low 2.7 percent, half the national average, and labor shortages had pushed wages at McDonald's to more than $7 an hour.

Then the bubble burst, and the Massachusetts Miracle became the Massachusetts Debacle. In reality, the fundamentals had been gradually eroding for years. By 1988, it became painfully clear that the growing power of microcomputers (that is, PCs) was allowing them to take over much of the minicomputer market, just as minicomputers had displaced many of the big mainframes of an earlier era—and microcomputers were a specialty of California's Silicon Valley, not Boston's Route 128. At the same time, the big Reagan defense budgets were beginning their long post–Cold

War slide. More generally, the high costs of doing business in Massachusetts had made it an increasingly unattractive place to manufacture, leading to a loss of market share across the board. This erosion was masked for a couple of years by the real estate boom, but at a certain point a collapse was inevitable. In 1988, like a cartoon character who walks four or five steps off a cliff before looking down, Massachusetts business took a look at the fundamentals and proceeded to plunge. By 1989, the unemployment rate reached almost 10 percent.

The slump hurt nearly everyone. Even middle-class people with secure jobs felt the pain if they tried to sell their homes, as many of them did: in 1989 it seemed as if every other home in the state had a "For Sale" sign, and the real estate pages of the *Boston Globe* had ballooned to three times their normal size. Tales of perfectly good homes that had gone unsold for more than a year were common.

By 1992, however, the housing market was more or less back to normal. "For Sale" signs were no more common than anywhere else, and houses turned over reasonably quickly. Admittedly, prices were down—maybe as much as 30 percent from their peak. But at least houses were moving.

Strangely, however, the restoration of normalcy in the housing market was not the result of any general recovery in the state economy as a whole. Unemployment in the Boston area remained near 10 percent; if it had not risen higher, in spite of a national recession, it was only because so many workers had left the state. The announcements of big layoffs had become less frequent, but there wasn't a lot of actual good news.

There was, of course, no mystery about why houses were selling again: their prices had finally come down enough to be realistic, given the state of the local economy. The question is, why didn't prices fall sooner? Why did the Boston housing market have to go through several years in which thousands of houses stood empty, and tens of thousands more were occupied by owners trapped by their inability to sell, when an early drop in prices could have quickly eliminated this apparent waste?

What I want to do now is try to convince you that the story of the Boston housing market shows us the puzzle of recession in microcosm. And when we try to explain how it was that for several years that market seemed stuck with a seemingly irrational inventory of unsold houses, we are led to the reasons why John Maynard Keynes is still alive and well.

Why is a depressed housing market like a national recession in miniature? For one thing, it is characterized by widespread "unemployment"—a house that stands empty, or is unwillingly occupied by a family that wants to move rather than by a family that wants to live there, is as much a wasted resource as a jobless worker or an idle factory. A city full of unsold houses is, on a smaller scale, as much a reproach to capitalism as a nation full of idle workers. If we can understand the smaller puzzle, we may have made significant progress on the larger one.

And as with a national recession, the question when the "For Sale" signs start sprouting is, why don't prices fall? Just because a local economy isn't prosperous doesn't mean that houses need to stand empty—they just need to sell cheaply. (That's why it's important to notice that the Boston area economy was no more prosperous in 1992 than it was in 1989; the housing market was "clearing," that is, supply was matched with demand, not because demand had increased but because prices had fallen to realistic levels.)

The short answer to why prices don't fall immediately is, of course, that sellers are reluctant to cut them. But that is true in any market. When the demand for wheat or for shares in General Motors falls, sellers would also prefer not to cut their prices, but that doesn't stop the market from driving the price down almost immediately to a level that matches supply with demand. Why is the housing market (or the labor market) different?

The answer is that houses are not a homogeneous commodity like wheat. A farmer who tries to demand a price that is even a penny per bushel higher than the prevailing rate knows that she will be unable to sell her harvest. The seller of a house, however, possesses an asset which is at least slightly differentiated in location, in decor, in amenities from any other house. The higher the price he demands, the longer he can expect the house to remain unsold, but there is no unique price at which the house can be sold at all; even if the asking price is a few thousand dollars above what similar houses are being sold for, a buyer just might come along who is in a hurry to close, or who is inexplicably drawn to the hot pink wallpaper. That is, there is a tradeoff between selling at a high price and selling quickly. There is in principle a best price for the seller to demand, a price that makes the best of this tradeoff, but it is not a catastrophe if the seller demands a bit too much.

And now we invoke the limits of rationality. A farmer who refuses to sell her harvest unless she gets a price 5 percent above what the market wants to pay is being wildly irrational—and economic behavior is rarely wildly irrational. But a homeowner who holds out for 5 percent more than the asking price that would optimize the tradeoff between selling high and selling quickly is making only a small error; and as George Akerlof pointed out, it is actually rational not to be excessively rational, so people not only can but even should make small errors like this.

So, when you think about it, you realize that the seemingly huge irrationality of a market full of unsold houses could be the result of thousands of "near-rational" decisions of potential sellers to hold out for just a little more than they should have. Given the difficulties of processing information and making decisions, they were not being foolish; but the collective outcome was nonetheless a very bad one.

It seems as if there are two kinds of markets: markets like wheat, where sensible behavior on the part of individuals leads to sensible behavior on the part of the market as a whole; and markets like housing, where "near-rational" behavior on the part of individuals can lead to highly irrational overall outcomes. What is the difference? It lies in the relative imperfection of competition.

A wheat farmer produces essentially the same good as thousands of other wheat farmers. This produces a "perfectly competitive" market, in which each farmer treats the price she receives as something given to her by the market; since she doesn't set prices, she can't set them wrong. Housing, by contrast, is a market with very imperfect competition: nobody's house is exactly the same as mine, and potential buyers have limited willingness to search over even the available alternatives. I therefore have some leeway in setting my price, including the leeway to get it wrong if I am a bit less than perfectly rational.

This, then, is the new Keynesian idea: What look like highly irrational outcomes in the marketplace are caused by the interaction between imperfectly competitive markets and slightly less than perfectly rational individuals.

THE NEW CASE FOR ACTIVE MONETARY POLICY[3]

We can now describe how the new Keynesian view of the economy can be used to revive the case for an active monetary policy.

Let's go back to the story offered in Chapter 1 of an economy that is initially chugging along at more or less full employment. We now realize, however, that markets in this economy are likely to be highly imperfect. For example, firms may often choose to pay wages that are well above the minimum necessary to attract workers, because otherwise the threat of dismissal will not be an effective way of punishing inadequate work effort. Many if not most firms will be "oligopolists," large players in industries in which each firm has a considerable ability to influence prices. In many markets, buyers and sellers will have difficulty finding each other, producing a costly and time-consuming process of search. As we pointed out in Chapter 1, even in the best of worlds, "full employment" will normally mean several percentage points of unemployment; in this not-best-of worlds the normal rate of unemployment will probably be a few points higher than this technical minimum.[4]

---

[3]Versions of this story may be found in articles by several economists, notably Greg Mankiw; George Akerlof and Janet Yellen; Olivier Blanchard and Nobuhiro Kiyotaki; and Laurence Ball and David Romer.

[4]By the way, saying that market economies are imperfect does not imply a longing for some

Suppose now that in this imperfect world we once again play the Keynesian experiment of positing an increase in the desire of people to hold cash. Recall that in Chapter 1 we saw how an attempt by everyone at once to increase cash holdings leads to a general fall in employment and incomes. The same will be true here.

At this point, the monetarist says that wages and prices will fall, increasing the real value of the cash in circulation and curing the recession. But will wages and prices really adjust?

What if firms are reluctant to cut their prices, either because there are measurable costs to putting on new price tags ("menu costs," in the jargon of the new Keynesians) or because they just don't want to be bothered with rethinking their pricing schemes? (The difference between real costs of changing stickers and subjective costs of thinking is actually quite blurry—that's why near rationality may in a way be regarded as a higher form of true rationality.) If markets were perfect, a firm that charges too high a price would lose all its business. In a world of highly imperfect markets, a firm that charges a price a little too high gains almost as much from that higher price as it loses in sales; a firm that fails to cut wages has a gain in higher leverage over its workers that almost compensates for its higher cost; and so on. In other words, the costs to an individual firm of being a little less than totally rational and not cutting wages and prices may be quite small, small enough that reasonable people just don't do it.

And yet the individually reasonable decision not to cut prices in the face of a recession can have collectively disastrous results. If prices don't fall when people decide to hold more cash, then the slump in output and employment is not self-correcting. In an imperfect world, senseless things can happen to groups of people who behave sensibly as individuals.

---

other system. Winston Churchill once said of democracy that it is the worst system of government known to man, except for all the others. Similarly, a real as opposed to an idealized market economy is a highly imperfect system which works better than anything else we have come up with. The point of emphasizing market imperfections is not to condemn the market system, but simply to explain how things can sometimes go wrong.

The case for an active monetary policy is now obvious. Suppose that we have slid into a recession, just as described. There is an easy way out: put more money into circulation, and spending, incomes, and employment will rise, just like that. (Well, usually. Sometimes it takes more money than you expect to turn things around, as the Federal Reserve discovered to George Bush's cost in 1991–92.)

Notice that this story doesn't require that anyone be confused about what's happening. Milton Friedman and Robert Lucas argued that monetary policy could work only by fooling people, and could therefore never add to stability. If, however, recessions persist even when people understand perfectly well what is happening, then increasing the supply of money can cure them even if it is a totally predictable action.

That is the new Keynesian story. It has its detractors. Economists raised in the school of rational expectations are bothered that it seems too open-ended: while there is only one way to be perfectly rational, there are many ways to be imperfectly rational; how do we know which one is most realistic? Or to put it another way, the style of argument that underpins new Keynesianism could conceivably be used to rationalize a lot of other stories about the economy as well; there seems to be an act of judgment in choosing this particular one, and many economists get nervous when theories are based heavily on judgments rather than derived rigorously from first principles.

Nonetheless, the new Keynesian idea serves a critically important purpose. During the 1970s, conservative macroeconomics had Keynesianism on the run with its assertion that it was a logically flawed theory—that it *could not* be right. The new Keynesian theory showed, on the contrary, that the idea that recessions represent a market failure that can be corrected by government action can indeed be right. This is useful, because in reality Keynesianism *is* basically right, so it's nice to have a theory that lets us admit it.

The Evidence

I just made an outrageous assertion: that Keynesianism is basically right. This assertion will raise howls of protest from many, so I'd better explain what I mean and what the evidence is.

When one says that Keynesianism is right, one does not mean that every word that Keynes the man wrote is correct, or even that traditional Keynesian policies like public works programs during recessions are a good idea. What is meant instead is that the general picture of what happens in a recession given in Chapter 1 is right—that a recession represents a failure of coordination in which the efforts of the public to hold cash play a central role. This picture depends crucially on the presumption that prices and wages will not quickly fall enough to restore full employment, even if everyone realizes that there is an economywide slump. It then implies as a consequence that government policy, in particular an increase in the money supply, can usually cure the problem.

What kind of evidence would support this view? It could be of two kinds. First, we could try to find evidence that the whole machine works as advertised—that monetary policy can cause or cure recessions. Second, we could look for evidence on the crucial point of difference between Keynesians and their critics, the relative inflexibility of wages and prices.

But we've already seen, in Chapters 4 and 7, respectively, evidence of both kinds.

For evidence of the power of monetary policy to affect the real economy, most policy-oriented economists needed no more evidence than the business cycle in the United States from 1979 onward. In 1979, the Federal Reserve decided to use tight money to fight inflation in the United States. The policy succeeded in bringing inflation down, but also generated the worst slump since the 1930s. When the Fed reversed policy in 1982, however, the economy obediently turned around and began a rapid recovery. The Fed's policy was not concealed; on the contrary, it was the subject of highly publicized discussions. Nonetheless, it had massive real effects.

Now supply-siders, of course, have a different explanation: the 1979–82 slump was somehow due to Jimmy Carter's policies, while Reaganomics created the boom. Even conservative economists, however, generally found this argument a bit hard to swallow. In any case, the experience of other countries seemed to exhibit the same Keynesian principles. We saw in Chapter 7 that disinflationary monetary policy in the United Kingdom in the early 1980s produced a sharp recession, just as in the United States. Moreover, the British, unlike the Americans, managed to illustrate the monetary nature of the subsequent recovery by overdoing it and getting into an inflationary boom.

If the evidence of business cycles were not enough, powerful evidence of the inflexibility of prices has come from another source: the movement of exchange rates.

If you thought that prices and wages in the economy were highly flexible, what would you expect to see happen if, say, the value of the dollar in terms of German marks falls 10 percent on the foreign exchange market? We already know the answer from Arthur Laffer, in his pre-curve days. Since nothing has happened on either economy's "real" or supply side, real quantities, including the price of German goods in terms of U.S. goods, should be unaffected. This relative price of goods may be calculated by multiplying the German consumer price index by the number of marks per dollar, then dividing by the U.S. price index; it is generally referred to as the *real exchange rate*. So a 10 percent depreciation of the dollar should lead to a mix of U.S. inflation and German deflation just sufficient to leave the real exchange rate unchanged.

In fact, nothing of the sort happens. Figure 11 shows that far from remaining unaffected by fluctuations in the dollar-mark rate, the real exchange rate has followed that exchange rate very closely. That is, American prices tended to remain stable in dollars, German prices in marks. This is prima facie evidence of exactly the kind of price stickiness that old Keynesians asserted and new Keynesians have tried to explain.

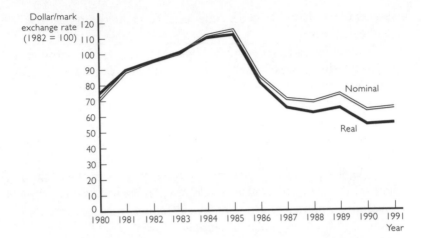

Figure 11. The real and nominal exchange rates of dollar against the mark have moved closely together.

This observation is not unique to the dollar-mark exchange rate: it applies across the board. Even the tiny Republic of Ireland, with a population smaller than that of Greater Boston, managed to demonstrate the potency of monetary policy when it joined the European Monetary System in 1977. Prior to that time, the Irish punt had been pegged to the British pound, an arrangement that made sense given that Ireland exports as much to the United Kingdom as it does to the rest of Europe combined. As a result, the real exchange rate between Britain and Ireland was fairly stable, while that between Ireland and Germany fluctuated sharply. Once Ireland had joined the EMS, however, it was in effect pegged to the mark. Nothing "real" had changed: Britain was still a far more important trading partner than Germany. Yet after 1977 Ireland's real exchange rate vis-à-vis Germany was much more stable than its rate against Britain.

There is a certain irony here. When we looked at the rise of supply-side economics, we learned that the central figures—Bartley, Laffer, Wanniski, and Mundell—were brought together by their views on international economics, specifically by their belief that devaluations of the dollar were reflected one-for-one in U.S.

inflation. In fact, however, the ratio is more nearly zero-for-one—and the fact that exchange rate changes are *not* reflected in prices is one of the best pieces of evidence for the Keynesianism the supply-siders so despised.

Theory and Policy in 1993

In early 1993 many countries faced macroeconomic policy dilemmas. In the United States, the Clinton administration was urging Congress to pass a mixture of tax cuts and public works programs to stimulate the economy, but critics argued that the recovery was already well under way. In Europe, Britain was waiting to see whether a depreciated pound and lower interest rates would produce recovery, while French policymakers quietly debated whether the strength of the franc was worth the cost in unemployment. In Japan, interest rates were cut to offset the effects of a bursting financial bubble, but the government agonized over whether a fiscal stimulus was needed as well.

Nobody really knew how all of this policy discussion would turn out. What was really striking, however, was that the terms of the discussion would not have been unfamiliar to an economist from, say, 1970. As a matter of practical policy analysis, Keynesianism was not only back, it was almost unchallenged. Monetarism had been swallowed up by the sands of time; rational expectations and the real business cycle had retreated to the upper stories of the ivory tower.

It would be nice to say that the rise of new Keynesian theory had greatly improved the quality of practical macroeconomic analysis. Unfortunately, it's not clear that it has. At least so far, the new Keynesians give much the same policy advice that old Keynesians might have, but with a better theoretical conscience.

But the mere fact that Keynes is still alive is major news. The prestige that gave conservative economics its sense of intellectual leadership, that convinced even moderates that the right was the party of ideas, rested largely on the brilliance and persuasiveness of macroeconomists like Friedman and Lucas. When their noisy attack on Keynes turned into a quiet retreat, the whole conservative claim to be the wave of the future lost its plausibility.

CHAPTER 9

The Economics of QWERTY

It is said that a true sage can see the universe in a grain of sand. Paul David is no sage, only a fine economic historian: the best he could do was see the nature of economic reality in the layout of a typewriter keyboard.

I am typing this chapter on a new, fast personal computer. The decal proudly proclaims, "Intel inside!", and indeed its 80486 chip allows it to carry out in a few minutes feats of computation that would have taken hours on a 1960s mainframe and that would have been simply out of the question in 1940. Yet the first line of my keyboard is the same as that on the clunky mechanical typewriter my mother used when she put my father through law school: QWERTYUIOP.

Why QWERTYUIOP? In the early 1980s, Paul David and his Stanford colleague Brian Arthur asked that question, and quickly realized that it led them into surprisingly deep waters. In a 1982 paper entitled "Clio[1] and the Economics of QWERTY," David made the QWERTY keyboard into a symbol for a new view about how the economy works, a view that had been quietly gaining ground even as conservative economic ideology was achieving its political triumph.

You can probably already guess the answer to the mystery of QWERTY. The standard keyboard layout of typewriters dates back to the nineteenth century. It is not the most efficient layout in terms of finger movement, but that was no disadvantage in the early days; indeed, given the tendency of keys to jam on early typewriters, there was some advantage to a layout that forced typists to work slowly. Eventually jamming keys became a thing of the past, and it would have made sense to shift to an alternative, more efficient design—but by then it was too late. Typists learned their trade on QWERTY keyboards, because that was what manufacturers produced; manufacturers made QWERTY typewriters, because those were what typists knew how to use. The standard keyboard, adopted more or less by accident, had become "locked in."

What Paul David, Brian Arthur, and a growing number of other economists began to recognize in the late seventies and early eighties was that stories like that of the typewriter keyboard are, in fact, pervasive in the economy. Some of these stories involve technology choices that bear an obvious resemblance to the QWERTY tale. For example, unless you are a fanatical movie buff who has invested in a laser-disk video player, your home VCR uses a tape cassette (VHS) system—not because VHS is a clearly better system, but because cassettes are what most video stores stock, which is in turn because most people have VHS systems in their homes. I write my books and articles in WordPerfect, not because I particularly like it, but because most of the editors I write for prefer to receive WordPerfect disks, since that's the word-processing software that most of their authors use.

Other stories sound a little different, but—as David and Arthur realized—they are at root the same. For example, where do you

---

[1] The Greek goddess of history.

live if you work in the film industry? Probably in Los Angeles. Why? Because the other film industry people you need to work with are there. But they are there because they need to be near people like you. If you are an investment banker, you probably work in New York for pretty much the same reason.

What does all this have to do with economic policy? Maybe quite a lot. What conservatives believe in, above all, is the effectiveness of free markets as ways to organize economic activity. Leave people free to make their own, individual choices, say conservatives, and they will be far more productive and efficient than if you try to plan or direct their activities. And as Milton Friedman showed, "Free to choose" can be a powerful slogan. But what if the collective result of those free choices is to lock in a bad result? What if we end up stuck with an inferior technology, or with an industry in the middle of a congested metropolis when it might function better in a new location?

And what if another country manages, with a little timely government intervention, to "lock in" an advantage in some major industry—and thereby to lock us out?

No, the story of the QWERTY keyboard is not just a cute piece of trivia. Like the description of the pin factory with which Adam Smith began *The Wealth of Nations,* it is a parable that opens our eyes to a whole different way of thinking about economics.[2] That different way of thinking rejects the idea that markets invariably lead the economy to a unique best solution; instead, it asserts that the outcome of market competition often depends crucially on historical accident. (Paul David calls this "path dependence": where you end up depends on what happens along the way.) And this conclusion is fraught with political implications, because a sophisticated government may try to make sure that the accidents of history run the way it wants.

In this chapter we will trace how this new way of thinking

[2]There is no single accepted name for the new approach to economics. Brian Arthur, drawing an analogy with physics, calls it "positive feedback." Many economic theorists, with a precision that is useful but not worth trying to explain in this context, prefer to talk about "strategic complementarity." I think, however, that Paul David's QWERTY is the most evocative phrase, and I will generally use it in this chapter.

emerged among professional economists during the very years of conservative political triumph. In Chapter 10 we'll see a less benign part of the story: the way that sophisticated economic ideas from the left were used, like the ideas of the sophisticated right, to provide cover for a simplistic policy agenda.

But before we get into all of that, let's start with a question: Why did it take until the late 1970s for anyone to take the economics of QWERTY seriously?

Seeing the Obvious

In the last few years there has been a surge of interest among economists in the field of "economic geography," which studies the location of industries within as well as between countries. As the examples above suggest, economic geography is a subject in which the role of historical accident in determining outcomes is often obvious. In the early nineteenth century Philadelphia was a more important port than New York. What tipped the balance in New York's favor was the opening of the Erie Canal. That canal has, however, been more of a tourist attraction than a serious transportation route for a century—yet New York is still the nation's largest city.

When I excitedly described some of the recent work in economic geography to a non-economist friend, he replied, "Isn't that all kind of obvious?"

Yes, it is obvious—but the fact that it is important isn't. The role of history and accident in determining the location of industry is not hard to see, once it has been pointed out. The problem is that there are lots of interesting things to say about the economy, which is after all an almost inconceivably complex system. The trick is to pick out the observations that get you somewhere. It is an undeniable fact that senior managers at large U.S. corporations tend to be tall men; but that fact does not seem to lead to any useful further insights about our economy. It is a less well-known fact that most of the carpets sold in the United States are made in or near the small Georgia city of Dalton. To many people this may seem a curiosity worthy of no more interest than the suit sizes of vice-presidents. But it is far more important, because it is an example of a broad principle. And that is *not* obvious.

Why are carpets made in Dalton—or more generally, why do many industries concentrate in only one or two locations? This is not a new question. The great turn-of-the-century British economist Alfred Marshall noted how many of his nation's industries were concentrated in particular industrial districts: cutlery in Sheffield, ironworking in Birmingham, lace in Nottingham, and the key cotton textile industry around Manchester. And Marshall offered an explanation of such concentrations that remains a classic of clarity.

First, a cluster of related firms in the same area provides a large market for people with specialized skills, which means both that workers have some insurance against unemployment and that firms have some insurance against labor shortages:

> [A] localized industry gains a great advantage from the fact that it offers a constant market for skill. Employers are apt to resort to any place where they are likely to find a good choice of workers with the special skill which they require; while men seeking employment naturally go to places where there are many employers who need such skill as theirs and where therefore it is likely to find a good market. The owner of an isolated factory, even if he has good access to a plentiful supply of labor, is often put to great shifts for want of some specialized labor; and a skilled workman, when thrown out of employment in it, has no easy refuge.

Second, a local industrial cluster supports providers of necessary specialized services:

> [S]ubsidiary trades grow up in the neighborhood, supplying it with implements and materials, organizing its traffic, and in many ways conducing to the economy of its material . . . the economic use of expensive machinery can sometimes be attained in a very high degree in a district in which there is a large aggregate production of some

kind, even though no individual capital employed in the trade be very large. For subsidiary industries devoting themselves each to one small branch of the process of production, and working it for a great many of their neighbors, are able to keep in constant use machinery of the most highly specialized character, and to make it pay its expenses. . . .

Finally, a grouping of firms promotes the exchange of information and thus the advance of technology:

The mysteries of the trade become no mystery; but are as it were in the air. . . . Good work is rightly appreciated, inventions and improvements in machinery, in processes and the general organization of the business have their merits promptly discussed: if one man starts a new idea, it is taken up by others and combined with suggestions of their own; and thus it becomes the source of further new ideas.

Despite the Victorian language (which is surely a relief compared with the dry technicality of modern economics and the even worse illiteracies of modern business jargon), this is a plausible story that remains as relevant as ever to such clusters as Route 128 in Massachusetts and Silicon Valley in California. As my friend would have said, however, it seems pretty obvious. What is not obvious, except to a great economist like Marshall, is that industry localizations illustrate some more fundamental principles.

First, they illustrate the importance of *increasing returns to scale*. Suppose that factories could be very small without any loss in efficiency. Then there would be no need to have a large pool of labor to offer workers and firms flexibility: even a small town could support a diversified mix of firms. You wouldn't need a large local industry to support suppliers of specialized inputs. And if even a small town could support a rich mix of production, you wouldn't need a big industrial concentration to facilitate the flow of information.

In fact, of course, it seems that we do need large local clusters to support many (though not all) industries. The traffic jams in the City (London's financial district) and the prices of real estate in Silicon Valley are the proof that increasing returns are important—important enough to make people willing to put up with a great deal of aggravation and expense.

Second, the example of industry localization shows that increasing returns apply at a level greater than that of an individual firm. The individual firms that make up Silicon Valley are not very big, but clearly the whole is greater than the sum of its parts. In economics jargon, there are *external economies of scale*. It is important not only that an individual business be large enough to compete, but that it be embedded in an industry—or cluster of industries—that is large enough to support the pool of skilled labor, the specialized suppliers, and the flow of knowledge that allow it to prosper.

Finally, as we have already seen, industry localization demonstrates *path dependence*—the powerful role of historical accident in determining the shape of the economy. Silicon Valley is where it is because of the vision of Frederick Terman, vice-president of Stanford, in supporting a few high-tech entrepreneurs in the 1940s, forming the seed around which the famous high-tech concentration crystalized. The carpet concentration in Dalton owes its existence to a teen-aged girl who made a tufted bedspread as a wedding gift in 1895, starting a local handicraft industry whose specialized skills turned out to be crucial when tufted carpets displaced woven rugs after World War II.

Now Alfred Marshall knew all this—the useful jargon about increasing returns and external economies comes from him. It was all there in his book *Principles of Economics*, published in 1890. Yet I have described QWERTY as a new trend in economics, which only became really influential in the 1980s. Why did it take so long to see the obvious?

The answer is, basically, that for most of the twentieth century economists found it convenient to ignore the QWERTYness of the world.[3] Economic theory is, in essence, a collection of models:

[3]This is actually unfair to several major branches of economics. Increasing returns and external economies played a major role in early models of economic development, al-

simplified representations of reality, which inevitably leave out some aspects to focus on others. And it happens to be easier to model a world in which increasing returns are not important, in which external economies are absent, in which the shape of a market economy is determined by its resources, not by the vagaries of its history.

In particular, it is tricky to build QWERTY into formal mathematical representations of the economy. (I use the word "tricky" advisedly; it isn't impossible, but you have to use some clever tricks to do it.) And economics has become increasingly mathematical over time. So, although many economists have been more or less aware of the importance of QWERTY, the main currents of economic discussion pretty much bypassed it until the late 1970s.

One could, by the way, read all of this as a condemnation of the narrow minds of academics. It seems that they were ignoring evidence that was right under their noses, simply because it didn't fit neatly into their preferred intellectual structures. Isn't this a case for preferring generalists, people who are not professors and are prepared to be less than rigorous? In other words, isn't this a classic lesson in why we need policy entrepreneurs?

Well, no. If it took a while for the professors to notice the obvious, the policy entrepreneurs didn't have a clue. One can look in vain at the works of non-economists for an appreciation of the implications of QWERTY for the economy. It is, of course, not there in the writings of the supply-siders—Jude Wanniski may have been prepared to explain *The Way the World Works,* but this particular piece of how it works escaped him. In general, the supply-siders wanted to praise free markets, not stress the ways they could go wrong; so it is no surprise that they failed to notice that markets can get stuck with the wrong technology or the wrong location of industry.

More surprising is the absence of much sense of the QWERTY-

---

though these models fell into disuse after about 1965. Urban economists have also, as a matter of necessity, kept their attention focused on these issues. But it is still true that for the most part economists put the effects that Marshall described in the back of their intellectual cupboard.

ness of the economy in the pundits of the left. For those who dislike the pretensions of the professors, it would be a nice story if the strategic traders, who challenged the orthodox views of the virtues of free trade, had been freed by their unorthodoxy to see what the professors had been ignoring. But, as we'll see when we come to the story of the competitiveness controversy, the initial manifestos by such key figures as Robert Reich and Lester Thurow showed no more awareness of the importance of QWERTY than the most orthodox of economic tracts.

In fact, the realization that QWERTY in all its manifestations could make a critical difference came not from outside but from inside the economics profession. And it began with a rethinking of traditional ideas about international trade.

Rethinking International Trade

Around 1978, several economists scattered around the world began to ask a seemingly naive question: Why is there international trade?

This may sound like a stupid question. The immediate answer is that countries trade because each country produces goods that other countries want. But on reflection this only pushes the question back a bit. *Why* do countries produce different goods?

Economists have long had a standard answer. Countries produce different goods because they are different from each other. These differences may involve natural resources—it's no mystery why Brazil exports coffee and Saudi Arabia exports oil—or such created differences in resources as differences in education or in the accumulated stock of capital per worker. In any case, countries have an incentive to specialize in producing the goods for which their resources and know-how best suit them, and to trade these goods for other goods produced elsewhere. The whole story goes under the name of the theory of "comparative advantage." Loosely, comparative advantage says that countries trade in order to benefit from their differences.

Of course that makes it sound trivial, when the idea of comparative advantage is anything but. In fact, as we'll see when we get to the debate over "competitiveness" in Chapter 10, comparative advantage turns out to be an idea that many self-styled experts fail to understand. And there is no question that comparative advantage explains a lot of international trade.

By the late 1970s, however, a number of economists working on international trade were coming to suspect that there was an important part of world trade that could not be explained by comparative advantage. Both the *direction* and the *character* of international trade seemed to suggest that not all exports were like Brazilian coffee.

THE DIRECTION OF TRADE

Suppose that I told you that international trade involves a matching between complementary countries. Countries at the same level of development, with similar resources, can basically make the same set of goods equally well, so they have no strong reason to trade with each other. Instead, what each nation needs is to find other countries that have what it lacks and lack what it has. In particular, rich countries, with their abundant capital and temperate climates, will find their most important trading partners in the Third World, whose abundant labor can take over the labor-intensive aspects of manufacturing and whose tropical agriculture will supply coffee, tea, sugar, and other necessities.

Sounds plausible? It sounded plausible to nineteenth-century statesmen; they looked at the British Empire and saw it as a sound business arrangement. (And if they weren't British, they decided that their own countries needed a few colonies too.) As late as the 1940s, political leaders still tended to think of international trade as running largely in a North-South direction; the Greater East Asian Co-Prosperity Sphere that Japan tried to carve out during World War II was not contemplated as a union of similar economies.

Yet something funny happened after World War II. There was a great surge in world trade—not between complementary nations, between North and South, but among the advanced nations them-selves. And this surge in trade among advanced nations took place even as those nations were becoming increasingly similar in their levels of technology, education, and capital.

In 1953, only about 38 percent of the exports of advanced countries went to other advanced nations—and if it had not been for the Marshall Plan, which allowed European nations to buy large quantities of American goods, the number would have been even smaller. By 1990, however, 76 percent of advanced country exports went to other advanced nations.

Familiarity breeds a false sense of understanding. Everyone knows that today's advanced industrial countries are similar in many ways. Hourly wage rates in Europe, the United States, and Japan are about the same. We all have highly educated work forces, working with technologies that are quickly diffused throughout the world. Our cities and ways of life become increasingly indistinguishable. Yet we take it for granted that there is a huge and ever-growing volume of trade among these increasingly similar societies. If we're all pretty much the same, why do we need to ship such huge volumes of goods back and forth across the oceans?

There is an old joke about how poor urban households used to make ends meet. "Oh, we make a living by taking in each other's washing," the women would explain. In effect, for a generation after World War II the advanced nations began taking in each other's washing on an unprecedented scale. Why?

THE CONTENT OF TRADE

A determined believer in the idea that trade always reflects underlying differences between countries might argue that the apparent similarity among advanced nations is only on the surface. At a deeper level, there may be differences that in the end determine trade flows. And she would surely be in part correct. But if these underlying differences are the main driving force behind trade among industrial countries, we ought to be able to "backcast" our way to the nature of those differences by looking at who exports what to whom.

The overwhelming conclusion from looking at the actual pattern of trade is, however, that exports from one industrial country to another *don't* give us much indication that they are based on any underlying national resource or characteristic.

Consider, for example, the strong U.S. presence in the world aircraft industry. Is there something about the U.S. mix of resources that makes Americans particularly adept at making aircraft? It is hard to argue that there is. Aircraft manufacture is a business in which the cost of capital is important, because investments in new generations of aircraft take so long to yield a return; but the U.S. cost of capital is no lower and often higher than the cost of capital in Japan or Europe. The aircraft industry requires highly skilled workers and engineers—but so does production of, say, autos, in which the United States runs massive trade deficits.

The United States does, of course, have a large pool of workers and engineers with the very specific skills and knowledge required to design and build aircraft. But where did this pool of skills and knowledge come from? Was it innate in the U.S. character? Of course not. U.S. workers developed the skills they needed to build aircraft because there was a large demand for those skills in the United States, arising from our dominant position in the world aircraft industry.

But of course our dominance in aircraft is in large part due to the fact that we have such a large pool of people with the right skills and knowledge. And you know where that puts us: squarely in the land of QWERTY.

Now there is a special reason why the virtuous circle that sustains the U.S. aircraft industry got started: the huge base of demand for aircraft that arose from the needs of the U.S. military during World War II and the early years of the Cold War. The interesting thing, however, is that even though that special advantage is long gone, the dominant position of the U.S. aircraft industry endures (indeed, it would be complete, were it not for

Europe's support of Airbus—which we will have to come to in a little while).

The point is that there are many industries like aircraft, industries in which an international competitive advantage can be self-reinforcing. And the presence of such industries explains why countries that are similar at a broad level do so much trade. American and German industry are nowadays very similar in their overall levels of technology and in the resources available to them. Time and chance have, however, caused the two countries to develop different competences at a more detailed level, with America leading in aircraft, semiconductors, computers, and Germany leading in luxury automobiles, cameras, machine tools. From a distance, the two economies look more and more alike; in close-up, we are sufficiently different to find reasons to engage in an ever-growing volume of international trade.

THE NEW TRADE THEORY

Not every industry is like the aircraft industry. The ability of a country to grow wheat cheaply depends mostly on climate and soil. A big subsidy can turn a wheat importer into a wheat exporter, as European nations have done with their Common Agricultural Policy, but it cannot create an advantage where none existed: remove the subsidies and European wheat output would crash. In other words, comparative advantage is still alive and well, and still governs much of trade.

On the other hand, not every industry is like wheat. Between 1978 and 1985, a group of economists hammered out what has come to be known as the "new trade theory," a theory that says, in effect, that a lot of world trade is in goods like aircraft rather than goods like wheat.

The new trade theory picture of the world looks something like this: Each country has, at any given time, a set of broad resources—land, skilled labor, capital, climate, general technological competence. These resources define up to a point the industries in which the country can hope to be competitive on world markets. Japan is not going to make it in the world wheat market; Canada will not be a successful exporter of tropical fruit; Brazil is not ready to compete in supercomputers. But a country's resources do not fully determine what it produces, because the detailed pattern of advantage reflects the self-reinforcing virtuous circles, set in motion by the vagaries of history.

At a broad level, then, trade reflects resources. A country with a highly skilled labor force will, in general, export goods whose production requires a high ratio of skilled to unskilled labor, and import goods for which the reverse is true. But precisely which goods the country exports cannot be determined from its resources alone. That final determination rests in the realm of chance and history, in the land of QWERTY.

This may sound a little vague, and if the ideas of new trade theory had only been expressed in this general way, they would probably not have had much impact. What the new trade theorists did, however, was to package this vision of trade in extremely sharply focused mathematical models. These models served two purposes. First, they helped to pin down the concepts in a way that dispelled a fog of confusion that had previously surrounded these ideas. Second, they legitimized QWERTYish ideas for other economists, by showing that they could be expressed with the same degree of clarity as more traditional approaches.

It's all a nice example of intellectual progress. Still, does it matter? Does knowing that much of world trade is in goods like aircraft, not goods like wheat, change our opinions about economic policy?

Yes—maybe. And then again, maybe not.

Strategic Trade Policy

It's possible to study the economy the way an entomologist studies an ant colony: dispassionately, trying to understand how it works rather than trying to change it. Indeed, if you want to do good social science, you should try to cultivate a certain amount of detachment, so that you get into the habit of seeing how things are rather than how you would like them to be.

The new trade theory as I have described it so far sounds fairly entomological. It is a description of how the world economy is, not a prescription about what to do about it. That is not a condemnation; like medical researchers, economists who add to our understanding may make a greater contribution in the long run than those proposing immediate cures.

Nonetheless, the temptation to try to apply theory to policy is irresistible. Sooner or later, the new trade theory was going to be given a policy spin. And it was not going to be a spin that conservatives would like. As I have already hinted, in the world of QWERTY one cannot trust markets to get it right. So it was inevitable that the new trade theory would be used to provide a justification for a departure from the principles of laissez-faire.

What kind of departure? In 1982, the Canadian economist James Brander and his Australian co-author Barbara Spencer pointed out that some of the basic ideas of new trade theory could be used to rationalize a policy that has long been anathema to economists: aggressive support by a nation's government of the international competitive position of home firms. Their concept has come to be known under the name of *strategic trade policy*. It's a concept whose practical usefulness can be and has been sharply questioned, but it represents a dramatic demonstration of the ways that QWERTY can undermine a conservative faith in the perfection of markets.

THE BRANDER-SPENCER MODEL

The Brander-Spencer concept can perhaps best be explained with a stylized example. (This example also gives you an idea of the way in which highly simplified models can help clarify thinking.) So here it is: Imagine a world in which the technology will soon be available to produce some new product, say a new kind of passenger aircraft. And suppose that there are two firms in a position to develop that technology, one American, one European. Let's call the two firms Boeing and Airbus. (Any resemblance to real firms is purely intentional.)

How profitable will it be to enter this market? It is not enough to ask about cash flow over a short period of time. Typically, introducing a new technology requires heavy initial spending on R&D and capital, followed by a period in which the firm continues to lose money while it works its way down the learning curve. Only then will the firm start to make profits. On the other hand, one cannot simply count future profits one-to-one against current losses, because a dollar tomorrow is worth less than a dollar today. So one needs to "discount" expected future earnings. In principle, a firm can collapse the whole expected stream of cash flows from a project into a "present discounted value" that summarizes the project's desirability.

So let's suppose that Boeing and Airbus have done that. And each reaches the conclusion that if it enters the market alone, that entry will be highly profitable—but that if both firms enter, both will end up losing money. That is, they conclude that the economies of scale in the global market are so large relative to expected sales that only one firm can profitably enter.

We can summarize the two firms' perceptions with a hypothetical table like Table 2. Each firm must decide whether or not to enter this new market; depending on what they decide, we get a matrix of possible outcomes. Each entry in the matrix is a pair of numbers. The first number represents Airbus's expected profit; the second Boeing's. If a firm chooses not to enter, of course, it makes zero—nothing ventured, nothing gained (or lost). In the table, we suppose that a firm that enters alone will make profits of 100 points; but if both firms enter, each will lose 10.

Table 2

AIRBUS	BOEING Enter	Don't enter
Enter	$(-10, -10)$	$(100, 0)$
Don't enter	$(0, 100)$	$(0, 0)$

What will happen? It is possible that through misjudgment both firms will enter. That's what happened to Lockheed and

McDonnell-Douglas in the 1970s, when they both introduced three-engine widebody jets (the L1011 and DC-10 respectively), with devastating effects on both firms. But in general each firm will either try to forestall entry by the other, if possible by making a credible early commitment to enter the market, or drop out if it becomes convinced that the other firm will enter.

Economists refer to the efforts of firms to deter potential rivals as *strategic* competition. It is a source of seemingly perverse behavior. For example, a firm may invest in capacity that it doesn't need in order to convince possible rivals that they will face a price war if they challenge its position; or a company may charge a lower price than the market will bear as a way of signaling rivals that its costs are too low for them to challenge.

Going back to our example, let's suppose that, for whatever reason, Boeing has a head start in this race, and is able to commit to enter the market before Airbus. Then what should Airbus do? It will lose money if it enters, so it stays out. The game ends up in the lower left-hand box of the matrix ("Boeing enter, Airbus Don't enter"), and Boeing reaps the rewards.

Now, finally, we get to the Brander-Spencer point. Suppose that at an early stage in the competition, governments get into the picture. Suppose, in particular, that a group of European governments promise Airbus a subsidy of, say, 20 if it enters the market, regardless of what Boeing does. Then, from the point of view of the firms, the payoff matrix now looks like Table 3, in which 20 has been added to the payoffs that Airbus receives when it enters.

Table 3

AIRBUS	BOEING Enter	Don't enter
Enter	(10,10)	(120,0)
Don't enter	(0,100)	(0,0)

This change in the payoffs alters the whole game. Now, whatever Boeing does, Airbus will find it profitable to enter. But this means that if Boeing enters, it will have to share the market; and lacking the Airbus subsidy, it will lose money. So Boeing doesn't enter and Airbus does. The outcome is in the upper-right box ("Boeing Don't enter, Airbus enter"). In effect, the promised subsidy has given Airbus a *strategic* advantage that allows it to win the game. Thus the subsidy is a *strategic trade policy*.

Now notice something interesting. Airbus's profits have gone from 0 in the case without subsidy to 120 in the case with a subsidy. Yet the subsidy was only 20. Where did the other 100 in profits come from? The answer, of course, is that it got taken from Boeing; in effect, it represents a shift of wealth from America to Europe.

This is only a hypothetical example, of course. But it suggests a broader principle: there are times when aggressive support of a domestic industry against its foreign competitors can be in the national interest. In this particular example, the policy involved supporting a single "national champion" in competition with a single foreign rival. Such examples of single combat are rare in world trade. But you can tell similar stories in which the combat is not between individual firms but between industries. If you really believe that we live in a QWERTY world, then there may be many cases in which a temporary policy of supporting an industry in international competition can create a virtuous circle of self-reinforcing, enduring competitive advantage—or, conversely, in which a foreign government, by supporting *its* industry, can either lock us out of a market or tip an established industry into a vicious circle of self-reinforcing decline.[4]

---

[4]Clear-cut examples of vicious circles in international trade are hard to come by, because there are always special circumstances. Consider, however, the decline of the British aircraft industry—which is the flip side of the rise of the U.S. industry. Britain was once a leading aircraft producer. During World War II, the Spitfire fighter was technologically superior to anything Germany or for that matter the United States could put in the air, and the first commercial jet aircraft was actually British rather than American. Nor was it inevitable that British technology would fall behind; in spite of a lagging economy, Britain has managed to retain a strong position in a number of high-technology industries, including pharmaceuticals and even jet engines (manufactured by Rolls-Royce). The aircraft industry itself, however, shriveled up in the 1960s. *(cont.)*

In other words, the strategic trade policy argument appears to open the door to a rigorous economic justification for international trade policies that are not only interventionist but involve an element of international confrontation.

And that is a potentially explosive conclusion, because it threatens to undermine one of the most dearly held dogmas of economists: their belief in free trade.

STRATEGIC TRADE VS. FREE TRADE

To understand why Tinkertoy examples like the one above created a major controversy among economists, you need to understand the special position that free trade holds in the profession's ideology and self-image.

International trade, more than any other area, is one in which the perceptions of the professors differ from those of the general public. When the public—and their elected representatives—look at international trade, they see it as a kind of competitive sport. America is trying to sell its goods on world markets; so are other countries like Japan, Germany, and China. To most people, the competition between countries looks a lot like the competition between companies; indeed, in many global industries a few American companies seem in effect to be acting as our national champions as they confront their European or Japanese rivals. And in competitive sports it's natural to root for the home team— especially if serious things like jobs are at stake.

If international trade basically means international competition, of course, it seems only common sense to do everything you can to help your side win. If import quotas that give our domestic industries the advantage of a protected home base or export subsi-

---

Why did Britain lose its aircraft capacity? As already suggested in the text, a likely culprit is the Pentagon. Huge orders by the U.S. military during the 1950s helped give American firms a decisive edge in jet technology. Once Britain had been driven out of the world aircraft market, it lacked the base of knowledge, suppliers, and skilled workers that would have allowed it to reenter.

dies that help them break into foreign markets help America compete, why not go ahead and use them?

Now, many people will concede that if every country follows such policies, the end result will be destructive, because world markets will end up fragmented. So they are willing to approve, grudgingly, of international agreements that limit import quotas or export subsidies. But free trade, to most people, looks like a good idea only if everybody practices it.

Economists who take the theory of comparative advantage seriously, however, don't see the world this way at all. In their view, international trade is *not* a competitive sport. It is essentially a process of exchange, which is usually mutually beneficial. Interfering with this process hurts our economy, even if other countries do not retaliate (and of course hurts us even more if they do). An import quota, for example, may seem to create jobs; but the jobs gained in the protected industry are lost through the indirect effects of the quota in crowding out employment throughout the rest of the economy, leaving us with nothing but higher prices and reduced competition. An export subsidy normally costs the government and domestic consumers far more than it benefits producers in that industry. (You sometimes hear advocates of policies for "competitiveness" complain that the United States favors consumers over producers. This is a meaningless statement: each of us is a producer, typically from nine to five, and a consumer the rest of the day. There is no such thing as a general preference one way or the other.)

The normal position of economists on international trade is therefore much stronger than the grudging "I'll play fair if everyone else will" that is the typical attitude of the man in the street. The economist advocates free trade *regardless of what other countries are doing*. The nineteenth-century French economist Bastiat once summed it up this way: Saying that our country should be protectionist because other countries do not practice free trade is like saying that we should block up our harbors because other countries have rocky coasts.

You might think that the conflict between what economists

think and the rest of the world believes would give the professors pause. But it doesn't work that way. Because comparative advantage is a beautiful idea that it seems only economists understand, economists cling to the idea even more strongly, as a kind of badge that defines their professional identity and ratifies their intellectual superiority. In effect, the statements, "I understand the principle of comparative advantage," and, "I support free trade," have become part of the economist's credo.

This may sound sarcastic. Yet in fact the economists are mostly right in their attitude. The lay view of international trade as a conflict with winners and losers is deeply wrong-headed—a wrong-headedness I'll have to discuss at some length in Chapter 10 when I tell the story of the rise of the strategic traders. In many sectors of world trade, from wheat to sugar to steel to shoes, the conventional wisdom of economists is exactly right; with few exceptions, the policy entrepreneurs and politicians who criticize that conventional wisdom do so not because they have achieved a deeper understanding but because they haven't even understood the simple things.

But here's the problem: the concept of strategic trade policy is a legitimate, well-reasoned theory of the kind that economists respect; yet it seems, at least on first sight, to yield conclusions that are similar to those of the non-economists. (Some of the more clever policy entrepreneurs were quick to notice this fact, and to use strategic trade arguments as a bit of protective cover; we'll talk about this more in Chapter 10.)

So, is everything that economists thought they knew about international trade wrong? No, not really.

LIMITATIONS OF THE STRATEGIC TRADE POLICY ARGUMENT

Brander and Spencer never claimed that they had offered a general argument for aggressive trade policies. What they provided was only an example of how such a policy *could* work. The important question, of course, is how realistic the example is—or, to put it differently, in how many cases will the conclusions be right? If the case for strategic trade policy applies to only a handful of industries, then the conventional view about free trade is still basically right.

What a number of economists argued, almost as soon as the idea of strategic trade began circulating, was that in most cases aggressive trade policies would simply backfire, for two main reasons.

First, they questioned the picture of international competition as a struggle between two national champions, with the winner assured of high profits. In most industries the choice is not so stark. Suppose that the competition is not between one firm from each country but between three or four firms from each. Then the payoff to winning the competition, at least in terms of profits, will not be all that large: even if our country wins, competition among domestic firms will tend to hold down prices and profits. So there won't really be a race to see who gets the global jackpot. Furthermore, any attempt to subsidize the domestic industry will be likely to encourage more domestic firms to enter, dissipating any potential gains in duplication of capacity.

Now this argument only applies to the profits that strategic trade policy may yield. There may be other benefits, particularly if there are external economies associated with the industry—that is, if entry of more firms lowers costs by supporting a wider network of suppliers, a larger pool of skilled labor, or a deeper knowledge base. Such benefits are, however, subtle and hard to evaluate, when the thing that made the strategic trade policy so attractive was precisely its seeming simplicity and concreteness.

Critics of the strategic trade policy idea were also quick to point out the crucial difficulty of deciding which industries to encourage. You can't promote all domestic industries; by subsidizing one, you help it bid capital and labor away from others. So a strategic trade policy on behalf of some industries is in effect a strategic policy *against* others. This immediately raises the question of whether governments are sophisticated or objective enough to do the job right.

Given these criticisms, how could economists tell how seriously they should take the strategic trade policy argument? The only answer seemed to be to get down to cases. But when it comes to deciding whether or not to pursue a strategic trade policy, looking at the facts is not as simple as it may seem. After all, just knowing an industry's history, or even knowing quite a lot about everything from technology to costs and market shares, does not automatically tell you anything useful about what policy is desirable. Inevitably, you want to ask "what if" questions—for example, if a subsidy of X percent is granted, will it deter foreign entry into sector Y, and will it lead another domestic firm to enter? You may think you know all about some industry; but when confronted with questions of this kind, you usually realize that you can only describe the industry, not predict what it will do.

Which is not to say that economists didn't try. During the 1980s, a number of efforts were made to produce simulations of industries that were potential targets of strategic trade policy. Nobody had much faith in these simulations—after doing several, I dubbed them Industrial Policy Exercises Calibrated to Actual Cases, so as to yield the acronym IPECACs. Still, they were the only game in town. And for what they were worth, they did not seem to suggest very much potential gain for countries that pursued aggressive trade policies.

Bold Ideas, Cautious Policy Recommendations

The rise of the economics of QWERTY felt like an intellectual revolution to those who participated in it; phrases like "paradigm shift" were used routinely. Yet when it came to actual policy applications, the professors were cautious.

There were at least three reasons for that caution. One is that while an acknowledgment of the importance of QWERTY refutes the near-religious faith of conservatives in free markets, it is not at all easy to decide which direction the government should pursue.

We've already seen how subtle the issue of strategic trade policy becomes once one tries to deal with real-world complications. So unlike, say, the rational expectations school, the new economic theorists did not find that their theory translated readily into simple policy recommendations. That does not devalue the significance of the theory: it is unreasonable to expect each intellectual advance to be ready for immediate policy consumption. Nonetheless, the failure of QWERTY to yield easy policy conclusions has been a real disappointment.

And yet it may also have been, to some extent, a bit of a relief. While this should not be overstated, a certain timidity may have contributed to the quietness of the QWERTY revolution. Although most economists are not doctrinaire believers in laissez-faire, an acknowledgment of the power and effectiveness of the market as a mechanism is a central part of the professional identity even of liberal economists. So they are understandably reluctant to come out too brashly against letting markets have their own way, especially when it comes to the almost sacred principle of free trade.

But perhaps the most important reason that economists were diffident about making policy pronouncements based on their new theory was their fear that it would be used, not to make better policy, but to rationalize bad policies. Concepts such as strategic trade policy can all too easily be used to rationalize good old-fashioned protectionism.

But politicians will get their ideas somewhere. If professors will not provide them with the slogans they need to win votes—as they often won't—it's always possible to find someone else who will.

The Strategic
Traders

Although a Republican White House tried to make an economic revolution in the 1980s, its occupants were surprisingly uninterested in talking about economics. Ronald Reagan was, of course, uninterested in the details of policy in general. He was a man of strong, simple ideas—he didn't like big government; he favored lower taxes; he believed that the private sector would respond to lower taxes by lifting all boats on a new wave of prosperity. Beyond that, he was prepared to leave the implementation up to his advisers. George Bush was more of a details man, but his interest in the fine points did not extend to economics; while he reveled in the jargon and acronyms of diplomacy and military strategy, when speaking he tended to stumble over even the most basic ideas in economics. For example, during one of the presidential debates he tried to refer to a recent study that showed that American productivity remains the highest in the world—but garbled the point by confusing the *level* of productivity (which is still highest in America) with its rate of growth (which has been faster abroad).

By contrast, the man who proposes to reverse their policies loves to talk about economic details—but then Bill Clinton loves to talk, period. By all accounts there is nothing he would rather do than spend all night discussing five- and ten-point programs. His friends speak reverently of "the Conversation," a more or less ongoing policy discourse that began when he was still a student and continues now that he and the friends he made twenty years earlier are in the White House.

What do Clinton and his confidants say in the Conversation? We have a pretty good idea, based both on the writing of those Clinton likes and admires, and on what he has said in his own speeches. Without doubt, some of the Conversation sounds like this (please ignore the numbers for now): "We need a new economic paradigm, because today America is part of a truly global economy (1). To maintain its standard of living, America has to learn to compete in an ever tougher world marketplace (2). That's why high productivity and product quality have become essential (3). We need to move the American economy into the high-value sectors (4) that will generate jobs (5) for the future. And the only way we can be competitive in the new global economy is if we forge a new partnership between government and business (6)."

This is not, of course, a real quotation. But it is instantly recognizable as the sort of thing that Clinton and some of his closest advisers say in public, and similar remarks can be found daily on the op-ed pages of the nation's newspapers. But where do ideas and phrases like this come from?

At a superficial level, this sounds quite a lot like the new economic analysis described in the last two chapters. The rebirth of Keynesian economics made it legitimate once again to call for an activist government role. The new economics of path dependence, of QWERTY, focused attention on the possibility that countries might get locked out of industries in which they could have competed on world markets, while the theory of strategic trade policy offered at least some rationale for an active government role in promoting the interests of domestic industries in world markets. Isn't this hypothetical excerpt from the Conversation simply a translation of those ideas into non-technical language?

No, not really. The words and phrases that I have put into the mouths of the Conversationalists come from an intellectual/political doctrine that bears about the same relationship to the professional economist's case for government activism that supply-side economics bore to the critique of government activism by Milton Friedman and Martin Feldstein. That is, it is a doctrine that comes from outside the mainstream of economic argument; that was largely created by journalists, and largely argued in the pages of newspapers and popular magazines; and that, like supply-side economics, rouses the intellectual ire of those who should be political allies of its proponents.

Unlike the supply-siders, who proudly adopted a label that had been dismissively pinned upon them by a (conservative) critic, the proponents of this new doctrine do not have a widely accepted name. Let me propose a fairly neutral one that I think gets at the essence of what they have to say: "strategic traders." This sounds like it has something to do with the strategic trade policy discussed in Chapter 9, and some of the strategic traders think that the economics of QWERTY justify their views. But they're wrong.

The Emergence of the Strategic Traders

It is mostly if not entirely true to say that the strategic trader view arose as a liberal response to Reagan's victory. In essence, a group of liberal policy entrepreneurs were looking for a set of ideas that would allow Democrats to promise economic growth in the same way that the Republicans had. Indeed, some of the early members of the group described themselves as "neoliberals," in deliberate parallel to the neoconservative intellectuals who had dominated much policy discussion in the 1970s. Thus from the beginning the movement was tied closely to the political world.

Nonetheless, the origins of strategic trade as a doctrine lie not in Washington but in Cambridge, Massachusetts. While there were forerunners, the doctrine was largely the work of two Cambridge academics: Lester Thurow of MIT and Robert Reich of Harvard's John F. Kennedy School of Government.

Thurow led with a best-selling book, *The Zero-Sum Society*. Published in 1980, the book actually predated Reagan's victory. Thurow had, however, caught the mood of disillusionment with traditional policies, and so his book was perfectly timed to play the role of anti-conservative bible. As one might guess from the title, it was not an optimistic tract; most of the book was devoted to discussion of the hard choices that had to be made on everything from energy policy to inflation. This no-free-lunch message was widely approved by conventional economists. But at the end of the book Thurow offered a vision of how to fix America's problems—by shifting resources from "sunset" to "sunrise" industries—that set bells ringing among ambitious politicians and their staffers. Here, many of them immediately thought, was just the thing with which to recapture the political high ground from the right.

Robert Reich, a lawyer with the Federal Trade Commission, moved to the Kennedy School in 1981. He quickly began advocating a U.S. industrial policy in op-ed pieces and magazine articles. These articles called for U.S. support for "high-value-added" industries, as well as for an array of policies to encourage the use of new technology in traditional sectors. In 1982 and 1983 he published, respectively, *Minding America's Business* (with management consultant Ira Magaziner) and *The Next American Frontier;* while neither was a best seller like *The Zero-Sum Society,* both had wide influence among politicians.

Although Thurow and Reich were the key figures in this movement, there were others contributing to the ideas and rhetoric of strategic trade. Some of these allies were based either in the academic world or in think tanks. At the Harvard Business School, a pro-industrial policy group formed around Bruce Scott and George Lodge; they pushed unabashedly for aggressive U.S. subsidies and protection to promote industries that they viewed as dynamic sources of growth. A somewhat similar, if more carefully worded, message came from the Berkeley Roundtable on International Economics, a think tank at the University of California, which warned that the United States was in danger of losing its industrial base and called for active government support of high-technology industries like semiconductors.

At least as important as these academic or quasi-academic sources of ideas was the Fourth Estate. *The New Republic* became a sort of house organ of strategic trade; one of its contributing editors, Robert Kuttner, became an unwavering propagandist for industrial policy. Arguably, indeed, both Lester Thurow and Robert Reich were more deeply rooted in journalism than in academia: Reich, in particular, was isolated from his colleagues at Harvard, who conspicuously refused to change his title from Lecturer to Professor, a serious academic snub. During the 1980s both men published exclusively in newspapers and in semi-popular magazines like *Foreign Affairs,* the *Harvard Business Review,* and *The New Republic.* Most surprising, perhaps, was the role of *BusinessWeek.* The nation's leading business magazine is almost as much a symbol of capitalism as *The Wall Street Journal,* and one might have expected it to have a strongly pro-market stance. Instead, it was *BusinessWeek* which, in June 1980, devoted an issue to the alleged problem of deindustrialization in the United States, and which kept up a steady drumbeat of concern about the issue of U.S. competitiveness throughout the 1980s.

And yet this was not totally strange, for strategic trade has nothing to do with traditional liberal concerns about equality and social justice. Its view of the U.S. economy and its problems is essentially that of a management consultant; its proposed solutions might well raise, not lower, the share of capital in national income.

Nonetheless, the early versions of strategic trade received an enthusiastic response from many Democratic politicians. The initial converts were a group of younger senators and congressmen (including Gary Hart, Tim Wirth, and Richard Gephardt) who came briefly to be known as "Atari Democrats," after the pioneering video game company. (The label was dropped after Atari moved its production to Asia in 1983.) As Walter Mondale began his steady march to the Democratic nomination, he too was converted. Indeed, in the summer of 1982, after reading a draft of Reich's *The Next American Frontier,* he is reported to have proclaimed to his wife, "This should do it for the Democrats in 1984."

And yet in the end Mondale did not run on Reich's or Thurow's ideas—largely because the traditional economic intellectuals of the Democratic Party, including some of those who were involved in developing the revival of Keynesianism and the new economics of QWERTY, united to denounce strategic trade as misleading nonsense. It was not until 1992 that the strategic traders would finally get their chance to put their ideas into practice.

But what was this doctrine that so attracted politicians yet repelled economists?

The Elements of Strategic Trade

The mock quotation above gives a pretty good sense of what strategic traders sound like. The rhetoric of competitiveness strikes a responsive chord with many businesspeople, journalists, and politicians; indeed, it seems so reasonable to many of them that they are startled at the suggestion that anyone might disagree. (More on that issue later.)

The reasons for the appeal of this kind of rhetoric are straightforward. In effect, strategic traders portray America as being like a corporation that used to have a lot of monopoly power, and could therefore earn comfortable profits in spite of sloppy business practices, but is now facing an onslaught from new competitors. Many companies find themselves in that position these days, and so the image rings true. In effect, the rhetoric of competitiveness says that what has happened to General Motors is what's happening to America.[1]

[1]President Clinton, who as we will see finally brought strategic trade into the rhetoric if not necessarily the policy of the U.S. government, said it bluntly in a speech early in his

There are a lot of problems with this diagnosis, not least the fact that by 1992 General Motors was a far less representative business than it had been in the days when an executive declared that what was good for GM was good for America. A growing majority of Americans work for small firms, not giant companies; even among the class of large American corporations in trouble, one could reasonably claim that the downward spiral of Sears in the face of purely domestic competitors like Wal-Mart was at least as significant as the problems that GM had with Japan. But leaving the question of the rightness of the competitive diagnosis on one side for now, we should also notice an odd thing about the solutions that strategic traders tended to propose for U.S. problems: the fact that they were rooted in a style of strategic business thinking that had become increasingly unpopular in the business world itself.

If you had to isolate one key idea in strategic trade thinking, it is that for a country to prosper, it must establish a leading role in the right sectors, somehow defined. Thurow called these good sectors "sunrise" industries; Reich preferred the term "high-value." The question of which sectors are better than others is crucial, but let's leave that aside for one moment. What all of the strategic traders agreed on was that the most essential thing for getting the U.S. economy growing was to make sure that the industrial mix moved toward these good sectors. "Our country's real income can rise only if (1) its labor and capital increasingly flow toward businesses that add greater value per employee and (2) we maintain a position in these businesses that is superior to that of our international competitors."[2]

Anyone who has followed the history of management theories knows where this idea comes from: it is straight 1960s Boston Consulting Group.

In the late 1960s and the early 1970s the Boston Consulting

---

administration: "The American economy today is like a big corporation competing in the global marketplace."

[2]Robert Reich and Ira Magaziner, *Minding America's Business* (New York: Harcourt Brace Jovanovich, 1982), p. 4.

Group (BCG) was America's hottest consulting firm. Traditional management consultants like McKinsey & Company tended to give nuts-and-bolts advice about organization structure or specific lines of business. BCG offered something much larger: strategic vision.

The classic BCG analysis went something like this: Place the businesses that a company owns into a matrix based on the anticipated growth rate of the business and your current market share. If a business is expected to grow rapidly, and you have a high market share, that's a "star"; if a business is growing slowly, but you have a strong market position, it's a "cash cow"; if a business is growing slowly *and* you have a low market share, it's a "dog." The last box, businesses that you expect to grow fast but in which you are weak, gets a question mark.

What you should do, according to the BCG analysis, is make sure that resources get transferred from your cash cow businesses to support the growth of your stars. You should get rid of your dogs; and you should decide if you want to try to break into a question mark business.

Substitute sunrise and sunset for stars and dogs, and you have essentially the Thurow-Reich industrial policy prescription. And indeed many of the advocates of strategic trade, including Thurow and especially the Harvard Business School group, were quite explicit that they were applying the concepts of business strategy to the economy as a whole.

What was strange, however, was that the business strategy concepts they were applying were ones that were going out of fashion in the business world itself.

By the late 1970s the BCG strategy matrix of cows, stars, and dogs had fallen into considerable disrepute, for several reasons. First, underlying the matrix was the belief that there were strong, predictable "learning curves" that would allow a firm to translate a dominant market share today into a sustained cost advantage over its rivals tomorrow; yet in practice these learning curves appeared to be much less reliable than the BCG had claimed.

Second, BCG had in effect assumed that "star" businesses

would always be profitable. In fact, however, since everyone tended to classify the same businesses as stars, they tended to attract so much investment that capacity got ahead of the market and profits were often disappointing.

Third, BCG had taken "cash cows" for granted. In fact, as companies like General Motors and Sears found out in the 1980s, a dominant position in a slow-growing market is no guarantee that someone will not enter that business with a new idea and savage your profits. (Looked at the other way around, what could be a more obvious "dog" from the point of view of a new player than small-town retailing? Tell it to Sam Walton.)

Finally, many executives blamed BCG-type analyses for the ill-considered wave of mergers and conglomerate building during the 1960s and 1970s. Suppose your company has a steady, traditional business with no obvious possibilities for rapid growth. What BCG and its imitators typically advised was that you acquire or merge with potential growth businesses, so that the traditional business's cash flow could finance the new business's growth. In practice, however, this led to many bad marriages—insurance companies trying to go into the software business, steel companies trying to sell electronics—in which the collision of corporate cultures and mind-sets proved deadly. And BCG strategy was used to justify the construction of too many unwieldy conglomerates with no common theme and no real reason to exist; one of the most profitable financial operations of the 1980s was breaking up these structures and selling off the pieces, because often the whole was less than the sum of its parts.

The business strategy gurus of the 1980s were, if anything, anti-BCG in their ideas. The decade's most influential business book was *In Search of Excellence* by Tom Peters and Robert Waterman; its advice was for businesses to "stick to their knitting," figure out what they did well and build on that rather than try to make abstract, high-level strategic decisions about what businesses to be in.

So strategic trade was, in effect, the business strategy concepts of the 1960s and early 1970s applied to the U.S. economy of the

1980s. One might have expected to see criticism of the approach from business strategy people themselves—people who would say, "Hey, we gave up on those ideas ten years ago; why are you trotting them out again?" If there was any such criticism, however, it was more than drowned out by criticism from the economists, who were horrified by the whole notion of trying to make national economic policy on the analogy of corporate strategy.

Economists vs. Strategic Trade

Think of it as the shootout at Jackson Hole.

Every August the Federal Reserve Bank of Kansas City holds a conference on international economic policy at Jackson Lake Lodge in the Grand Tetons. It's a clever idea. The setting is spectacularly beautiful; the conference schedule is relaxed, with mornings of meetings followed by afternoons of hiking, whitewater rafting, and side trips to Yellowstone. Early-rising conference participants can see elk and moose roaming across the flats that lie beneath the windows of their comfortable rooms. It's just the right kind of setting to entice finance ministers and central bank governors, who of course inform their governments that their attendance at the meeting is crucial to their effectiveness. It also attracts senior economics and business correspondents from major newspapers and magazines, who invariably give the meetings good press as a way of justifying their own expense accounts. Over time, the natural appeal of the site has been reinforced by a bit of QWERTY: the officials come, not only to enjoy themselves, but to get the publicity, while the high rank of the officials who attend turns the whole thing into a real journalistic event as well as an excuse for a vacation.

What makes it work, however, is not just the setting but the good judgment of the organizers. Jackson Hole conferences aren't just shmoozing sessions: each conference is structured around a currently hot topic in economic policy. A few academics are asked to present background papers on that topic; then the discussion takes off.

In August 1983, the topic was industrial policy and international competitiveness.

It was, of course, the third year of the twelve-year winter of the Democratic Party. Nobody knew at that point how long the winter would be, but Democrats knew they had a problem. The Republicans had found in supply-side economics a powerful political idea; while some Democrats were willing to wait until the failure of that idea had become apparent, others felt that they needed an equally appealing idea. And at least some of them believed that an industrial policy, a deliberate policy of supporting future winners in America's industrial mix, was that idea.

In other words, that summer the strategic traders were riding high.

What happened at Jackson Hole was that the economic intelligentsia of the Democratic Party got together to gun down the industrial policy idea. The assembled economists included many established figures. They also included some younger figures: notably a brilliant Harvard professor, still in his twenties, named Lawrence Summers, who had just finished a year on the staff of the Council of Economic Advisers. And one of the background papers, a critical survey of the case for industrial policy, was written by a new trade theorist who had also just spent a year at the Council, by the name of Paul Krugman.

Young and old, the economists denounced the industrial policy proposals of Reich and others. Summers dismissed Reich's ideas as "economic laetrile." The Krugman paper, while admitting that new trade theory offered a limited case for industrial policy, filed the ideas propounded in Magaziner and Reich's *Minding America's Business* under the category of "popular misconceptions."

The professors won that round. Walter Mondale didn't run on an industrial policy platform in 1984, and Michael Dukakis (who chose Larry Summers as his chief economic adviser) didn't run on one in 1988. But strategic trade did not go away, because it filled a vital need. The Republican Party found the modest proposals of a Boskin or a Feldstein too subtle to provide a political rallying cry, and the supply-siders filled the void. The subtle and qualified arguments of the theorists of QWERTY, of the new trade and new growth economics, were equally inadequate to the demands of politics. Politicians needed people who would say simple things.

But why did economists feel the need to speak out so strongly against strategic trade ideas? Maybe it sounded a bit like slightly stale business strategy, but what brought such unified disapproval?

The short answer is intellectual outrage. The ideas of the strategic traders seemed to the economists to be a set of crude misconceptions, presented as if they were sophisticated insights. Like medical researchers who go wild when they are equated with chiropractors (an analogy also used by Summers), or astronomers confused with astrologers, the professors were furious to find the strategic traders taken seriously.

But what was it that bothered them so much about strategic trade?

What's Wrong with Strategic Trade?

To understand why strategic trade drives economists into a fury, let's go back to the imaginary quote from the Conversation that began this chapter (p. 245). It is, of course, a fake, but a very carefully constructed one: it is designed to illustrate in a brief space a number of what seem to economists to be fundamental misconceptions in the strategic trade view. To be precise, there are six such misconceptions; they are indicated by the mysterious numbers in parenthesis within the quotation.

Let's do the numbers.

1. *"We need a new paradigm . . ."*: The essence of the strategic trade view is the analogy between the economy as a whole and an individual corporation competing in the marketplace. If the United States were a largely self-sufficient economy, as it was during the 1950s, this analogy would obviously make no sense—an economy that produces for itself is clearly not competing with anything except its own aspirations. So it is clearly essential for the strategic traders to argue that now that the United States is more open to international trade, everything is different.

But is it? Economists tend not to think so, on at least two grounds. One is a matter of principle: making an economy international does *not* change the basics; trade is just another economic activity, subject to the same principles as anything else. The other is a factual issue: the U.S. economy is not as dependent on international trade as strategic traders seem to think, nor is its position without any historical precedent.

One textbook on international trade (by James Ingram) contains a clever parable designed to illustrate this point. It imagines that an entrepreneur starts a new business that uses a secret technology to convert U.S. wheat, lumber, and so on into cheap high-quality consumer goods. The entrepreneur is hailed as an industrial hero; although some of his domestic competitors are hurt, everyone accepts that some dislocations are the price of a free-market economy. But then an investigative reporter discovers that what he is really doing is shipping the wheat and lumber to Asia and using the proceeds to buy manufactured goods—whereupon he is denounced as a fraud who is destroying American jobs. The point, of course, is that international trade is an economic activity like any other, and can indeed usefully be thought of as a kind of production process that transforms exports into imports.

Turning to the factual issues, what the rhetoric of strategic trade seems to imply is both that the typical American business or worker is now producing for global markets, and that the extent of "globalization" is historically unprecedented. In fact, neither of these is true.

In 1991, exports were 10 percent of U.S. gross domestic product, imports were 11 percent. This was substantially more than the 4 percent on both sides of 1960. (Somewhat surprisingly, however, the numbers hadn't changed much since 1980; as Figure 8 in Chapter 5 showed, the big increase in the importance of international trade to the U.S. economy took place in the 1970s, not the 1980s.) Still, the numbers remain modest. Think of the supposed analogy between the economy and an individual corporation. How many companies sell 90 percent of their output to their own workers and owners?

One might argue that while most U.S. output is still sold to ourselves, a much larger proportion is sold in markets subject to international competition, such as automobiles or computers. This is, however, only a little bit true. In 1991, 76 percent of U.S. output consisted of services rather than goods; and most services are effectively insulated from international competition by the fact that they are hard to transport. (Despite their dominant role in the economy, services account for only about 20 percent of U.S. trade.) At a rough estimate, at least two thirds of the output of the U.S. economy is in so-called non-tradeables.

Nor is the degree of U.S. dependence on world trade something without precedent. In fact, the importance of international trade to today's U.S. economy is *not* unprecedented, or even unusual, by historical standards—although many people, including the President of the United States, seem to think that it is. "When I was growing up, business was mostly a local affair . . . [b]ut now we are woven inextricably into the fabric of a global economy."[3]

Most historians of the international economy date the emergence of a truly global economy to the forties—the *1840s*, when railroads and steamships reduced transport costs to the point where large-scale shipments of bulk commodities became possible. International trade quickly surged. The leading economy of the day was Great Britain, and by the mid-nineteenth century it was exporting more than a third of its GDP—about three times as large a fraction as the U.S. exports today.

Nor was this some kind of primitive trade based on natural resources or incidental to domestic markets. Britain's leading industry was cotton textiles—an industry totally dependent on imported raw materials (try growing cotton in England) that exported about 60 percent of its output, more than the export ratio of the U.S. aircraft industry, our export leader today.[4]

Nineteenth-century trade was accompanied by massive international capital movements, which were much larger relative to

[3]Speech by President Bill Clinton, February 26, 1993.
[4]The Civil War in America severely disrupted the British economy by cutting off its major source of cotton. British statesmen seriously contemplated military intervention to break the Union blockade.

the size of the world economy than anything seen since World War I: in a typical year in the late nineteenth century, Britain invested about 40 percent of its savings overseas. And of course an era of mostly open borders was marked by international migration that dwarfs anything recent. (Where was your great-grandmother born?)

It is a common remark among economic historians that the U.S. economy is not now, and may never be, as integrated with and as dependent on the global economy as Britain has been since the reign of Queen Victoria.

Why does this matter? Think about it from the point of view of a professor. The strategic traders reject conventional economic wisdom on the grounds that it is no longer relevant in a global economy—but even classical economic theory, developed mostly by English economists in the nineteenth century, was developed for an economy that was actually more dependent on international trade and investment than the U.S. economy is today. So what looks like wisdom to the unwary lay consumer looks like ignorance and shoddy thinking to the professor who knows some economic history.

2. *"Competing in the world marketplace"*: The strategic trade view is that countries are in competition with each other in the same way that companies are; the long stagnation of middle-class standards of living is attributed to a failure to compete effectively.

What's wrong with this? Like the claim that globalization changes everything, it seems to economists to combine a conceptual confusion with an apparent lack of knowledge about the data.

At a conceptual level, the most basic point about trade—already illustrated in the parable of the fraudulent factory—is that it is a process of exchange. Any country is both a seller and a buyer on world markets, and indeed market forces will always guarantee that over the long run, sales (exports) and purchases (imports) are roughly equal. And the purpose of international trade, the reason why it is useful, is to import, not to export. That is, what a country gains from trade is the ability to import things it wants. Exports are not an objective in and of themselves: the need to export is a burden that a country must bear because its import suppliers are crass enough to demand payment. So the whole idea that "competitiveness" is crucial, or even that it means anything, is usually rejected by economists.

But isn't it a fact that the stagnation of U.S. living standards has been in large part due to a failure to compete effectively on world markets?

No, it's not a fact. From 1979 to 1989 the real compensation of all U.S. workers in terms of a price index that excludes housing rose 5.8 percent, while productivity in terms of consumption goods rose 5.1 percent.[5] These are purely domestic variables—that is, productivity is not measured relative to other countries, and no data about global market shares or anything else that involves the global economy are taken into account. Yet the series rose by almost exactly the same (disappointing) amount. What this shows is that we got almost exactly the growth in living standards we would have gotten if we had no international trade at all—if the United States were alone in the world. Difficulty in competing with other countries had nothing to do with it.

3. *"High productivity"*: Strategic traders believe that productivity is important because it helps you to compete on world markets. The standard economics view is that productivity is important because it lets you produce more, and that this would be just as true in an economy with no international trade.

The rhetorical association of productivity with competitiveness has pervaded public discussion to such an extent that many people are unaware that it can even be disputed. In 1992, I wrote an op-ed piece for *The New York Times* emphasizing the importance

[5]Overall productivity in the U.S. economy rose 10.5 percent from 1979 to 1989, but much of this gain was in the production of investment goods such as computers that do not enter directly into the standard of living. Real compensation rose only 1.5 percent in terms of the overall consumer price index, but this was largely due to a sharp rise in the price of housing, which presumably had nothing to do with international competition. The importance of excluding both housing and investment goods from the calculation has been made in a recent study by Robert Lawrence of Harvard University and Matthew Slaughter of MIT: "Trade and U.S. Wages: Great Sucking Sound or Small Hiccup?" (forthcoming), *Brookings Papers on Economic Activity*, 1993.

of raising productivity. The editorial assistant I dealt with insisted that I should "explain" that we need to be productive "to compete in the global economy." He was reluctant to publish the piece unless I added the phrase; he said it was necessary so that readers could understand why productivity is important.

This is a fairly large subject. Rather than try to sort it out here, I walk through the issue in the appendix to this chapter.

4. *"High-value sectors"*: One of the most effective parts of the strategic trade doctrine is the idea that the nation's real income can be raised by encouraging a shift to industries with high value added per worker. These high-value sectors are generally assumed to be advanced, high-technology sectors like computers and aerospace.

Once again, this seems conceptually wrong to economists. Why is value added per worker in some sectors higher than in others? It isn't enough to assume that those sectors are just better. If they were, wouldn't capital and labor flood into them, competing the high returns away? (Markets may be imperfect, but they aren't stupid or sluggish.) In fact, the usual reason why value added per worker is high in some industries is because other inputs, such as capital or skill, are high there as well. Since the economy has limited supplies of capital and skill, encouraging industries that use those scarce resources intensively may well lower instead of raising per capita income.

What was most striking to economists, however, was that the advocates of "high-value" industries, like Reich, apparently hadn't bothered to check which industries actually *do* have high value per worker. Table 4 (on the following page) shows the results of such a check. It turns out that the real high-value industries are extremely capital-intensive sectors like cigarettes (!) and oil refining. The high-technology sectors that everyone imagines are keys to the future, like aircraft and electronics, are only average in their value added per worker.

5. *"Jobs"*: One major subgroup within the strategic traders blames American failure in international competition for the loss of "good jobs" in manufacturing, with the unfortunate workers

Table 4

VALUE ADDED PER WORKER, 1988 (THOUSAND DOLLARS)

Cigarettes	488.3
Petroleum refining	283.4
Autos	98.5
Iron and steel	96.7
Aircraft	67.8
Electronics	63.9
All manufacturing	65.9

forced either into unemployment or into much lower-paying service jobs. The image of the former steelworker now earning minimum wage flipping hamburgers is deeply embedded in popular perceptions, and is a central theme of many journalistic overviews.[6]

The economists had conceptual problems with this idea, too, but their objections in principle are almost unnecessary compared with the gross facts. The U.S. economy has not been unsuccessful at creating jobs compared with its foreign rivals; on the contrary, the United States has been the great job engine of the advanced world, with a 38 percent increase in employment from 1973 to 1990, compared with 19 percent in Japan and only 8 percent in Europe.

Now it is true that real wages have stagnated. Is this because workers have been forced out of the good jobs in manufacturing into low-paying service jobs? No, for two reasons. First, manufacturing jobs are not all that well paid (the hourly wage in manufacturing is only 10 percent higher than that in the non-manufacturing sector). The stagnation in real wages was not because the good jobs in manufacturing were lost, but because real wages for *all* jobs that didn't require a college education stagnated or fell. And second, the widespread belief that the United States has lost its manufacturing base in the face of foreign competition is simply wrong.

[6]See, for example, Barlett and Steele, *America: What Went Wrong?* (Kansas City: Andrews & McMeel, 1992).

This last assertion is so far removed from the conventional wisdom of journalists and policy entrepreneurs that it sounds shocking. It is often taken as a matter of proven fact that the United States suffers from "deindustrialization," a loss of the supposedly crucial manufacturing base—also known as the "hollowing out" of the economy, with the implication that manufacturing is the real heart of the economy, without which it becomes an empty shell. Many of the "deindustrialists" think that their only opponents are a supposed faction that believes that America can prosper as a service economy alone.

It is a peculiar debate, because deindustrialization never happened.

Let's start with what didn't happen. It is, of course, true that the share of manufacturing in U.S. value added and employment has been falling for many years. As Figure 12 shows, however, this trend is common to all industrial countries; while Germany and Japan have larger manufacturing sectors relative to their economies than the United States, the manufacturing share has declined as fast as or faster than that in the United States. Nor is there any mystery about the trend. Essentially, it is driven by the combination of relatively fast productivity growth in manufacturing and

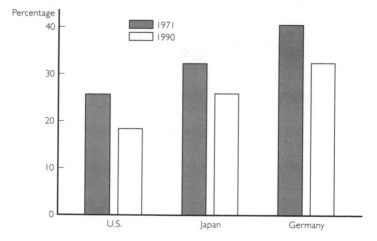

Figure 12. Employment in manufacturing, as percentage of non-agricultural employment.

limited demand for manufactured goods. U.S. factories have become steadily more productive over time, at a rate considerably higher than service businesses; but the general public prefers to spend most of the annual increase in its income on services rather than manufactures. So the rate of increase of demand for manufactures has been fairly slow, while productivity has risen quickly. The result: demand can be satisfied by a static or even falling number of factory workers.

This story should sound familiar: it's exactly what happened to the agricultural sector fifty years earlier. Very few Americans now live on the farm, not because our farmers are uncompetitive, but because they are so productive that we don't need many of them. And America's "deagriculturalization" has proceeded in spite of consistent trade surpluses in farm products.

What appears to make the manufacturing story different is that since 1980 the United States has consistently run trade deficits in manufacturing, and that there is no question that some U.S. industries (e.g., shoes, apparel) have shrunk under the impact of import competition. Has a failure of competitiveness in manufacturing been a major cause of deindustrialization?

The answer is an overwhelming no. It is fairly easy to calculate the approximate net impact of international trade on the size of the U.S. manufacturing sector, and it's not very large.

Table 5 shows such a calculation for 1991. The first line shows the U.S. trade deficit in manufactured goods, which was $47 billion that year. By definition, total sales of manufactures produced in the United States equal total domestic sales of all manufactures, plus exports, minus that part of domestic sales satisfied by imports. So we might suppose that the net impact of international trade on the size of our manufacturing sector can be approximately measured by the trade balance: exports add to domestic value, while imports displace domestic production.

This calculation, however, overstates the impact of international competition on the size of our manufacturing sector. The reason is that much of a dollar of "manufactured" exports indirectly represents services such as health care purchased by the

Table 5: Impact of Trade on U.S. Manufacturing, 1991

Exports of manufactures ($billion)	345
Minus:	
Imports of manufactures ($billion)	392
Equals:	
Trade balance in manufactures	– 47
Implies:	
Reduction in manufacturing value added:	– 28.2
(60% of trade balance)	
Value added in manufacturing:	1,000
Implies:	
% reduction in manufacturing:	2.8

manufacturer rather than value added by manufacturing firms. (General Motors' largest supplier is not a parts manufacturer or a steel company but Blue Cross/Blue Shield.) Thus only part of an extra dollar of manufactured exports adds to the size of our manufacturing sector, and conversely much of a dollar of manufactured imports in effect displaces service rather than manufacturing employment.

Fortunately, input-output studies of the U.S. economy give us a pretty good estimate of the hidden service component of manufactures trade: only about 60 percent of a dollar of manufactures sales represents manufacturing value added. Thus we should scale down the trade deficit by 40 percent to get an estimate of the overall impact of trade on the industrial base. To a first approximation, competitive problems in U.S. manufacturing, as measured by our trade balance, reduced value added in our manufacturing sectors by 60 percent of $47 billion, or $28 billion, in 1991.

That may sound like a big number, but whenever you talk about the U.S. economy it is essential to keep in mind its sheer overwhelming size. "Deindustrialized" America in 1991 still had a value added in manufacturing of about $1 trillion. We have just suggested that in the absence of a trade deficit that number would have been about $28 billion larger; that's a difference of only 2.8 percent.

To put this in perspective: in 1991, 17 percent of U.S. workers were employed in manufacturing, compared with 27 percent in

1970. If the United States could have eliminated its manufacturing trade deficit—if it could have made the rest of the world disappear—its manufacturing sector would have been 2.8 percent bigger—that is, its share of employment would have been about 17.5 instead of 17 percent. Of the 10-point decline in the share of manufacturing in employment since the late 1960s, less than 10 percent could be attributed to the effects of international competition.

A careful study by Lawrence and Slaughter concludes flatly that "international factors contributed nothing to America's wage performance in the 1980s."[7] International competition had nothing to do with it.

6. "A new partnership": This is, of course, the bottom line. Where the economists who developed the new economics of QWERTY were cautious and diffident about policy conclusions, the strategic traders were anything but. At least in the early 1980s they were willing to promise politicians that by following their recipe, by promoting high-value or sunrise industries, they could not only improve the economy but actually solve its problems.

Strategic Traders in the White House

As we saw, in 1983 and 1984 the political momentum of the strategic traders was broken by opposition from liberal economists. By the early 1990s, however, strategic trade—involving pretty much the same people—was back in force. In 1991 Robert Reich published a new book, *The Work of Nations,* which was rapturously reviewed and sold well; in 1992 Lester Thurow's new book, *Head to Head,* became a huge best seller. And with the election of Bill Clinton, the strategic traders went to Washington. Reich became Secretary of Labor; Ira Magaziner, co-author of *Minding America's Business* and the author of his own manifesto, *The Silent War,* was put in charge (under Hillary Rodham Clinton)

---

[7]Lawrence and Slaughter, "Trade and U.S. Wages."

of health care reform; and while Thurow did not go to Washington, the new President made a point of being seen reading *Head to Head* and referred to it frequently.

How did this happen? To some extent there was an element of sheer chance: Magaziner and Reich had attended Oxford with the President. Yet one should not have in mind a picture of the President being sold a set of ideas that he did not fully understand. He and those friends had in effect come to those ideas together, over the years of the Conversation. That is, Bill Clinton wasn't captured by the strategic traders: he was a strategic trader himself. He was in one person both policy entrepreneur and politician.

And in any case the times were right. The public was thoroughly disillusioned with the promises of the supply-siders, but it still wanted answers. As usual, the answers from the professors were too mild or too complicated, if not for the public, certainly for the press. (As we saw in Chapter 8, the retreat of conservative macroeconomics and the revival of Keynes went virtually unreported.) What public and politicians needed was a new set of policy entrepreneurs; and strategic trade filled the bill.

Unfortunately, as we've seen, strategic trade was excruciatingly bad economics—as bad, in its own way, as the supply-side doctrine. As the Clinton administration got under way, its economic policy was already headed in the wrong direction.

Appendix to
Chapter 10
Productivity and
Competitiveness

Just about everyone now agrees that the U.S. economy needs higher productivity. Most people, however—including people who should know, like newspaper reporters specializing in economic issues—are confused about why. Probably the most popular explanation is that we need to be productive in order to compete in the global economy. That was the explanation a *New York Times* editorial assistant tried to force me to include in an op-ed piece in the summer of 1992; it was also the explanation that President Clinton gave in February 1993, when he tried to justify an economic package that included painful tax increases. But it's wrong. We need to be more productive in order to produce more, and this would be true even if the United States were completely without foreign competitors or customers.

If so many intelligent people get the logic of productivity wrong, however, it must not be obvious. So this appendix is an effort to illustrate, using some simple hypothetical examples, why productivity and competitiveness have very little to do with each other—and, indeed, why the whole concept of "competitiveness" is at best problematic, at worst misleading.

Three Questions and Their Answers

As a starting point, let's consider three questions that bear on the relationship between productivity and international competition. You should think about what your instinctive answers are, and (what is probably the same thing unless you have studied economics) what you usually hear when these or similar questions arise in public. Then I'll give the right answers, after which I'll run through why these are in fact the right answers. As we'll see, by the time we are done we will have arrived at a view about the relationship between productivity and competitiveness that is very different not only from the popular view but even from that of many people regarded as experts.

So here are our three questions:

1. *What happens to a country whose productivity is inferior to that of the countries it trades with?*

2. *What happens to a country whose productivity growth lags behind that of its rivals?*

3. *Which is more important: productivity growth in sectors that must compete with foreigners, or productivity growth in sectors that produce for sheltered domestic markets?*

Let's start with question 1. Surely the common view is that a country will suffer if its productivity is inferior across the board to that of its competitors. After all, if you aren't better than your rivals in *something*, how can you sell anything on world markets? The right answer is that being less productive than your trading partners poses no special problems. Of course, a country whose productivity is low across the board is not going to have a high standard of living; but that has nothing to do with the fact that it must coexist with more productive nations. In fact, the possibility of trading with more productive "competitors" mitigates, rather than exacerbates, the consequences of low domestic productivity.

Question 2 is, in a way, the same question, but shifted from a discussion of levels to one of rates of change. The common view here is, surely, that a country whose productivity growth lags that of its rivals is in big trouble—after all, a corporation that systematically fails to match competitors' productivity gains is not going to stay in business. This suggests that a crucial determinant of U.S. economic health is our rate of productivity growth relative to that of other nations. The right answer, however, is that to a very good approximation the rate of growth of the U.S. standard of living equals the rate of growth of U.S. productivity—*period*. How fast productivity is growing abroad, and whether we are ahead of or behind the pack, is irrelevant.

Finally, most people would answer question 3 with the assertion that productivity growth in sectors that must compete internationally is more important—after all, they are the sectors that must keep up with foreign rivals. The right answer is that, again to a very good approximation, what matters for the U.S. standard of living is the overall productivity of U.S. workers. It doesn't matter whether they are competing with foreigners or producing only for the domestic market. This has one particular implication that runs counter to much conventional wisdom: service productivity matters more than manufacturing productivity. To be more exact, since about 70 percent of the value added in the U.S. economy takes place in the service sector, while only 20 percent takes place in manufacturing, a percentage point gain in service productivity is worth about three and a half times as much as an equal gain in manufacturing.

These are so far just bald assertions. Let's see what they are based on.

Low Productivity and the Consequences of International Trade

To answer question 1, it will help if we lay out a stylized numerical example. This will take a little time, but why should you imagine that something like international trade can be understood without a little arithmetic?[1]

Imagine, then, a grossly simplified world in which there are only two countries—call them East and West—and two goods—call them autos and buses. To make things even simpler, we'll suppose that labor is the only input into production, and ignore any differences in skill or education. So the only thing that matters is differences in the productivity of labor across sectors and countries.

To answer the question, let's imagine that East is more productive across the board than West. In particular, let's suppose that the number of hours required to produce a single car or a single bus in the two countries is as shown in Table 6. East is better at both activities, but unequally so: it is 6 times as productive in the auto industry, but only 1.5 times as productive in buses.

Table 6. Hypothetical Labor Requirements

HOURS PER:	AUTO	BUS
East	100	200
West	600	300

What will happen if these two countries trade with each other? The exact result depends on the relative demand for autos and buses, but one thing is clear: workers in West will have to receive lower wages than workers in East; if not, it would be cheaper to produce everything in East, and West would simply go out of business, something that does not happen to whole countries. On

---

[1]Readers who have taken some economics will recognize the exercise as a version of David Ricardo's original exposition of comparative advantage, first published in 1817.

the other hand, wages in West cannot be too much lower—otherwise it would be cheaper to produce everything there in spite of lower productivity. So the wage ratio must end up somewhere in between the productivity ratios in the two industries, i.e., 6 and 1.5. Let's suppose that Western workers end up being paid only one third as much as Eastern workers.

You can see right away what will happen. It is cheaper to produce autos in East, in spite of higher wages, because of the large productivity gap; but it is cheaper to produce buses in West, in spite of lower productivity, because of its lower wages. West is at an *absolute* disadvantage in productivity everywhere, but it manages to export the good in which it has a *comparative* advantage, that is, in which its productivity relative to that of East *compared with its relative productivity elsewhere* is highest.

This example suggests immediately that just because a country is less productive than its trading partners doesn't mean that it will be unable to find something to export. But isn't that just theory? What happens in the real world?

The answer is that in the real world, as in our stylized example, the success of a country in exporting depends not on absolute but on comparative productivity advantage.

The classic real-world example that shows the principle of comparative advantage at work comes from the early postwar comparison of Britain and the United States.[2] At that time, British productivity was far less than that of the United States—labor productivity in manufacturing was below U.S. levels in all major industries, and on average was less than half that of the United States. The British economy, however, was much more dependent on foreign trade, and therefore was obliged to generate approximately the same dollar value of export earnings. If you look at the comparative pattern of exports, you see a clear picture of compar-

[2]A similar relationship between relative productivity and exports applies between the United States and Japan today. The United States–United Kingdom comparison from the early postwar period, however, remains a particularly revealing example, because Britain was able to export about as much as the United States in spite of an overwhelming U.S. productivity advantage across the board.

ative advantage at work. Table 7, using data for a set of thirty-nine industries in 1950, compares the ratio of American to British productivity with the ratio of American to British exports. There is a clear-cut association between relative productivity and relative exports. U.S. productivity was higher in all cases; but only in industries in which U.S. productivity was more than 3.4 times UK productivity did the United States have larger exports. That is, the United Kingdom did not have an absolute advantage in anything, but it had a comparative advantage in those goods in which its productivity exceeded 30 percent of the U.S. level.

Table 7

	Industries in Which:	
Ratio of U.S. to British Productivity:	U.S. EXPORTS LARGER THAN BRITISH	U.S. EXPORTS SMALLER THAN BRITISH
greater than 3.4	22	4
less than 3.4	3	10

Britain's ability to outsell America in industries in which its productivity was inferior depended, of course, on the fact that British workers were paid much less than U.S. workers—a pay differential that was greatly widened by the 1949 devaluation of the pound from $4.80 to $2.80. Doesn't that mean that Britain was forced to accept a lower living standard than the United States to compete with America?

Yes, it does. But while the British standard of living was lower than that in America, it was nonetheless higher than it would have been in the absence of trade.

Consider our example again: if West were isolated from international trade, it would have to produce autos for itself, and each auto would require 600 hours of labor. In a trading world, West can instead concentrate on making buses and trade them for autos. An imported auto requires the input of 100 hours of Eastern labor, which is three times as expensive as Western, but the overall labor cost for West is still only 300 hours, half what it would cost to produce the auto at home.

The moral of our discussion, then, is that while low productivity is a shame, international trade does not make it any more of a problem. Instead, the option of exporting the things you don't make too badly, and importing the things you do, reduces somewhat the costs of being unproductive on average.

We can also extract one more surprise from the example. Suppose that East were only half as productive as we have supposed, i.e., that it took Eastern workers 200 hours to make an auto and 400 to make a bus; and correspondingly, suppose that the wage ratio were 1.5 instead of 3 to 1. How would this affect West's position?

The answer is that it would not affect West at all. An imported auto would still cost West 300 hours of labor. All that matters to West is the rate of exchange between its export good (buses) and its import good (autos)—that is, its terms of trade. Given that fact, the comparative productivity of East does not matter at all.

So, while low productivity is a problem, low productivity relative to other countries is not only not a disaster; it is irrelevant.

Lagging Productivity Growth

We can firm up our grip on question 2 by returning to a thought experiment presented in the text. We first imagine a world in which productivity rises by 1 percent annually in all countries. Few would disagree that in that case the U.S. standard of living would also rise by 1 percent annually. Next, suppose that while the United States continues to raise its productivity by only 1 percent per year, the rest of the world manages to achieve 3 percent productivity growth. What is the trend in our living standard?

A surprising number of people who should know better immediately respond that the U.S. standard of living will now *decline* at 2 percent per year. Most people find it natural to suppose that there is at least some negative effect on the United States from our failure to keep up with the rest of the world.

But the right answer is that our living standard will still increase by 1 percent per year. To see why, let's spin out the example a bit further, by adding some hypothetical trends in wages, prices, and exchange rates.

Suppose, then, that wages in the United States (measured in dollars) and abroad (measured in foreign currency) both rise steadily at, say, 4 percent per year. Assume that prices rise in proportion to unit labor costs. In the case in which productivity rises at 1 percent everywhere, this will mean that the prices of goods produced both at home and abroad will rise by 3 percent annually.

Since productivity and wage performance are the same at home and abroad in this case, there is no reason to expect any trend in the value of the dollar. With a constant dollar, the only reason for U.S. import prices to rise is because of general inflation abroad; so prices of imported goods, like those of domestic goods, will rise at a 3 percent annual rate. Given 4 percent wage growth, this means that real wages will rise 1 percent per year—at the rate of productivity growth.

Now suppose that productivity growth in the rest of the world accelerates to 3 percent. How does this change the picture?

Obviously something has to give. If U.S. wages were to continue to grow at the same rate as foreign, and if the exchange rate were to remain unchanged, then U.S. goods and services would rapidly be priced out of world markets. Either U.S. wages must grow more slowly, foreign wages grow more rapidly, or the dollar start declining. It makes no difference to our point which happens; so let's suppose that the dollar begins to slide. It seems natural to assume in particular that it must slide on average by 2 percent per year to offset the 2-percent-per-year lag in U.S. productivity.

But if the dollar must have a downward trend in order to offset lagging U.S. productivity, doesn't this depress our standard of living? Let's work it through.

In the United States, 4 percent wage growth minus 1 percent productivity growth translates into a 3 percent inflation rate for domestic goods. In the rest of the world, 4 percent wage growth less 3 percent productivity growth means an inflation rate of only 1 percent in terms of foreign currency. But the dollar is declining at 2 percent per year, so in terms of dollars, the prices of foreign goods rise 3 percent annually. Thus the prices of imports into the United States, like the prices of domestic goods, rise at 3 percent. Real wages in the United States therefore rise by 4 − 3 = 1 percent—the same rate as in the case of equal productivity growth everywhere.

What happened here? Why didn't a declining dollar translate into a reduced standard of living? Because the acceleration in foreign productivity growth that was responsible for the declining dollar was also passed on in lower prices of foreign goods, offsetting the dollar's decline. The terms of trade were unaffected.

Again, you may be tempted to dismiss this as abstract theory, and to rely on the common sense feeling that falling behind in the productivity race must be a bad thing. But let's look at the facts.

The era of stagnating U.S. living standards began in 1973; the modern era of floating exchange rates began in the same year. On average over that period U.S. productivity growth has lagged that of other advanced nations, and the dollar has depreciated. Over the whole period from 1973 to 1991 the dollar fell an average of 2.6 percent per year against the German mark, 3.9 percent against the Japanese yen. But what happened to the terms of trade?

The answer is basically nothing. On average, the prices of U.S. exports rose 5.2 percent annually; the prices of U.S. imports rose 6.0 percent; so the terms of trade declined, but only by 0.8 percent per year. Since exports averaged less than 10 percent of national income over the period, the drag on U.S. real income growth from this slight terms of trade decline was less than 0.1 percent annually.

It is unclear whether the U.S. terms-of-trade decline, such as it was, should be attributed to our relative productivity lag. It is possible that increased foreign competition in sectors of traditional U.S. leadership did contribute to a fall in our export prices. But even if we accept for the sake of argument the proposition that faster productivity growth abroad was responsible for declining

U.S. terms of trade, any loss on this account is dwarfed by the purely domestic consequences of the productivity slowdown. In the period from World War II until 1973, productivity in the United States rose at 2.8 percent annually. After 1973, it rose at only 0.9 percent annually. If the United States had had no competitors, if the rest of the world did not exist, this slowdown would have reduced the rate of growth in income by 1.9 percent per year. Any effects from the lag in U.S. productivity behind other nations contributed only at most another 0.1 percentage points.

The moral, then, is that what matters is our domestic rate of productivity growth—end of story. Comparisons between our productivity growth and productivity growth in other countries are essentially irrelevant for the trend in the U.S. standard of living.

Competing versus Non-Competing Sectors

Our third question gets at a very widely held notion: that the really important thing for our economy is selling goods and services on world markets, with producing goods and services for ourselves a secondary and derivative activity. Certainly the overwhelming bulk of writing on the problem of U.S. competitiveness focuses on manufacturing, even though manufacturing is only about 20 percent of our economy, essentially because it is the manufacturing sector that must go "head to head" with foreign rivals.

But this is wrong. To see why, let's first lay out a stylized "round number" description of the U.S. economy, then try another thought experiment.

Imagine, then, an economy in which 20 percent of employment is in manufacturing, a sector exposed to international competition, and 80 percent is in services, which are non-tradable and thus sheltered from world markets. We suppose that manufacturing and services must pay equal wage rates. (In the real U.S. economy, services are a little smaller than this, because there are some sectors that are neither manufacturing nor services, like agriculture, construction, and mining. Also, wages and value added per worker are a little bit higher in manufacturing than in services, though not as much as many people suppose. Adding these real-world complications would make the story messier but not change its bottom line.)

As in the real U.S. economy during the 1980s, let's suppose initially that manufacturing productivity rises at an annual rate of 2.5 percent, while service productivity rises at an annual rate of only 0.5 percent. Since manufacturing includes only 20 percent of the labor force, this means that the overall rate of productivity increase is only $0.2 \times 2.5 + 0.8 \times 0.5 = 0.9$ percent, which is just about the actual rate of increase during the 1980s.

What would be the trend in real wages in this economy? Obviously the real wage in terms of services will rise at a glacial 0.5 percent annually. The real wage in terms of domestically produced manufactures will rise faster, at 2.5 percent per year. And given our discussion of question 2, you should be able to convince yourself that the real wage in terms of foreign manufactures will rise at the same rate, because on average the dollar's exchange rate will just offset any difference in domestic and foreign manufacturing productivity growth.

The trend in the overall real wage rate depends on the relative importance of manufactured goods and services in consumption. If trade in manufactures is almost balanced—and as we saw in Chapter 10, for the United States it is, in the sense that eliminating our trade deficit would add only a few percent to the size of the manufacturing sector—then the share of manufactures in spending will be the same 20 percent as their share in output. In that case, the average gain in real wages will be the same weighted sum of sectoral rates of productivity growth as the rate of productivity growth for the economy as a whole: 0.9 percent.

Now let us ask the following question: Which would the United States rather have, an increase in manufacturing productivity growth, from 2.5 to a torrid 5 percent annually, or a more modest increase in the rate of growth of service productivity, from 0.5 to 1.5 percent?

The answer is: Whichever raises overall productivity growth more, and this turns out to be the extra service growth. Since manufacturing is only 20 percent of the economy, an extra 2.5 percentage points of manufacturing productivity growth would raise overall productivity growth by only 0.5 points, to 1.4; since services are 80 percent of our simplified economy, a single extra point of service productivity raises the growth rate by 0.8 percentage points, to 1.7.

But isn't there some extra "competitive" gain from faster productivity growth in manufacturing? No; we've already taken it into account. Higher productivity growth in manufacturing will strengthen the dollar, but only by enough to ensure that real wages rise in terms of imported manufactured goods at the same rate at which they rise in terms of domestic manufactures.

It's not quite as easy to offer some factual backing for our answer to question 3 as it was for the other two questions. It may be useful, however, to point out that the shift from rapidly rising living standards before 1973 to near stagnation afterward was primarily due to a slowdown in service rather than manufacturing productivity. Indeed, during the 1980s productivity in U.S. manufacturing rose at 2.7 percent annually, almost as fast as during the prosperous 1960s, and faster than the 2 percent productivity growth rate in West Germany. Nonetheless, the American economy in the 1960s and the German economy in the 1980s both delivered much larger real wage growth, thanks to rising service productivity. (And services led the surprise surge in productivity in 1991 and 1992.)

Why Does It Matter?

The examples presented in this appendix are intended to demonstrate that the general belief that productivity is important because it is crucial for international competitiveness is completely misguided. Productivity *is* important, but international competitiveness has nothing to do with it. Indeed, I hope the examples have convinced you that the whole concept of competitiveness is at best elusive, at worst meaningless.

But why does it matter? If productivity is important, why object if some people try to raise the urgency level by claiming that the reason that it is important is because we are in some kind of international race? If Bill Clinton can finally get a real deficit reduction plan by warning of the necessities of facing international competition, why not let him have his rhetoric?

There are, I think, two answers.

The first is that a misplaced belief that the United States needs higher productivity primarily to face international competition can lead to substantive errors in policy. For example, there has been some talk of trying to focus government-sponsored research on improving productivity in U.S. manufacturing—as opposed to services, which are deemed less important because they do not face foreign competition. Since an extra percentage point of service productivity is worth 3.5 times as much as an extra point of manufacturing productivity, this would be a serious mistake.

More important is that the prevalence of fashionable misconceptions about the relationship between productivity and competitiveness provides a kind of test of the reliability of supposed experts. The issues involved are not hard to sort out—we're not talking quantum mechanics here. Certainly anyone who wants to be considered an expert on economics has no excuse for not getting the arguments and facts just described straight. So, if you hear someone say something along the lines of "America needs higher productivity so that it can compete in today's global economy," never mind who he is, or how plausible he sounds. He might as well be wearing a flashing neon sign that reads: "I DON'T KNOW WHAT I'M TALKING ABOUT."

Epilogue

n the 1970s, conservative ideas forced the pace in serious discussion of economic issues. The leading conservative economists offered powerful arguments against government activism, arguments that liberals had trouble answering. It was in a way only fair that the advocates of these clever and often deep conservative ideas should get their chance at power in 1980.

The ideas embraced by the Reagan administration were, however, anything but deep. To the astonishment of the serious conservatives, the real winners of 1980 turned out to be the supply-siders—ideologues whose economic concepts were cartoonlike in their simplicity, who dismissed conventional economics because they could not be bothered to understand it.

For the next twelve years, even while conservatives controlled the White House, the pendulum of sophisticated economic thinking was swinging the other way. Keynesian ideas experienced a revival; new arguments for an active government role to improve the functioning of markets gained in influence.

The liberal revival was not as cohesive a movement as the conservative thrust of the 1970s, but by 1992 the cutting edge of serious economic thinking was arguably on the moderate left. Bill Clinton's election victory seemed to offer a chance to put that thinking into practice.

At least in the early months of the Clinton administration it seemed, however, that once again the real winners of the election had been the advocates of a crude, simplistic set of ideas: the strategic traders, who if anything understood even less about the economy than the supply-siders.

It's a disappointing story. Instead of facing up seriously to the problems of the U.S. economy, both conservative and liberal politicians sought easy ways out. In so doing they delivered the policies of a great and sophisticated nation repeatedly into the hands of the peddlers of economic snake oil.

We've already seen the consequences of the reign of the supply-siders. While they did not bring disaster to the country, they did create an unnecessary problem—the budget deficit—that has weakened the U.S. economy and preoccupied American politics to the exclusion of almost everything else. They also helped to make America a harsher, meaner place with tax and social policies that favored the rich and hurt the poor.

But what will the strategic traders do? They may offer a deeply misleading diagnosis of America's economic problems, but will this translate into seriously destructive policies?

To answer this we first need to ask what America *should* be doing, then make a guess at what the nation *will* do.

What Should Be Done?

America has two great economic problems: slow growth in productivity, and rising poverty (which is the consequence both of inadequate productivity growth and of increasing income inequality). Everything else is either of secondary importance or a nonissue. For example, the budget deficit matters only to the extent that it is a drag on our productivity growth; we saw in Chapter 6 that this drag is significant but not overwhelming. America's alleged problem of international competitiveness is almost completely a non-issue.

So the big question is: How should the U.S. government set about solving these two great problems? And the answer is straightforward: It shouldn't.

That is, it is a mistake for the U.S. government to base its policies on the idea that it can solve the problems of productivity and poverty in the sense of eliminating them—raising productivity growth back to pre-1973 levels and eliminating poverty or reducing it to insignificance. The reason it is a mistake is the simple fact that nobody knows how to do either of those things. The roots of inadequate productivity performance are deep and poorly understood; the causes of growing inequality and poverty hardly less so. If the President insists on finding advisers willing to claim that they can really solve these problems, he will inevitably find himself listening to men and women whose certainty is based on ignorance.

While the government cannot promise to *solve* the nation's problems, however, it can do many things that can help *diminish* them.

Here's a partial list of sensible things to do about productivity growth. It makes no sense for the United States to complain about low growth (and trade deficits) while continuing to run large budget deficits; so let taxes be raised and truly wasteful government programs (like farm subsidies) be cut. Rising health care costs are a significant burden both on the federal budget and on real earnings in the private sector; let us consider a serious reform of our deeply distorted health care system. Much regulation in the United States is simultaneously less effective and more costly than necessary; let's make greater use of innovative schemes like taxes on pollution and congestion that exploit the power of market incentives (and incidentally let's end the strange policy of allowing private interests to mine and graze on federal land for nominal fees).

None of these proposals would involve a radical change in the shape of American economic policy, even though some of them would be very difficult to push through politically. Nor is it likely that they would bring back the magic of economic growth (although that magic might return in any case). They would, however, leave the U.S. economy a few percent richer than it would otherwise be.

What about poverty? Again, we can make a list: Let's spend more on programs that help poor children, from nutrition and medical programs for poor mothers up through to aid for distressed school districts. Let's also raise the support given to poor families with children (international comparisons show that the main though not the only reason the United States has so many more poor children than other industrial countries is that it spends less public money keeping children out of poverty). All of this will cost money—but not that much, because our poor are so poor that it only takes a moderate amount of spending to make them much better off.

Like the growth proposals, these anti-poverty proposals would not solve the problem. They would not end the social collapse of the underclass; they would not transform minimum wage workers into highly paid symbolic analysts. They would, however, make the lives of millions of people somewhat less miserable, and give at least a few of the children of the poor a chance at escape.

No doubt there are desirable policies that have been left off these lists, and perhaps some of the proposals can be argued against. The point of the lists, however, is to show that there is no shortage of ways in which to improve our economic policy. Other things equal, it would be better to seek fundamental solutions than to look for a number of ways to make things somewhat better. But it's no use insisting that economic policy face the big issues when you have no good idea what to do about them. As Raymond Chandler once pointed out, there have been some very bad books written about God, and some very good ones about trying to make a living while staying fairly honest.

So here's what the federal government should be doing: It

should be trying to get it right on as many policy issues as possible, seeking to increase productivity in the ways that we understand, seeking to help the poor with the tools available.

Now, in fairness, in its early months the Clinton administration did try to do some of the things listed above. Above all, it proposed a reasonable package of measures to reduce the budget deficit. The problem was that at the same time it appeared to be in the process of getting some other major things wrong, through a misplaced belief that America's economic problem was one of "competitiveness" rather than essentially domestic.

The Fixation on Competitiveness

In the movie *The Music Man,* Robert Preston plays a traveling salesman who specializes in selling musical instruments and uniforms for marching bands to small towns. To make his sale in River City, he needs to convince local leaders that they have a problem he can solve. And so he manages to turn the formerly innocuous pool hall into a symbol of gathering social danger, to which the answer is, of course, the healthy town spirit that only a properly equipped school band can provide.

Many policy entrepreneurs (and to be honest, not a few professors) play a similar game. They have a solution; now they have to convince the politicians and the public that there is an appropriate problem. Often they fail: despite his best efforts, Robert Bartley of *The Wall Street Journal* never managed to convince many people that monetary chaos looms unless we put America back on the gold standard. Sometimes, however, policy entrepreneurs and the politicians who make alliance with them are spectacularly successful at creating imagined problems to which their favorite policy prescriptions are the answer.

The imaginary problem that galvanized the supply-siders and Ronald Reagan was the danger of Big Government: a government that taxed people too much, then wasted the money on legions of useless bureaucrats and generous welfare handouts to the undeserving poor. Big Government is not, of course, wholly imaginary. Taxes *are* a significant burden on all of us, and there are indeed useless bureaucrats and undeserving welfare recipients. But as a diagnosis of what was wrong with the American economy, it was deeply misleading; and the myth of Big Government both distracted America from coming to grips with its real problems and created new difficulties.

The supply-siders have now retreated to their think tanks, though they still hope to return for revenge. For the time being, Big Government is no longer an effective slogan, and middle-class Americans are angrier at the undeserving rich than the undeserving poor. But the policy entrepreneurs now riding high have convinced many Americans that we have a new kind of trouble in River City: trouble with a capital "C" that stands for "Competitiveness."

The strategic traders have now sold the American public (and for the most part themselves, for only a few policy entrepreneurs are entirely cynical) on the idea that our most crucial economic problem is our struggle with other advanced nations for global markets. The subtitle of Lester Thurow's *Head to Head* is "The Coming Economic Battle Among Japan, Europe, and America"; the jacket entices readers by saying, "The most decisive war of the century is being waged right now . . . and we may have already decided to lose."

Unfortunately, the alleged competitive problem of the United States is as much a fantasy as Reagan's myth of wasteful Big Government. The United States has some real problems in international competition, just as it really has some unproductive bureaucrats and welfare cheats. But in the image it conveys of what's really wrong with the economy, Clinton's rhetoric is as far off as Reagan's.

Economic rhetoric based on the myth of international competition as war has some advantages. It is easier to mobilize voters to support painful policies like tax increases and cuts in popular programs by claiming that the goal is national security—and President Clinton did just that in his highly effective 1993 State of the

Union address. But ultimately the rhetoric of competitiveness will be destructive, because it can all too easily lead both to bad policies and to a neglect of the real issues.

The rise of the strategic traders poses two main risks. One is that in their effort to win global markets, they will destroy them instead. The other is that the commitment to a foolish ideology in one area will undermine economic policy across the board.

THE RISK OF TRADE WAR

There are two kinds of trade war: the imaginary ones that protectionists and strategic traders claim we are fighting all the time, and the real ones that happen when they get their way.

The fantasy of the strategic traders is that international trade is by its nature international competition—that countries that trade with each other are in a struggle over who gets the spoils. In reality there is almost nothing to this view: what a country gets depends almost entirely on its own performance, and there is nothing competitive about it. But when countries *believe* that they are in a competitive struggle, or when they become captive to the special interests that benefit from trade conflict, they can fall into what is generally known as a trade war.

A trade war in which countries restrict each other's exports in pursuit of some illusory advantage is not much like a real war. On one hand, nobody gets killed. On the other, unlike real wars, it is almost impossible for anyone to win, since the main losers when a country imposes barriers to trade are not foreign exporters but domestic residents. In effect, a trade war is a conflict in which each country uses most of its ammunition to shoot itself in the foot.

And yet once a trade war is started, it can be very difficult to stop. Each country finds it politically impossible to free up its trade without corresponding "concessions" from other countries, and these may be very hard to negotiate. In other words, once the world has gotten caught up in a wave of tit-for-tat protectionism, it can take decades to undo the damage.

Consider the lessons of the interwar period. A trade war among the advanced countries erupted after the United States passed the infamous Smoot-Hawley tariff in 1929, and intensified as countries made desperate efforts to find ways out of the Great Depression. Yet most people, even including the senators who voted for Smoot-Hawley, soon realized that protectionism had gone too far. The United States began trying to negotiate tariffs down again as early as 1934, and after World War II both the political and the economic environment were very favorable for trade liberalization. Once the global trading system had been shattered, however, it was very hard to put back together; trade among industrial countries didn't regain its 1914 level until 1970.

In the 1990s, the world is ripe for another outbreak of trade war. The key economic ingredients that led to protectionism in the interwar period—slow growth, persistent high unemployment—are back again, especially in Europe. Meanwhile, the political strengths that helped make the freeing up of trade after World War II possible—a strong leading nation and a common purpose—are gone with the relative decline of the United States and the end of the Cold War. It wouldn't take much miscalculation to start a round of tariffs, countertariffs, and mutual recrimination that could repeat the interwar experience of shrinking trade.

Would this be a catastrophe? No, but it would add significantly to our problems. Big, largely self-contained economies like the United States, the European Community, and Japan could take restricted global trade in stride. Even a quite nasty trade war would reduce their real income only a percentage point or two. But smaller countries, more dependent on world markets to help them make up for the small size of their internal markets and their limited resources, would either have to scramble to form commercial alliances with the big players or be left dangerously out in the cold. It would not be surprising if a world of trade conflict among the big advanced countries was a world of political instability, and maybe growing anti-Western feeling, in smaller and poorer countries from Latin America to the former Soviet Republics.

World trade, then, is in an endangered state, in which we could easily stumble into an era of trade conflict that would be at least as hard to get rid of as Ronald Reagan's deficit. Yet it is at this of all moments that strategic traders in the United States think that we need to get tough with other countries in pursuit of "competitiveness."

Imagine the following scenario: Clinton administration officials—ignoring advice from conventional economists—decide that Japan's trade surplus is the root of many of America's economic difficulties, and decide to demand that Japan not only take measures to reduce that surplus but agree to meet specific numerical targets. The Japanese are indignant: they point out, correctly, that it is perfectly reasonable for a country with a very high savings rate to invest a significant fraction of those savings abroad, and that Japan's trade surplus is simply the other side of its capital account deficit. Besides, they say, what are they supposed to do— run huge budget deficits to soak up all that private saving?

The strategic traders in the Clinton administration nonetheless present their demands at an economic summit—and the Japanese reject them. At this point the U.S. government faces a dilemma. To drop the issue would look like weakness; but there is no real policy option other than to close U.S. markets to Japanese goods. And so protectionism it is—a protectionism that is matched by Japanese retaliation and European emulation. Within two years the results of four decades of negotiations to open world markets are reversed.

An unlikely scenario? At the time of writing, much of it had already happened. The Treasury Department is usually a bastion of free trade thinking, but in May 1993 Lawrence Summers, now the Undersecretary of the Treasury for International Affairs, asserted in a speech that "Japan's surplus is the major asymmetry in the global economy" and that this surplus was a "significant drag on global growth"; he followed this assertion with the statement that "The United States will focus less on process and more on results, and results have to be measurable." Everyone knew what he meant: the U.S. Trade Representative had for several weeks been telling reporters that the United States was likely to demand that Japan impose a ceiling on its trade surplus at the next meeting of the Group of Seven industrial countries. Meanwhile, Japanese officials and the Japanese public were furious and defiant in the face of American pressure.

One hopes that by the time this book is published this particular scenario will turn out to have been a premature alarm. As long as the administration is committed to the ideology of strategic trade, however, the risk of trade war will remain high.

So the direct threat from the ascendancy of strategic traders is that their fixation on the supposed problem of competitiveness will set off a trade war. Like the budget deficit created by the supply-siders, a trade war will not destroy the U.S. economy; but also like the budget deficit, it will be very hard to get rid of.

There is also, however, another kind of risk from the ascendancy of strategic traders, a more subtle one. When a government is committed to an ideology that all real experts know to be wrong, this tends to exert a chilling effect on its ability to get anything else right, even in areas in which that ideology seems to have no bearing.

WHEN BAD IDEAS DRIVE OUT GOOD

International economic policy is not everything. Indeed, one of the essential misperceptions of the strategic traders is that they overrate the importance of international as opposed to domestic issues. So one might imagine that an administration misguidedly dedicated to the pursuit of "competitiveness" could be otherwise sensible, doing the right things on the budget, health care, environmental policy, and so forth.

But matters are not that simple. Once an administration has decided to accept a set of basically bad ideas in one place, there is a sort of Gresham's Law in which these bad ideas drive out good ones even in seemingly unrelated areas.

An example came early in the Clinton administration, in what one might have thought was the thoroughly non-international field of health care. If you had asked most people in the field to list the leading experts on the economics of health care, almost all of them would have mentioned Henry Aaron of the Brookings Institution, an economist with solid liberal credentials and a strong backer of Clinton during the election. But when the Clinton administration formed its health care task force, a huge effort involving more than five hundred people, Aaron was not involved. Why? The answer appeared to involve a sort of guilt by association. The health care task force was headed by Ira Magaziner, a business consultant by profession but a strategic trader by inclination, whose views on international competition were summed up by the title of his 1990 book on the subject, *The Silent War*. Now, in the great confrontation over industrial policy in 1983 and 1984, economists from Brookings had been highly critical of strategic traders in general and Magaziner in particular. It was not too surprising that Magaziner would exclude a Brookings economist from his deliberations, or even that he would, as appeared to have been the case, have excluded virtually anyone with prior background in health care economics.

The general principle that this example illustrates is the following: If there is an economic dogma that is simply, flatly, demonstrably wrong, then good economists are likely either to have said that it is wrong or to be associated somehow with other economists who have said that it is wrong. If this wrong-headed dogma is then adopted as the official ideology of an administration, it therefore tends to drive out good economic ideas in general, even where they do not on the surface conflict directly with the dogma.

At the time of writing it was too soon to judge, but the early indications from key areas like health care were that the foolish simplicities of strategic trade were damaging the ability of the Clinton administration to make good policy decisions across a surprisingly broad front.

The Role of the Economist

An experienced and therefore cynical government economist once described to me his vision of his job. "It's mostly a matter of getting rid of bad ideas," he explained, "but it's like flushing cockroaches down a toilet—sooner or later they just come back." The role of the economist who cares about policy can be dispiriting: one may spend years devising sophisticated theories or carefully testing ideas against the evidence, then find that politicians turn again and again to ideas that you thought had been discredited decades or even centuries ago, or make statements that are flatly contradicted by the facts.

It's tempting to give up—either to retreat to the ivory tower, or to start to play the policy entrepreneur game. After all, what is the use of sophisticated policy thinking or careful examination of the facts if simplistic ideas win every time?

One answer is simply that it would be wrong to give up. If the people with good ideas do not fight for them, they have no right to complain about the outcome.

But good ideas will still often lose to convenient nonsense. When that happens, every serious economist is ultimately sustained by a faith that the right ideas will eventually prevail. Unlike the simplicities of the policy entrepreneurs, good thinking about economics is cumulative. A generation from now, the supply-siders will be of purely historical interest, but the valid insights of serious conservatives will remain. Strategic trade will be remembered as a defunct doctrine, but the economics of QWERTY will still be a vital part of the intellectual tradition.

Or so we hope. In the long run we are all dead, but one must have faith that good ideas live on.

Index

293